DEADLY DEVELOPMENTS

War and Society

A series edited by S. P. Reyna and R. E. Downs

Volume 1
Feuding and Warfare: Selected Works of Keith F. Otterbein

Volume 2
Studying War: Anthropological Perspectives
Edited by S. P. Reyna and R. E. Downs

Volume 3
Troubled Times: Violence and Warfare in the Past
Edited by Debra L. Martin and David W. Frayer

Volume 4
Roots of Violence: A History of War in Chad
Mario J. Azevedo

Volume 5
Deadly Developments: Capitalism, States and War
Edited by S. P. Reyna and R. E. Downs

This book is part of a series. The publisher will accept continuation orders which may be cancelled at any time and which provide for automatic billing and shipping of each title in the series upon publication. Please write for details.

DEADLY DEVELOPMENTS

Capitalism, States and War

Edited by

S. P. Reyna

and

R. E. Downs

University of New Hampshire, Durham, USA

GORDON AND BREACH PUBLISHERS

Australia Canada China France Germany India
Japan Luxembourg Malaysia The Netherlands
Russia Singapore Switzerland

Copyright © 1999 OPA (Overseas Publishers Association) N.V. Published by license under the Gordon and Breach Publishers imprint.

All rights reserved.

No part of this book may be reproduced or utilized in any form or by any means, electronic or mechanical, including photocopying and recording, or by any information storage or retrieval system, without permission in writing from the publisher. Printed in Singapore.

Amsteldijk 166
1st Floor
1079 LH Amsterdam
The Netherlands

Front cover: *Untitled head*, 1997, A. N. Reyna.

British Library Cataloguing in Publication Data

Deadly developments : capitalism, states and war. – (War
  and society ; v. 5 – ISSN 1069-8043)
  1. War 2. War – History 3. War – Economic aspects 4. Violence –
  Political aspects
  I. Reyna, S. P. (Stephen P.) II. Downs, R. E.
  303. 6'6

ISBN   90-5699-589-8

CONTENTS

Introduction to the Series vii
Acknowledgments ix

Introduction: Deadly Developments and
Phantasmagoric Representations
S. P. Reyna 1

Part I

ONE   The Force of Two Logics: Predatory and
Capital Accumulation in the Making of
the Great Leviathan, 1415–1763
S. P. Reyna 23

Part II

TWO   Colonialism and the Efflorescence of Warfare:
The New Ireland Case
Abraham Rosman and Paula Rubel 69

Part III

THREE   Insurrection in the Texas Mexican Borderlands:
The Plan of San Diego
Candelario Sàenz 87

FOUR   War in Uganda: North and South
Joan Vincent 107

FIVE   Warfare in the Lower Omo Valley, Southwestern
Ethiopia: Reconciling Materialist and
Political Explanations
David Turton 133

SIX	Requiem for the Rational War	
	Carolyn Nordstrom	153
SEVEN	The Politics of Ethnic Conflict in a Transboundary Context, the Senegal River Valley	
	John Magistro	177
EIGHT	Ethnicity and Land Tenure in the Sahel	
	Pierre Bonte	213
NINE	Detour onto the Shining Path: Obscuring the Social Revolution in the Andes	
	William P. Mitchell	235
Index	....	279

INTRODUCTION TO THE SERIES

The *War and Society* book series fosters studies of organized violence and its consequences in all forms of society, from deep in the past until the present. It encourages different intellectual traditions from different disciplines. Its goal is to expand theoretical understanding of the causes and effects of war, thereby to provide intellectual tools for constructing a more peaceful world.

ACKNOWLEDGMENTS

There has been at the University of New Hampshire, for some years now, a lively anthropological community whose members tolerate the most diverse opinions, but who share the belief that anthropological projects need to be advanced with rigor because, after all, such ventures matter. In different ways, at different times, the voices of Bolian, de Munck, Fields, Goodby, Larson, Lugalla and Schiller have been heard in this community and in this volume's editing.

John Magistro's article (chapter 7) appeared in *Cahiers d'Etudes Africaines* (XXXII–2, 130, 1993). David Turton's paper (chapter 5) was published in *Disasters* (15:3, 1991). Both are included with the publishers' permission, Societe des Africanistes and Blackwells, respectively.

INTRODUCTION

Deadly Developments and Phantasmagoric Representations

S. P. Reyna

"**phantasmagoria**:...a constantly shifting, complex succession of things seen or imagined as in a dream or fever state" (Webster's 1966: 1693).

Classical nineteenth century social theory arose as an attempt to understand the emergence of modernity. Theorists thought that modern society was "civilized," and that this quality was related to economic developments. So thinkers proceeded by formulating economic dichotomies that distinguished the uncivilized from the civilized. Saint-Simon made the main dichotomy one between feudal and industrial economies; Comte and Spencer distinguished military and industrial societies; Marx emphasized the transition from pre-capitalist to capitalist modes of production; and Durkheim believed that segmental societies, integrated by mechanical solidarity, evolved into industrial ones, integrated by organic solidarity. Not only Comte and Spencer, but Marx and Durkheim as well believed that war dominated the earlier societies and that it would become infrequent, or die out entirely, in states with industrial capitalism.[1] Classic social theory, then, to a considerable degree, represented modern social order to be one of pacific, capitalist states developing out of some warring uncivilized Other.

This book's goals are to introduce readers to the rich variety in anthropological analyses of modern war and, in so doing, to give them some understanding of the intimacies between capitalist states and war.[2] The present introduction contributes to the realization of these goals by providing some analytic tools helpful when studying wars and states, by offering previews of the articles' arguments, and by raising the alarm that certain scholarly traditions peddle phantasmagoric representations that darken comprehension of modern war. The volume includes nine articles by ten anthropologists who investigate warfare in different times and places during the evolution of modern governments and capitalism. Included are studies from what came to be the crucible of modern society, Atlantic Europe, to what came to be its peripheries in the Third World. Certain findings of these articles provide a basis for evaluating different representations of capitalism, states, and wars. It turns out that classic social theory's insistence that capitalist states were pacific is a phantasm, a chimera that hides deadly developments.

I

The articles that compose this book analyze warfare in societies with states. So it is important to begin by specifying an understanding of this social form. The "state" is a territory within which there are two sets of institutions, those of government and those of civil society. "Government" is understood to be a roughly hierarchical organization of offices with different amounts of power and authority in executive, legislative, and judicial domains. Modern governments are distinguished from their premodern counterparts, among other things, by the enormous variety and amounts of resources at their disposal as well as by the prodigious differentiation of their offices that allows them to utilize these resources. Both of these differences contribute to the vastly superior powers of modern vis-à-vis premodern governments. "Civil society" includes the economic, kin, religious, and other non-governmental institutions found in states.

"Capitalism" refers to the nature of institutions that have increasingly come to dominate the civil society of modern states. Capitalist institutions exhibit five attributes: 1. ownership of the factors of production by private persons (who are the capitalists); 2. provision of labor by workers who are politically free to dispose of their labor as they wish; 3. the orientation of workers' and capitalists' activity to the objective of the maximization of profit; 4. the realization of profit through the operation of the market; and 5. the appropriation of profit by the capitalists. Capitalism, because it exhibits these five attributes, is a process of capital accumulation. Two forms of capitalism have been important. Most capital accumulation in the early modern period (c.1415–c.1760) resulted from the maximization of profits of mercantile enterprises. After this time, capital accumulation increasingly resulted from the maximization of the profits of manufacturing enterprises that utilized machine technologies. These two varieties of capitalism have been respectively called "commercial" and "industrial." A "capitalist state" is one in which either of the two forms of capitalist enterprise dominate the civil society's economic life. The essays constituting this book analyze different forms of warfare in capitalist states or in populations influenced by such states. A brief précis of these articles is in order.

The volume is divided into three chronological parts. The first part consists of an essay by myself that is concerned with warfare between Portugal, Spain, Holland, Britain, and France during the development of commercial capitalism in the early period. The second part of the book also consists of a single essay: that of Abraham Rosman and Paula Rubel dealing with an outburst of "tribal" fighting among certain islanders in the south Pacific during the nineteenth century.

The third part of the volume, by far the largest, investigates twentieth century conflicts. First, there is a piece by Candilario Sàenz exploring little known ethnic fighting in the United States southwest at the dawn of the century. This is followed by five articles analyzing warfare in postcolonial Africa. Three articles consider the eastern portion of the continent. Joan Vincent analyzes Ugandan government attacks upon various elements of its civil society, warring that has plagued Uganda almost since Independence. David Turton contemplates an instance of "tribal" war, one involving the Mursi and their neighbors in Ethiopia. Carolyn Nordstrom seeks to understand war in Mozambique between the government and a guerilla movement whose brutality has seemed to epitomize "savagery." Two articles are set in West Africa. Although wars between states have been rare in postcolonial Africa, John Magistro seeks to explain one such case that erupted between Mauritania and Senegal in the late 1980s and early 1990s. A comparative piece by Pierre Bonte looks at the relationship between land and ethnic conflict in the Sahel, the arid savanna immediately south of the Sahara. The last article in the third section deals with Latin America. William Mitchell seeks to explain the war between the government and the Shining Path guerillas in Peru.

Elsewhere (Reyna 1994) I have suggested that the term war is applied properly only to societies with states. Specifically, war involves practices of organized violence performed by institutions within states. These articles explore two types of war: international and internal. "International" war is that waged between the military institutions of the governments of different states. Reyna considers a case of international war. "Internal" war is that conducted within a state. There are two major sorts of internal war. First there is "civil" war, which happens when the military institutions of a state's government wage war against different institutions in that state's civil society. Then there is "civil society" war that arises when different institutions in a civil society fight each other in the absence of government intervention.

A further distinction might be made between "ethnic" and "non-ethnic" internal wars. Civil or civil society wars between religious groups or gangs are non-ethnic internal wars. Those between groups such as the Sioux and Cheyenne in 19th century United States are ethnic internal wars. Rosman and Rubel, Sàenz, and Turton concentrate their analyses upon ethnic civil society war. Magistro and Bonte investigate instances of ethnic civil war. Nordstrom and Mitchell explore cases of non-ethnic civil war.

The articles tend to identify determinants or accelerants of the different types of wars. By "determinant" is not meant the sole cause of a conflict. Rather, a determinant is understood in the context of this volume to be a phenomenon that played a role in bringing about, in the sense of "making occur," organized violence. "Accelerants" are like gasoline on a fire, for they are phenomena that, in the presence of existing conflict, make the violence occur more frequently and/or intensely.

Further, the articles generally explore structural and subjective categories of determinants or accelerants. "Structural" phenomena are those involving the actions of organizations that, in the cases analyzed, are largely those of the governments and civil societies of capitalist states. "Subjective" phenomena are those having to do with peoples' thoughts and emotions. People are born with neuro-physiologies that allow them to experience an enormous variety of cognitions and sentiments. Their subjectivities are what they actually think and feel in different contexts. Subjectivities, however, are "constructed." Construction involves the activities of organizations that embody — i.e., literally put-in-the-body, in the sense of placing within neuro-physiologies — systems of cultural meaning, so that people will experience different cognitions and affects as they have been constructed to experience them. It is time to look a bit more closely at what the articles identify as structurally and subjectively important in the determination and acceleration of modern warfare.

II

Most anthropological analyses of modern war are concerned with conflict over short periods of time in global peripheries. A long period of time is considered in my article, the three and a half centuries during which the modern capitalist state emerged. Further, the scene of the action is the core, the five European Atlantic states most directly involved in the making of modernity.

I begin with a discussion of the properties of the modern state and suggest that foremost among these is its extraordinary power, a property sensed by Hobbes when he imagined the state as a "great Leviathan," the most powerful thing he could envision. This means that an important question to pose is: did anything happen during the time of increasing commercial capitalism to make the Leviathan so powerful? I believe that what happened was the gradual emergence of a "military-capitalist" complex. This was a number of inter-related institutions that allowed the accumulation of capital by commercial capitalists in civil society to accelerate the accumulation of violent force in government and vice versa. The Leviathan grew so powerful because the military-capitalist complex made the accumulation of profits and militaries mutually reinforcing, thereby accelerating the accumulation of capital and violent force. It was the concentration of ever increasing amounts of these forces within the state that made it so powerful a behemoth.

Analysis of the histories of the European Atlantic states in the early modern period reveals that seventeenth century England learned how to make a better military-capitalist complex than did its

Portuguese, Spanish, Dutch, and French competitors. Armed with its better military-capitalist complex, Britain blasted and traded its way through the eighteenth century, accumulating violent force and capital, with the result that by 1763 it had amassed sufficient power to exercise truly global domination.

Abraham Rosman and Paula Rubel take us to the periphery and expand upon Ferguson and Whitehead's approach to the anthropological analysis of war, which studies "the transformation of indigenous patterns of warfare brought about by the proximity or intrusion of expanding states" (1992:1). Specifically, they describe an efflorescence of "tribal" war among Melanesian peoples living on the New Ireland islands subsequent to their first "contact" with Europeans in the 1880s. It is the nature of this contact that is critical. Copra is the dried meat of coconuts. When processed, copra yields an oil that has been used since the 19th century as an ingredient in a wide range of industrial capitalist products including soaps and margarines. Rosman and Rubel make clear that agrarian capitalism was penetrating Melanesia during the late 1800s, often taking the form of copra plantations. Trading stations were set up throughout Melanesia to facilitate the copra sector. Employees of the trading stations bartered guns to those who would provide them with labor for the plantations.

Those New Irelanders who had acquired guns used them against their usual adversaries, which created, in Rosman and Rubel's words, an "imbalance" in relations between opponents, one that provoked them to war more fiercely. Thus what appears to be an instance of "traditional tribal" war turns out to be nothing of the sort. Rather, the search for labor by agro-capitalist enterprise, supplying products demanded by industrial capitalist enterprise, turns out to be a structural accelerant of violence. At the end of their essay, Rosman and Rubel suggest parallels between what happened in New Ireland at the end of the 19th century and what has happened recently in Somalia.

Sàenz's piece, which opens the third section, considers an episode in the "winning" of the West. In 1915 a document was found upon a gentleman in Texas that came to be known as the *Plan de San Diego*. The "Plan" called for the formation of a military unit, the "Mexican Liberation Army of All Races and Peoples," to be composed of Mexican-Americans, Japanese-Americans, African-Americans, and Native Americans, that would fight to create an independent republic in the southwestern portion of the United States. A Mexican-American insurrection started in the summer of 1915 as an attempt to implement this plan. Sàenz, whose family were active participants in the events leading up to it, weaves a tale that accounts for the passions driving the formulation of this plan.

A lesson of Sàenz's tale is that ethnic groups like the *Tejanos* and Anglos do not war because of "natural" bloodlusts or because it is an essential aspect of their ethnic identities to massacre each other. In fact, the *Tejanos* were an amalgamation of Mexican and older Anglo families who had inter-married and lived in peace. Rather, Sàenz's point is that structural phenomena, changes to the global capitalist system involving the production of wool were at the heart of the ethnic conflict.

Kay Warren has recently argued for the "'centrality of cultural issues' in the study of organized violence" (1993: 1). Joan Vincent's contribution shows readers how such issues can be central in an analysis that links cultural to political and economic factors. She seeks to understand the civil war that has plagued Uganda almost since Independence. Specifically, she is interested in accounting for differences in the ferocity of the conflict, for she finds that the fighting conducted in more southerly areas was in a number of instances less brutal than that in the north. In an analysis blending Foucauldian and Gramscian insights with her own rich ethnography, Vincent shows how colonialism resulted in a cultural hegemony, one of whose properties was what might be termed a geographic consciousness, a consciousness that helped legitimate different levels of violence.

The concept of cultural hegemony, with a genealogy deriving from Antonio Gramsci via Raymond Williams and John and Jean Comaroff, is a useful tool for the analysis of the role of subjectivities in domination. Hegemony in Williams' influential definition is a "...system of meanings and values — constitutive and constituting — which as they are experienced as practices appear as reciprocally confirming" (1977: 118).[3] Specifically, hegemonic meanings, which tend "...to be taken for granted as the natural and received shape of the world..." (J & J Comaroff 1991: 23), construct peoples' subjectivities so that they will be more likely to consent to their domination. Colonial officials, according to Vincent, were interested in introducing agro-capitalist enterprises into Uganda to satisfy the needs of English industrial capitalism at home. These officials and their minions introduced a cultural hegemony in which things associated with capitalism were valued, while those not associated with it were devalued. Agro-enterprises introduced by the British were largely located in more southerly areas and included such export cash crops as coffee. More northerly areas were less touched, except as reservoirs of cheap labor.

Given the prevailing hegemony, people living in these two areas came to be conceptualized differently. Those in the south were seen as more modern and civilized, while those in the north were understood to be less modern and rather uncivilized. Here is the crucial point. This constitution of values, a veritable hegemonic geography of where the British had introduced capitalism, persisted into the postcolonial times. So when southern Ugandan commanders and soldiers campaigned against northerners in the north, they fought with greater fury, a ferocity in some measure determined by their consciousness of what awaited them in the heartland of the uncivilized. Vincent, thus, shows how a certain type of subjective phenomena, the cultural hegemonic geography, introduced to facilitate the introduction of capitalism into Uganda, acted to accelerate violence in certain regions of that country.

Turton takes readers to the isolated Omo River valley in Ethiopia, to a people called the Mursi. His analysis explores the effect of the acquisition of automatic weapons upon Mursi "traditional" warfare. A key question, however, is why do the Mursi, who live in an outback beyond the outback, suddenly find themselves massacring clan rivals with AK 47s and the like?

An answer to this question has to do with threats to industrial capitalism due to Communist expansion. Many people came to resist the domination they experienced under capitalism. One way they did so was to develop Communist ideologies, which helped to construct the subjectivities of those opposing capitalism. Such opposition was effective. Russia fell in 1917, much of eastern Europe went after 1945, and China was lost in 1949. Such events closed off enormous areas of the globe to capitalism and threatened to deny still more. This meant that by 1950 *the* primary threat to continued capitalist accumulation was Communist expansion. Such a threat had to be addressed on many levels, one of which was to call upon the assistance of governments to harass Communism politically.

One way this was done throughout the Third World was to arm opponents of the Communists, which, of course, motivated Communists to arm their supporters. One area where such an arms race was prosecuted vigorously was in the Horn of Africa. As a result, Ethiopia in the 1970s and 1980s became awash in weapons, some of which eventually trickled down to the Mursi.

Turton notes that when the Mursi finally got their guns, "tribal" warfare in the Omo River valley was part of a regional, inter-ethnic system of reciprocity involving the exchange of violence as well as goods. In such fighting an act of violence by a group must be reciprocated by those attacked. Once this reciprocation has occurred, it becomes the basis for restoring peace. Turton is especially insightful in showing how the introduction of automatic weapons acted as an accelerant to this system, one that, as was the case among the New Irelanders, unbalanced it. When the Mursi's opponents got machine guns, the Mursi had to get them or be annihilated. When all groups get these weapons the killing may be so inflated that they all will be threatened with extermination. However, should the Mursi be exterminated, it will not be because they were acting upon primordial antagonisms. Rather, it would be an unintended consequence of political decisions taken by officials of capitalist Great Powers to defend capitalism.

Mozambique became independent in 1975 as a result of a decade of war against Portuguese colonial rule. This anti-colonial revolt was conducted by a Marxist oriented Frelimo (*Frente de Libertação de Moçambique*). In the years immediately after independence, Frelimo instituted a Marxist-Leninist government dedicated to assisting liberation movements in Rhodesia and South Africa. Southern Africa, in general, is an area that has enormous quantities of natural resources. Moreover, the regional hegemon, South Africa, then operating under a racist Apartheid regime, was a country that both supplied a wide range of raw materials to U.S. and European capitalist enterprise and benefited from their substantial investments in its developing industrial sector. So capitalism stood to suffer big losses if southern Africa fell. Mozambique, then, in the late 1970s directly threatened capitalism in a region where losses would be great. Mozambique had to be neutralized, which was, of course, a task for governments in the region that favored capitalism.

Rhodesia formed and controlled a terrorist movement called Renamo (*Resistência Nacional de Moçambique*) with the covert, but strong, support of Great Britain and Portugal. After the white regime fell and Rhodesia became Zimbabwe with a left-leaning government, the prospects for capitalism in southern Africa seemed even more threatened. As a consequence, South Africa, encouraged by the Reagan administration, began an anti-Communist war throughout the region. Mozambique, of course, became one theater in this war. The South African military greatly strengthened Renamo around 1980, using it as their weapon in Mozambique.

Renamo's strategy was one of "dirty war," i.e., the use of terrorism against civilian populations. Nordstrom provides a phenomenology of such violence. She seeks to understand the experience of unimaginable butchery. For example, Renamo forced children to watch, or on occasion to perpetrate, the murder and cannibalism of family and friends. It commonly asked husbands and children to watch their wives and mothers being gang raped and murdered.

Nordstrom interprets such cultures of terror as rituals that are destructive of life-world viability. "Life-world" is a central subjective notion of the philosopher Husserl and is his concept of the everyday, unreflected upon experience of the way things are.[4] It is that part of a person's psyche that is like a computer's operating system. Without an operating system a computer cannot connect with its external environment. Without a life-world a person cannot connect with, in the sense of having experience of, reality. Nordstrom shows how eating one's mother, a horrific perversion of normal experience, tends to obliterate one's life-world; as one of her informants says, "Who am I? I am nothing." Such persons, with their subjectivities literally "deconstructed," and wandering in a world chaotic experience, simply cannot fight and hence could not oppose Renamo and their South African patrons.

Nordstrom suggests that Renamo's dirty war was waged more by "habit" than by "rational" strategy. This may well be true in certain instances. However, South African security forces took Renamo over in 1980 to suppress Communist threats to South African dominance and a whole way of life that had a capitalistic bias. Renamo made life so miserable in Mozambique that Frelimo backed off the business of exporting Marxist-Leninism to other countries and, for that matter, it pretty much curtailed anything that smacked of Communism in Mozambique. Dirty wars are cheap wars. So it seems that for relatively little money South Africa got Renamo to help contain the spread of Communism in a big region. This seems perfectly rational if one's goal is the maintenance of capitalism. It is, however, the rationale of savagery.

Mobs of one ethnicity have butchered those of other ethnicities in the Senegal River Valley since 1980. This fighting has pitted Maures from Mauritania against sub-Saharan ethnicities, especially Toucouleurs, who reside on both sides of the river in Senegal and Mauritania. Magistro explores the causes of this violence, which, however, appear to have little to do with ethnicity *per se*.

Since the 1970s there have been massive donor lending and foreign capital investment in the Senegal River valley. These funds have been used largely to construct an irrigation infrastructure. Once, while on a development mission to this region in 1980, a natty European Community official confided to me that such lending would give a "nice little boost" to European and other core nations' agro-industries. It turns out that he was right. The lending has stimulated sales for these firms. Such donor lending might be seen as a mechanism that allowed core governments to lend money, derived to a considerable extent from the taxes of their middle classes, to Mauritania and Senegal, which then spent it largely upon the products of European industry owned by wealthy capitalists. This is a public subsidy of private, capitalist enterprise. Ultimately such structural action helped provoke ethnic war.

Certain Maures are called *bidan* (white). Wealthy *bidan* control the Mauritanian government. They have lived in the recent past in the Sahara. However, they have come to realize that the enormous irrigation investments have conferred great value on the southern riverine areas. Consequently, *bidan* have used their government connections to expropriate lands from those who formerly exploited it. The latter are often Toucouleur, and the loss of their lands is a fighting matter to them. It is this expropriation that is at the heart of the ethnic conflict.

No person, or persons, consciously planned for Maure and non-Maure ethnicities to butcher each other. However, some officials did consciously plan river basin development, which they expected would provide, among other things, a "boost" to EC business. Unfortunately it was the unintended consequences of this rational planning that produced the irrational mob butcheries that have characterized the ethnic violence in the Senegal River valley.

Bonte extends Magistro's analysis of the Senegal River Valley to include other areas of the Sahel. His article reminds readers of the crucial roles of the postcolonial state and land tenure in the construction of ethnic identities and conflict; especially between herders and farmers. Specifically, he investigates countries — Mauritania, Niger, and Mali — whose governments are dominated by officials from either pastoral or agricultural ethnic groups.

In the Séno Mango region of Mali he shows that, as the commercialization of food production has occurred, it has for the most part benefited the agricultural Dogons at the expense of pastoral Fulani. This has allowed wealthier Dogon to purchase Fulani lands. Mali's government is dominated by people from farming ethnicities, and their national development projects in the Séno Mango have added to the expropriation of Fulani lands. The result has been an increased potential for Dogon/Fulani conflict as the latter have been increasingly marginalized.

Bonte reports on a somewhat similar situation in the interior delta of the Niger River. This is an area that has been a major source of dry-season pasture for herders throughout the central Sahel. Here the Malian government has again favored development programs that privilege farming. This has resulted in a situation where former pastoral areas are being given over to different forms of commercial farming, tending to marginalize people from herding ethnicities.

Bonte's third case comes from Tuareg areas of Mali and Niger. The Tuareg, of course, are the most famous of the saharan camel pastoralists. However, both Niger's and Mali's governments are dominated by farmers and have followed policies that have tended to expropriate Tuareg pastures. This ethnic marginalization has created a situation of conflict, one that has evolved to the stage of armed revolt.

The final region Bonte investigates is that of the Senegal River Valley. Mauritania is the only sahelian state whose officials derive predominantly from a herder ethnicity, that of the Maures. The Mauritanian government has used its powers to help wealthy *bidan* Maures expropriate the land of riverain farmers, especially the Toucouleurs, which they then use to set up commercial farming operations. This ethnic marginalization of riverain folk, as we already know from Magistro's piece, has produced inter-ethnic fighting.

A crucial point to grasp is that ethnic conflict does not result from deeply embedded, "traditional" pastoralist/farmer rancor. Rather, in the particular instances discussed it is derived from structural changes in the access to productive land that come about as governments seek to aid their supporters to get into the business of capitalist agriculture.

Shining Path, or *Sendero Luminoso*, is the popular name of the Peruvian Communist party, which, until the capture of its head, Abimael Guzman, had led an effective war against governmental regimes fighting to defend, among other things, Peruvian capitalism. Shining Path, perhaps because of its effectiveness, has inspired a considerable literature, mostly critical of its brutality. Mitchell argues that focusing attention purely upon the Shining Path has prevented an understanding of the social revolution of which it is but a part.

Since the 1940s Peru has evolved in the direction of an industrial capitalist society, one integrated into United States dominated trade and finance. This transformation, Mitchell's social revolution, has been accompanied by the ruin of peasant farming. This, in turn, has produced a high rural exodus, with former peasants becoming underemployed proletarians. Unfortunately, capitalism simply has not worked, at least in the sense of providing rising incomes and living standards to the vast majority of the population. In part this is because the Peruvian development is a late blooming, not especially competitive, form of industrial capitalism. In sum, Peru has experienced protracted economic crisis since the 1970s.

This crisis has obliged capital and labor to compete more vigorously for their respective shares of the national income. Capital, of course, has had the better of this competition, with its profits representing an increasing proportion of the national income. This means that labor's share, wages, has declined. A few wealthy capitalists have gotten still wealthier, while the vast bulk of the population has been impoverished. A society-wide escalation of both crime and violence has been a consequence of increased poverty. The Shining Path was but one manifestation of this violence. Thus the changes involved in the development of Peruvian capitalism have increased inequality and poverty. This has resulted in violence — be it that of criminals against their victims, the state against its people, or of the Shining Path and other revolutionary groups against the state.

Is the Peruvian case a portent of the future of much of the rest of the world, especially the part that got a late start on capitalism? Such states are obliged by the International Monetary Fund or the World Bank to develop capitalism in ways that decrease equality and increase poverty. Peru has been down this "shining path," and it has descended into an inferno of violence. It is time to move out of this realm of hell and into that of phantasmagoric representation and then, perhaps, out of the phantasmic into a clearer apprehension of modern war.

III

Remember, from the beginning of the introduction, that a phantasmagoria is "...a...sucession of things...imagined (as in a dream...)." The articles just discussed provide grounds for separating dreaming from fact and suggest that three commonly held approaches to understanding modern war do strain towards the phantasmagoric.

Let us begin with the oldest, most persistent, at least in the Western intellectual tradition, approach to the explanation of war, which was first articulated in ancient Greece by Thucydides in his *The Peloponnesian War* (1949) to account for wars between Athens and Sparta in the fifth century B.C. It was introduced into modern discourse by Thomas Hobbes in *Leviathan* (1968 [1651]) during the seventeenth century. Thinkers hewing to the Thucydides-Hobbes line believe that warfare — any warfare, modern or otherwise — is an expression of natural human impulses, with "natural" here understood to mean pertaining to biology. War occurs, according to this view, as Hobbes pungently put it, because the natural state of people is "...warre of every man against every man..." (1968: 188). This approach might be called "naturalist," and it is so tenacious because for many people it is hegemonic. Of course, there will always be war: "It is human to hate" (Huntington 1996: 130).

Since the 1950s this position has been given an explicitly evolutionary biological twist, of which there are now two variants. One of these, argued by Ardrey (1961) and Lorenz (1966), has it that selective pressures favored the evolution of pugnacious humans, "natural born killers," whose innate ferocity provoked wars. Another view, the most recent, proposed by Ehrenreich, has it that before people were predators they were prey, and that war is an expression of going from the hunted to the hunter. Specifically, she argues that "...the emotions we bring to war are derived in an evolutionary sense from..." what she terms "...a primal battle...," the prey-to-predator transition (1997: 95). These emotions are "ecstasy" (ibid.: 14) and "thrill" (ibid.: 17). Further, war is pretty much a religious ritual of blood sacrifice, and such rituals — whipping celebrants up to thrilling heights of ecstasy — "...both celebrate and terrifyingly reenact the human transition from prey to predator, and so...does war..." (ibid.: 22).

The evolutionary biological versions of the naturalist approach to war have been roundly criticized within sociocultural anthropology (see Alland 1973 and Montagu 1973 and 1976). There have been a number of lines of criticism. The most fundamental is that evidence supporting evolutionary biological accounts tends to be weak. For example, Ehrenreich's argument depends, among other things, on having those who are involved in war feeling the thrill of ecstasy. However, none of the articles in this volume reports the faintest hint of rapture among combatants and non-combatants in the conflicts they analyze. Further, the vast bulk of the literature dealing with war fails to report that people experience war as ecstasy. It might be countered that none of the contributors to this volume was looking at the emotions of war and so did not mention them. However, if war was such a big thrill it might be expected that its observers would report it.

They don't. Rather, what they do mention are facts like that narrated by Nordstrom for Renamo, that it obliged children to cannabalize their parents. Where is the bliss in such ingestion? Or they brag, as did one Assyrian ruler, that,

> I felled 3,000 of their fighting men with the sword. I carried off prisoners, possessions, oxen (and) cattle from them. I captured many troops alive: I cut off some of their arms (and) hands; I cut off of others their noses, ears, (and) extremities. I gouged out the eyes of many troops. I made one pile of the living (and) one of the heads. I hung their heads on trees around the city. I burnt their adolescent boys (and) girls. I razed, destroyed, burnt (and) consumed...(Grayson 1972: 176).

Realities of daddy and mommy for lunch, gouged eyes, heads decorating trees, with the teen population roasting in merrily, crackling fires evoke dread. Is it any wonder that Ehrenreich informs her readers that her "...standards of proof...are hardly as firm as those that prevail in the natural sciences..." (1997: 4); or that one reviewer, Ignatieff, commenting on her work should hail it as "a tour de force" of *"hypothetical* anthropology" (1997: 12; emphasis added).

How do the findings of our essays bear upon the naturalist position in general? *None* of the articles supports it. In each case institutions of the capitalist state, institutions influenced by the capitalist state, or subjectivities constructed by these institutions, do the job of provoking war. The determinant or accelerant of violence is never biological. A final point to appreciate concerns Ehrenreich's scholarly representation of war. Popular culture in novels, television, and movies portrays war as exciting and glorious. *Star Trek, Aliens, Independence Day*, and the like, teach viewers to thrill to the kill of the alien Other. The U.S. is an advanced capitalist state. Such states, our contributors show, are deeply involved in war. Ehrenreich's scholarly cultural views converge with those of popular culture. She, and the movies, are in the business of constructing subjectivities in which it is pretty much taken for granted that war is a glorious rush. The existence of such subjectivities would seem to help the U.S. go about its military activities. Let us consider a second popular approach to explaining contemporary wars.

Officials, journalists, and scholars, as they contemplate the Northern Irelands and Bosnias of this world, often blame contemporary war upon "essentialist" tribal or ethnic antagonisms. Essentialist views of social groups are those that specify that groups have primordial, in the sense of immanent, attributes that are their fixed and unchanging essence.[5] Many believe that the current spate of ethnic or, more journalistically, "tribal" wars have resulted because these groups, today's savage Other, are essentially antagonistic towards each other. This is a second "ethnic essentialist" approach to the explanation of modern war.

However, the New Irelanders and Mursi did not start killing ethnic enemies at higher rates because of essentialist antipathies. Rather, more prosaically, they got guns, which allowed them to kill more. Sàenz's evidence shows that *Tejanos* and Anglos did not always hate each other. Rather, for a considerable period the reverse appears to have been the case. However, violence erupted when the position of the *Tejanos* rapidly deteriorated in the capitalist world economy. Similarly the ethnic groups described by Magistro and Bonte that are at each other's throats in the Sahel have been made competitors over land. The case of Mozambique is the most striking. Its utter bestiality has nothing to do with tribal antagonisms, and everything to do with the governments of capitalist states fighting threats to capitalism, and doing this fighting through dirty wars devised by agents of these states.

Additionally, there is a considerable literature arguing that the spate of "ethnic" wars since the 1980s in Bosnia, India, Sri Lanka, Central Asia, Sudan, Rwanda, and Somalia are the result of the deliberate construction of antagonistic ethnic identities by political leaders seeking to control these states, often with the conivance of agents of advanced industrial capitalist states.[6] This suggests that those marketing ethnic essentialism — dreaming that all ethnic groups hate each other as the savage Other — peddle a phantasmagoria.

Let us end by considering a particular contention of a third approach, that of classic social theory's insistence upon the pacific nature of capitalist states. Reyna's article, however, argues that what gave the modern state its distinctive quality was the evolution between 1415 and 1763 of a military-capitalist complex — military institutions in governments co-dependent with those of capitalism in civil society — that warred to assist in capital accumulation, and then used this capital to increase military capabilities, i.e., to facilitate predatory accumulation. Rosman and Rubel document how the accelerated war in the tribal zone of New Ireland was the result of the arrival of capitalist institutions from an expanding German state. Sàenz believes the rebellion in early twentieth century Texas was in part determined by competition between two form of capitalist agro-enterprise. Turton's data suggest that the acceleration of Mursi fighting was, in part, a consequence of the operation of government institutions protecting capitalist interests during the Cold War.

Magistro's argument may be interpreted as suggesting that Senegal River valley ethnic fighting has been partially determined by European Community government operations in support of the profits of their agro-enterprises. Bonte accounted for heightened ethnic tension throughout the Sahel as a result of African governments' taking sides between ethnic groups, helping some at the expense of others, especially with access to land that could then be utilized for capitalist farming. Mitchell sees the civil war in Peru as in part the effect of the increased poverty and inequality resulting from its late, industrial capitalist development. Vincent and Nordstrom deal with the realm of subjectivities. They show how colonial government (in the case of Uganda) and postcolonial government (in that of Mozambique) took actions that constructed their peoples' subjectivities by creating cultural hegemonies or life-worlds. These subjectivities, then, disposed peoples to greater violence.

Thus, the conclusions of the different articles support the following generalization. Structural and subjective factors found in, or associated with, capitalist states help determine or accelerate the types of war found in the modern world. This means that any representation of capitalist states as pacific is delusional. Additionally, I have shown how naturalist and ethnic essentialist accounts tend to induce the sweet dreams of phantasmagoria.

IV

Let us place these generalizations within a broader context, that of the history of modern war since the emergence of industrial capitalism, in order to draw a broader conclusion. The capitalist states that had developed in Atlantic Europe by the eighteenth century were killing machines. Roughly seventy to eighty percent of their budgets were spent to pay the expenses of ongoing wars and the debts of past wars (Mann 1986). Industrial capitalist states began to emerge outside of their original crucible in Atlantic Europe during the nineteenth century. One of these, Germany, developed a different version of the military-capitalist complex, based in part on a vastly more lethal industrial weaponry, and fought its way to territorial conquest throughout central and western continental Europe. Two other newcomers, the U.S. and Japan, joined Great Britain and France toward the end of the century in the use of the new weaponry to butcher non-capitalist peoples in North America, Africa, the Middle East, East Asia, and the Pacific. The term "butcher" in the previous sentence is appropriate. Enormous numbers of peoples fighting with spears and swords were slaughtered by those with automatic weapons and heavy artillery. Some of these wars, especially those against native Americans, were genocidal because they led to the extermination of whole peoples (see Stannard 1992 and Todorov 1984). They made it possible, however, for capitalist states first to free lands for capitalist development and then to supply raw materials and markets needed for this development.

The first half of the twentieth century was dominated by the most cataclysmic war the world has seen. World Wars I and II were a Second Thirty Year War that ran from 1914 to 1945. In it, younger capitalist states, Japan and Germany, fought older capitalist states, Great Britain and France. Perhaps as many as ninety million people were killed as a result of the conflict (Mandel 1986: 169). The U.S. emerged from it with by far the most powerful military-capitalist complex. It, not Germany or Japan, became the greatest of the Great Leviathans, and ever since there have been wars for the U.S. to fight and people to kill. Between 1946 and 1976 there were 120 wars. The U.S. intervened, overtly or covertly, in roughly 42% of these (Kende 1978).

It is time to step back and smell the daisies. First remember that many works in popular culture strive to convince folk that war is thrilling, while, at the same time, many contributors to scholarly culture labor to persuade us that it is natural, a natural high, or a product of the unchangeable reflexes of ethnic, alien Others. Such popular, naturalist, and ethnic essentialist representations construct subjectivities that take a kindly view of war as a natural thing, a good thrill, or a regretable necessity in a world of antagonistic, ethnic Aliens. Such representations make notions of war hegemonic, because, though they quibble over the nature and causes of war, they are based upon an unreflected upon, taken-for-granted, premise that people should be disposed towards war. Of course, such hegemonic notions help furnish capitalist states with a supply of culturally constructed killers.

Remember, however, that popular, naturalist, and ethnic essentialist depictions of war are phantasmagoric representations that hide an actuality. The reality is that there have been deadly developments along the highways and byways of capitalist states. These states — sometimes intentionally, often unintentionally, through intricate webs of causation involving government and capitalist institutions and the subjectivities they have constructed — have been instruments of internal and international war. The savage Other is (capitalist) us. The grossest delusion may be to ignore this reality, for if one does, one may not be around to smell the daisies.

NOTES

1. Comte said, "no enlightened mind disputes the continual decline of the military spirit, and the gradual ascendency of the industrial" (1957: 166).

Spencer made Comte's observation a central part of his theories (1896). Engels believed that war would negate itself when capitalism evolved into socialism (1955: 239–40). Durkheim stated that war became "...more intermittent and less common" (1957: 53) in industrial societies. Giddens has noted classic social theory's faith in the pacificity of capitalist states (1985).
2. Ferguson and Farragher (1988) have written a useful guide to the literature of the anthropology of war. Nagengast (1994) has reviewed studies concerned with violence as it pertains to the state.
3. There is a considerable literature concerning Gramscian hegemony, to which an especially useful introduction is Lears (1985). A distinction should be made between cultural and other forms of hegemony. "Cultural hegemony" is about cognition that reproduces domination *within* a state. Other forms of hegemony refer to situations where one state has the power to influence other states. This latter notion is about domination *between* states.
4. Husserl's life-world is, perhaps, best first approached in *The Crisis of European Sciences and Transcendental Phenomenology* (1970). It was introduced into social thought by Schutz (1972). Life-worlds are, in part, a product of past cultural traditions. Absent in the notion of life-world, as opposed to that of cultural hegemony, is any sense that a life-world might help to reproduce the domination of certain groups within a society.
5. The view of essentialism offered in the text is that of Aristotle (Fetzer and Almeder 1993: 47). Essentialist views of ethnic violence are expressed more often than not by those in governmental and journalistic communities. However, the political scientist A. D. Smith believes that "ethnicity is largely 'mythic' and 'symbolic,' and..., once formed,... exceptionally durable..." (1986: 16). This is a rather essentialist view of ethnicity. An essentialist view of ethnic conflict in the former Yugoslavia, based upon Smith's understanding of ethnicity, might assert that part of the myth of what it is to be a Serb is that Serbs hate Croats and so the two groups fight frequently.
6. For alternatives to ethnic essentialist accounts readers might consult Denich (1993) and Kideckel and Halpern (1993) on Bosnia; Lessinger (1994) on India; Schoeberlein-Engel (1994) on central Asia; Tambiah (1986) on Sri Lanka; Erny (1994) on Rwanda; Deng (1994) on Sudan; and Ahmed (1995) on Somalia.

REFERENCES

Ahmed, A. J. (1995). The Invention of Somalia. Lawrenceville, NJ: Red Sea Press.

Alland, A. (1973). The Human Imperative. New York: Columbia University Press.

Ardrey, R. (1961). African Genesis. New York: Bantam.
Comaroff, J. and J. Comaroff (1991). Of Revelation and Revolution. Chicago: University of Chicago Press.
Comte, A. (1975). The Foundations of Sociology. New York: Wiley.
Denich, B. (1993). Dismembering Yugoslavia: Nationalist Ideologies and the Symbolic Revival of Genocide. The State Under Siege Conference. New York: New York Academy of Sciences.
Deng, F. (1994). Conflicts of Identities in the "War of Visions." Washington: Brookings.
Durkheim, E. (1957). Professional Ethics and Civic Morals. London: Routledge.
Engels, F. (1955). Anti-Dühring. London: Lawrence and Wishart.
Ehrenreich, B. (1997). Blood Rites: Origins and History of the Passions of War. New York: Holt.
Erny, P. (1994). Rwanda, 1994. Paris: Harmattan.
Ferguson, R. B. and L. Farragher (1988). The Anthropology of War: An Annotated Bibliography. New York: Harry Frank Guggenheim Foundation.
Ferguson, R. B. and N. Whitehead (1992). Warfare in the Tribal Zone: Expanding States and Indigenous Warfare. Santa Fe: School of American Research.
Fetzer, J. A. and R. F. Almeder (1993). Glossary of Epistemology/Philosphy of Science. New York: Paragon House.
Giddens, A. (1985). The Nation-State and Violence. Los Angeles: University of California Press.
Grayson, Albert (1972). Assyrian Royal Inscriptions. Wiesbaden: Harrassowitz.
Hobbes, T. (1968 [1651]). Leviathan. Harmondsworth, UK: Penguin.
Huntington, S. M. (1996). The Clash of Civilizations. New York: Simon and Schuster.
Husserl, E. (1970). The Crisis of European Sciences and Transcendental Phenomenology. Evanston, IL: Northwestern University Press.
Ignatieff, M. (1997). The Gods of War. New York Review of Books XLIV: 10–13 (Oct. 9).
Kende, I. (1978). Wars of Ten Years (1967–76). Journal of Peace Research 3: 227–241.
Kideckel, D. A. and J. M. Halpern, eds. (1993). War Among the Yugoslavs. Special Issue: Anthropology of East Europe Review 11.
Lears, T. J. J. (1985). The Concept of Cultural Hegemony: Problems and Possibilities. American Historical Review 9: 567–593.
Lessinger, H. (1994). Hindu Nationalism, Fascism, and Anti-Muslim Violence in India. The State Under Siege Conference. New York: New York Academy of Sciences.
Lorenz, K. (1966). On Aggression. New York: Harcourt Brace.
Mandel, E. (1986). The Meaning of the Second World War. London: Verso.
Mann, M. (1986). The Sources of Social Power. Vol. 1. Cambridge: Cambridge University Press.

Montagu, A., ed. (1973). Man and Aggression. Oxford: Oxford University Press.
———— (1976). The Nature of Human Aggression. Oxford: Oxford University Press.
Nagengast, C. (1994). Violence, Terror, and the Crisis of the State. Annual Reviews of Anthropology 23: 109–36.
Reyna, S. P. (1994). A Mode of Domination Approach to Organized Violence. *In* Studying War, Anthropological Perspectives. S. P. Reyna and R. E. Downs, eds. Newark, NJ: Gordon and Breach.
Schoeberlein-Engel (1994). Toppling the Balance: The Creation of "Interethnic" War in Tajikistan. The State Under Seige Conference. New York: New York Academy of Sciences.
Schutz, A. (1972). The Phenomenology of the Social World. London: Heineman.
Smith, A. D. (1986). The Ethnic Origins of Nations. Oxford: Blackwell.
Spencer, H. (1896). The Principles of Sociology. New York: Appleton and Co.
Stannard, D. (1992). America Holocaust. Oxford: Oxford University Press.
Tambiah, S. (1986). Sri Lanka: Ethnic Fratricide and the Dismantling of Democracy. Chicago: University of Chicago Press.
Thucydides (1949). The Peloponnesian War. Oxford: Oxford University Press.
Todorov, T. (1984). The Conquest of America: The Question of the Other. New York: Harper Row.
Warren, K. B. (1993). Introduction. *In* The Violence Within: Cultural and Political Opposition in Divided Nations. K. B. Warren, ed. Boulder, CO: Westview.
Webster's International Dictionary (1966). Springfield, MA: Merriams
Williams, R. (1977). Marxism and Literature. Oxford: Oxford University Press.

Chapter ONE

The Force of Two Logics: Predatory and Capital Accumulation in the Making of the Great Leviathan, 1415–1763

S. P. Reyna
Anthropology Program
University of New Hampshire

Have you ever wondered, how do you build a "great Leviathan;" with it recognized that Leviathan was Thomas Hobbes' term for the state; and with it further understood that the most successful modern variant of it has been the *capitalist* state. This article builds the Leviathan for readers by bringing them to the places where (Atlantic Europe) and the times when (1415–1763) the capitalist state was first constituted. It argues that Great Britain developed a military-capitalist complex that allowed it, more effectively than was the case with its competitors, to conduct war so that greater profits would be made, and to use these profits so that more war could be waged. The operation of this complex allowed England by 1763 to become a behemoth with global powers.

Thomas Hobbes published *Leviathan* in 1651, beginning modern English discourse concerning the state. Hobbes' state consisted of the "Soveraigne" and the "Subject" in a dominion (1968: 228). I accept this Hobbesian notion of a state as a sovereign government and a subject civil society, and my concern in the present article is to introduce an approach that helps to explain the emergence of the modern version of this Leviathán. So, in a sense, I tell a whale of a story, but do so using the logical approach introduced below.

The "logics" of what I call the new social anthropology, as opposed to those of mathematics, concern directions taken as a result of complex actions, with it understood that "complexes" are groups of institutions in which force is concentrated.[1] There have been logics of "capital accumulation" that move in the direction of increasing and concentrating capital force in capitalist complexes. There have also been logics of "predatory accumulation" that move in the direction of increasing and concentrating violent force within government complexes. Scholars have recognized that changes internal to Atlantic European states' capitalist complexes increased their capital accumulation and were influential in the emergence of the modern state. Few scholars have contemplated any such role for predatory accumulation, and systematic analysis of the relationships *between* the two logics in the making of the Leviathan has been virtually ignored. I argue in this article that a military-capitalist complex, based upon two mutually reinforcing logics of predatory and capital accumulation, contributed to the formation of the modern state because the complex allowed the reciprocating logics to produce more violent and capital force than was possible when they operated alone. The military capitalist complex, then, might be imagined as a sort of structural steroid that bulked up stately whales into Hobbes' "great Leviathan," a creature with the forces of a "mortal God" (1968: 227) that — luckily for England — turned out by 1763 to be England.

The plausibility of this view is established by documenting just how England became a "great Leviathan." The documentation proceeds in four parts. The first section shows how medieval states employed a form of predatory accumulation between A.D. 950 and A.D. 1400. It also explains why predatory and capital accumulation were not mutually reinforcing during this time. The second section relates how the Iberian expansion (A.D. 1415–A.D. 1566) involved a new variety of predatory accumulation that stimulated capital accumulation. Further discussed is why Spain, the senior partner in this expansion, was unable to make the two accumulations mutually reinforcing. The third and fourth sections document the history of the original formation of the military-capitalist complex. The third section proposes that a military-capitalist complex was instituted in Holland, ironically in part due to Spain's own attempt to make the two accumulations mutually reinforcing in the period 1566 through 1648. Then, the fourth section specifies how England in the late seventeenth century instituted a better military-capitalist complex that allowed it by the end of the eighteenth century to become the first modern "great Leviathan." A goal of this article is to demonstrate how the anthropological approach used in the text can nudge anthropology out of an obsession with the exotica of particular cock-fights and into more general and frankly more important questions like, how did the Leviathan of modernity originate? A reply to this question is offered in the conclusion, an answer that is an elaboration upon a penetrating insight of Eric Wolf.

I

Historians have conventionally dated the beginning of European expansion at around A.D. 1500. Such dating is dated. R. Bartlett notes that "...between 950 and 1350 Latin Christendom roughly doubled in area..." due to "...conquest, colonization and associated cultural change..." (1993: 3).[2] This expansion largely originated from the area of the old Carolingian empire. It included the conquests by Norman nobility in the British isles and the Mediterranean; by Burgundian and other French nobility, allied with different Iberian dynasties, in the *reconquista* of the Iberian peninsula; and by German-speaking nobles eastward into the Baltic and Polish regions. Finally, the crusades were the eastern-most, and least enduring, expression of this expansion. Bartlett has suggested that this growth involved "...a process of..." societal "replication..." (ibid.: 307). I agree, though I believe that

Barlett's "replication" may be reinterpreted as an expansion of fiscal domination in feudal fields through predatory accumulation. It is necessary when documenting this assertion first to introduce the concepts of fields and domination, then to discuss the distribution of violent force in feudal fields, and finally to consider how fiscal domination augmented that force.

"Fields" are distributions of complexes of institutions with force. The fields explored in this article are those of states. Violent force in feudal fields was decentralized because of the existence of lord/vassal relationships. A higher noble, the lord, would grant land, a fief (or estate), to a lower noble, who as a result became a vassal. Vassals in return paid homage and swore fealty to their lord, which meant that they owed them services, especially military ones. Feudal military units were called "hosts," and consisted of lords and their vassals. Vassals sometimes had their own vassals, who had their own fiefs. Lords and vassals had wide authority (administrative, fiscal, and judicial) within their fiefs, so that these, in effect, were mini-governments. A collection of vassals who swore fealty to a particular overlord was spoken of as the realm of such and such a sovereign. Feudal fields were a topology of mini-governments in realms. Violent force in such fields was decentralized and distributed among "...the...small armies of wealthy and powerful lords" (Thompson and Johnson 1937: 297).

It is time now to explore how violent force was augmented in feudal fields. Notions of regimes and fiscal domination need to be introduced in order to understand this augmentation. Force is only concentrated in certain institutions within a complex. Violent force, for example, is only concentrated in military institutions in a governmental complex. "Regimes" are institutions in complexes that help the force-concentrating institutions in the complex to acquire or exercise that force. "Domination," in the context of the present analysis, is a situation where a complex possesses the force to have regularly some power over other institutions in the former complex's field. "Fiscal regimes" are those that help governmental complexes acquire forces that can be derived from revenues. Different forms of domination can be named after the force ultimately conferring domination. "Fiscal domination," for example, refers to powers resulting from revenue flows to government complexes.

Four attributes distinguish fiscal regimes in feudal fields. First, the revenues were uncentralized. There was no procedure that sent the realm's revenues to the king or queen at the center. Rather "rulers," as Strayer notes, "...drew the supplies they needed from their own estates..." (1982: 28). Second, most revenues were extracted from agricultural workers within the fief and were either in the form of agricultural labor or products. Third, the revenues went to feed and outfit soldiers who were the lord's retainers, his or her vassals, and the vassals' retainers. Fourth, commerce and manufacturing tended to be taxed lightly. This was because medieval fiscal regimes evolved prior to A.D. 1000, when there was little in the way of trade or crafts, so little effort was made to collect what were then unimportant revenue sources. In the later Middle Ages, commerce and industry developed in towns. However, urban areas often remained untaxed or lightly taxed. This was the situation, for example, in the medieval Netherlands, where the seventeen provinces that roughly corresponded to contemporary Holland, Belgium and Luxembourg could only be taxed with their concurrence. Thus nobles had no automatic way of securing revenues from merchants and manufacturers.[3]

Because the main service the lord's retainers and vassals provided was military, the more vassals a lord had, the more violent force he had available, and hence the more power. This meant, as Perry Anderson recognized, that the "classical object" of medieval war was the acquisition of "geographical territory" (1979: 58), since new lands allowed a lord to make new fiefs and thus to acquire new retainers and vassals. So wars of geographic conquest accounted for Bartlett's expansion. These worked as follows. A lord would recruit a host, usually from the lesser nobility who would not inherit or marry into land. Often these followers included the personal retainers of the host's leader as well as others hoping to be enfeoffed for their labors. Once organized, this host would conquer new territory, usually on some frontier. The newly acquired land would then be distributed. Some of it might go to enlarge the domain of the overlord who led the venture. This would give him more food-producers from whom he might exact additional dues. Other newly conquered lands would be given to the followers as their new fiefs. William's conquest of Anglo-Saxon England (A.D. 1066) was perhaps the most famous of such operations.

What was happening here was that an initial increase in violent force, due to the original recruiting of warriors for the host, led to the seizure of new land. This allowed the lord who directed the host to have more personal land and more vassals with fiefs. This increased his or her revenues, leading to increased fiscal domination. These additional revenues meant more personal retainers and vassals who formed the basis of still larger hosts. The logic, then, of this medieval expansion was clearly one of predatory accumulation where accumulations of the lords' violent force were exercised to expand fiscal domination to increase violent force.

Capital accumulation was brisk by the end of the Middle Ages in part because lordly conquests created new commercial opportunities. Capital domination, powers resulting from capital flows to capitalist complexes, began to expand, especially in urban areas where the capital flowed. However, it should be appreciated that this capital accumulation was not mutually reinforcing of predatory accumulation, because "urban economies" in feudal fields were "freed" from the "...direct domination by a ruling class" (Anderson 1979: 21). This was manifest in the fact that merchants went either un- or undertaxed in medieval fiscal regimes. This meant that increased incomes for merchants did not invariably become increased revenues for nobles. It is now time to consider the beginning of the expansion of European fiscal and capitalist domination beyond Europe.

II

"In Spain...the ruling classes managed the Conquest as they had the *reconquista*, namely, *in the feudal manner*" (Vilar 1974: 105; emphasis in the original).

A first phase of this expansion, largely an Iberian affair, ran between 1415, the year of Portugal's first conquests in Morocco, and 1566, when the Netherlands revolted against Philip II of Spain. This expansion, as the above quotation makes clear, has been thought of as "feudal." My sense is that such an assertion is only partly correct and that it is important to distinguish what was new from what was old in order to ascertain what was actually feudal in the Iberian expansion. Below I suggest that a new type of predatory accumulation — more deadly and more costly — in a newly emerging type of fields greatly stimulated capital accumulation, but that an older, more feudal, fiscal regime frustrated making the two logics mutually reinforcing.

The violent force exercised in the Iberian expansion was organized in something of a "feudal manner." De Oliveira Marques, speaking of the Portuguese Prince Henry, famous for organizing the voyages of discovery during the first half of the fifteenth century, says that the Prince's interest in these voyages was that of an overlord who "...primarily regarded [the voyages] as a way of increasing his patrimony and rents..." (1972: 143–44). Further, Spanish *conquistadores*, according to the 16th century historian Valdes, "...were vassals of the Kings..." (in Stein and Stein 1970: 12) who tended to be drawn from the lower levels of the noble, *hidalgo* class. Hernando Cortes, the conqueror of Mexico, was of a noble but impoverished family. Elliot says that he, "...like any *caballero* of medieval Castile, aspired to obtain a fief and vassals, to secure a title..." which he did, and so "...ended his life as *Marqués del Valle de Oaxaca*..." (Elliot 1964: 54). Thus by conquering Mexico, Cortes achieved his aspirations and became, according to his friend and confidant Bernal Diaz, a "*gran senor*" (a "great noble") (Elliot 1964: 54). The preceding seems to support Vilar. Prince Henry and Cortes, lord and vassal, were acting out the old, feudal logic of predatory accumulation in the New World.

However, the fields that were being built were *not* feudal. Rather, they were what might be termed "centralizing" because in both Spain and Portugal, territories added by conquest, or other means, became part of a central government organized around the crown, a ruling dynasty. Consider, for example, the case of Spain. During the reign of Ferdinand and Isabella (1479–1516), Castile, Aragon, Navarre, and Granada in Iberia, as well as parts of North Africa and the New World came to be ruled, though in different ways, by the throne. Ferdinand, towards the end of his reign, would claim that "the crown of Spain has not for over 700 years been as great or as resplendent as it now is" (in Kamen 1991: 9). Then, under Charles V (1519–1556), grandson of Ferdinand and Isabella and inheritor of the Habsburg dynasty, territories that included much of the Austrian empire, Italy, France, and the Netherlands were joined to the Spanish throne. It seemed to Charles' Grand Chancellor, Gattinara, as if a "world monarchy" had been created (in Kennedy 1987: 545).

To some degree, all the different regions in Charles' realm were permitted to conserve their own, medieval forms of governance. This has led one commentator to assert that there "never was" a Spanish empire (Pagden 1990: 3). Such an assertion is deceptive, because Ferdinand and Isabella, and later Charles, overlaid local institutions with a single central government.[4] It was equally true that they strove mightily to increase the power of this government against all others within their realm. Such centralization might be called institutional transformation by bricolage; keep the old, add the new. Nevertheless, a trend was unmistakable. This was a return to the sort of centralized government that had occurred in Spain during Roman times, where a single central government extended its domination throughout an expanding governmental complex. Stately fields, then, during the time of Iberian expansion were characterized by the gradual elimination of the lord/vassal mini-governments and their replacement by centralizing dynastic monarchies, such as the Tudors in England, the Valois in France, and — most successful of all — the Habsburg in Spain. It was for this reason that Ferdinand bragged about the size of his kingdom and others spoke of "world monarchy."

Centralization of power in these fields of dynastic monarchies involved the mobilization of military forces and the attacking of some area in Europe, Asia, or the New World. The resulting conquests resulted in increased crown revenues, which made it possible for the crowns to mobilize still greater military force. This was predatory accumulation. However, it was a new variety of such accumulation distinguished from that in the Middle Ages by the nature of its violent force and the manner in which this force was increased. These novelties are considered below.

Three attributes define the nature of violent force in dynastic monarchies. The first of these had to do with the means of destruction. Medieval violent force had largely relied upon hand-held weapons — lances and swords — whose ability to hurt was dependent on the prowess of the noble wielding them. There is agreement that there was a "military revolution" at the end of the Middle Ages based on gunpowder.[5] My sense is that what made this violent force so revolutionary was that it made prowess obsolete. A lowly villein firing a canon could pulp a lord of the noblest prowess and then, for good measure, blast his castle into smithereens. The remaining two attributes of this violent force pertained to how it was acquired. Weapons in the Middle Ages were for the most part fashioned by artisans on the lord's manor. Soldiers, already armed by these artisans, were supplied as part of the vassal's obligations to the lord. No money changed hands. Violent force did not have to be purchased. This had all changed by the time of the Iberian expansion. The crown had to go out into the market to purchase canons, ships, and soldiers who now, for the most part, were mercenaries. Additionally, there was a "price revolution" in Europe during the first half of the sixteenth century that involved rapid and great price inflation (Hamilton 1932). The second and third attributes of early modern violent force, then, were that the vastly more violent means of destruction were acquired through purchase and were increasingly expensive.

The fact that governments could only acquire violent force by purchasing it had great implications for how violent force was expanded. Predatory accumulation occurred entirely *within* the complex of governmental institutions in the Middle Ages. This was impossible in early modern times. When government officials bought weapons they did so from merchants who had themselves spent money to make, or purchase, them, and who fully intended to sell their weapons to officials at prices that exceeded their costs. These merchants, then, planned to make a profit and thereby to accumulate capital. Predatory accumulation could not occur within the complex of governmental institutions. For the first time a governmental complex was linked to a capitalist complex: such that for the former to get what it had to have, violent force, the latter had to get what it had to have, capital force.

So, unlike the feudal lords, who fought to acquire land to acquire serfs from whom agricultural surplus could be extracted to arm and feed soldiers, the Iberian crowns fought to get their hands on anything they could sell. By the mid sixteenth century, Portugal had "...fought the naval engagements..." that allowed it to create "...the one new major artery of world trade from Asia to Europe" (Modelski and Thompson 1988: 157). Thus was born "...a fruitful partnership between trade and conquest..." (Rahn-Phillips 1990: 48), because the crown, by the middle 1500s, controlled much of the world spice trade (Oliveira Marques 1972: 217–218). Spain also used war to generate trade (Lang 1975). There was an eightfold increase in Spanish trans-Atlantic trade between 1510 and 1580 and a threefold increase again between 1550 and 1610 (Wallerstein 1976: 117). Much of this commerce was in bullion.

This trade, as was that of Portugal, was in principle a crown monopoly, which meant that it was not part of the early modern capitalist complex. Rather it was part of the Spanish and Portuguese complex of governmental institutions. Portugal created the *Casa da India* as part of the central government. The *Casa* purchased spices in the east and resold them, largely to merchants in Antwerp, for money that became crown revenues. Similarly, Spanish officials created the *Casa de la Contratacion de las Indias* to perform the same function as the Portuguese *Casa*. However, once the two *Casa* had sold their merchandise they entered the complex of capitalist institutions, because merchants took the crown products and resold them for their own profits. Here, then, was a second way that the early modern Iberian governmental complex was linked to the capitalist complex.

There was a third way in which the Spanish governmental complex, in particular, was linked to that of the capitalists. The *Casa de la Contratacion de las Indias* was "...merely a vast contracting out system..." (Pearson 1991: 81) that would license private enterprise — Genoan, French, or, most often, Netherlander financiers or merchants — to do the crown's work in exchange for a percentage of the sales. The royal cut might be quite high. Roughly 25% of royal revenues came from bullion in the sixteenth century (ibid.: 82). Thus, what was supposed to be a governmental trade, at least for the Spanish, never really was.

It is important to grasp how well this new form of predatory accumulation worked. Portuguese crown revenues expanded enormously during the sixteenth century (Godinho 1944). The revenues of Charles V tripled during his reign, while those of his successor, Philip II (1556–98) doubled in the period 1556–73 alone (Lynch 1991: 128). Increased revenues permitted royal accumulation of the new violent force. Especially significant was the development of naval force in which Portugal took the lead, developing in the years between 1430 and 1515 the caravel, the carrack, the *nau*, and finally the galleon. Portugal had no large warships in service in 1470; by 1537 it had a total of 40 such ships distributed from Lisbon to the Indian ocean and beyond to the straights of Malacca (Modelski and Thompson 1988: 173). The number of soldiers in armies of the Spanish crown increased roughly tenfold during the sixteenth century, growing from about 20,000 soldiers in 1470 to 150,000 by 1550 and 200,000 by 1590 (Kennedy 1987: 56). Clearly, this was a logic of predatory accumulation, one where expenditures of violent force led to increased fiscal domination which allowed increases in the crown's violent force. However, as we have seen, predatory accumulation was impossible without capital accumulation. This means that war was good for those doing business, which poses the question: was business good to those doing war?

An answer to this question depends on the discussion of two matters: where business was being conducted and what happened to Spain's fiscal regime. The geographic locus of capital accumulation in Europe during this time was not Iberia. Spain's commercial capitalists in Iberia occupied a "weak position" compared to those in the Mediterranean, the Netherlands, and Germany (Kamen 1991: 170). There were a number of reasons for this, of which perhaps the most significant was that much Iberian commerce and finance had been in the hands of Moorish and Jewish populations, both of whom had been expelled by A.D. 1500. This initially "weak" position was further "...rapidly undermined in the sixteenth century..." (ibid.: 170).

There were two major reasons for this. The first pertained to who conducted Spain's finance and commerce. The second concerned the terms-of-trade characteristic of this commerce. Most of those trading and providing financial services in Spain were not Spanish, because of the destruction of the indigenous commercial capitalist class. Rather they were either Germans, Netherlanders, Italians, or French. A 1566 law allowed these merchants to export bullion from Spain. This meant that a considerable portion of the profits of commercial capitalism in Spain were accumulated elsewhere, increasingly throughout the 1500s in Antwerp. Furthermore, Spain exported raw materials and agricultural products in the fifteenth and sixteenth centuries, and these were commodities of lesser value than the manufactures Spain imported from the rest of Europe at that time. This pattern of international trade meant that Spain experienced a severe balance-of-payments problem such that "vast amounts of specie" left the country (Reitzer 1960: 223). Such capital flight meant that those merchants who remained in Spain were left with even less capital to compete with other merchants in more capital rich areas, which were increasingly in the Netherlands. The Habsburgs thus faced a great fiscal problem: how to tap the capital accumulating elsewhere than in Spain.

Charles V created a Council of Finance (*Consejo de Hacienda*) in 1524 to serve as the central fiscal institution. This Council suffered from a number of problems, not the least of which was that its system of bookkeeping was incapable of accurate accounting (Thompson 1976: 67–100). Thus the Council could not efficiently collect revenues. However, a more serious problem was that the empire had expanded enormously between 1500 and 1560, and sixty years was simply too brief a period to transform a medieval into a modern fiscal regime. So Charles governed each part of the empire "...by its own traditional laws in its own traditional manner" (Elliot 1964: 157). This meant that revenues were largely based upon "...the same principles for the collection of taxes and levies..." that had been present in the different late medieval fiscal regimes of the component territories of the empire (Vives 1972: 52).

There were four major sources of revenue: the different provinces of the European empire (e.g. those in Austria, the Netherlands, Aragon, etc.), the Americas, the church, and public credit. The medieval principles governing these revenues were varied and complex. Castile was very heavily taxed. However, Aragon gave according to its medieval *fueros* ("privileges"), which meant a "relatively small share" (Elliott 1964: 193). Similarly, the Austrian territories by custom gave little, and after 1556, when Charles ceded these lands to his brother Ferdinand, they gave nothing. In Milan, Naples, and Sicily revenues "...were progressively absorbed by local needs" (Braudel 1976, I: 534). The Netherlands gave according to its "liberties", of which there were over seven-hundred (Parker 1977: 34), and only if their parliaments agreed to pay. Church taxes were similarly complex and generally light. Taxes arriving from America, the bullion, were treated as if they were the property of a feudal entity, the crown of Castile.

This fiscal regime was not well centralized. Regions like Aragon never contributed very much to the center. The Netherlands gave what its parliaments, not the center, decided. Not a great deal arrived from Italy. Nobles throughout the empire tended to be "...exempt from taxes" (Vives 1972: 52). Similarly, commercial wealth tended to be under-taxed. Hence, Spain's fiscal regime was inefficient and only semi-centralized. Koenigsberger has said this regime was the "...fundamental weakness" of the Spanish government because "...Castile and the silver financed and defended the empire...," while "...the other dominions were, to a greater or lesser degree, onlookers" (in Wallerstein 1976: 123).

Now we are in a position to distinguish old from new in Iberian expansion. There was a novel form of predatory accumulation that reinforced capital accumulation. But there remained something old. This was the fiscal regime, which remained essentially medieval, especially in its inability to transform private capital into public revenues. So while war was good for business, business — like a frosty lover — was indifferent to war. Nevertheless, the need to make predatory and capital accumulation mutually reinforcing was becoming increasingly urgent for the Habsburgs.

The revenues Charles had at his disposal provided him "...with a wealth of resources that no other European power could match" (Koenigsberger 1971: xi). However, such revenues were simply insufficient because the Habsburgs made more war than any state in the field of centralizing European monarchies. Spain fought with France constantly from 1494 through the 1540s, especially over Italy. It fought the Ottoman Empire throughout this same period, especially in central Europe and the Mediterranean. Finally, it attacked Protestant princes in northern Germany from the mid 1540s through the 1560s. Military costs vastly exceeded revenues. By 1560 the government's debts had reached twenty million ducats (Braudel 1972, I: 533); but it still "...urgently needed more ships..." (Elliott 1964: 224) to confront Turkish advances in the western and central Mediterranean. As a consequence the Habsburgs were involved in a continual "struggle for solvency" (Kennedy 1987: 46). This quest for solvency was one in which they *had* to expand their fields of fiscal domination. I shall show in the following section how the Habsburg's use of violent force to expand their fiscal domination in the Low Countries had them like Don Quixote, tilting at the most ghastly of windmills. This tilting, we shall see, would have revolutionary consequences.

III

"From experience, your lordships ought to know very well that in
India trade is driven and maintained under the protection of your own

weapons, just as the weapons are furnished from the profits of trade, in such wise that trade cannot be maintained without war, nor war without trade" (J. P. Coen, 1614: in Tracy 1991: 1).

During the years roughly between 1566, when the Netherlanders rose in revolt against their Spanish rulers, and 1648, when the Peace of Westphalia finally ended the eighty or so year war that ensued, Holland became an independent state and the Dutch managed to integrate predatory with capital accumulation. This was done in a manner, as Coen, a proconsul in the Dutch East India Company realized, that married war with trade and vice versa in a manner that produced a military-capitalist complex.

Charles V reigned from 1516 until he abdicated in favor of his son Philip II in 1556. Philip continued his father's policies. The Netherlands at this time corresponded roughly to modern Holland and Belgium and consisted of seventeen provinces that in the Middle Ages had come into the hands of the Dukes of Burgundy, from who they were inherited by Charles V. These provinces were small in area, so they were not places of enormous noble fiefs. Rather they consisted of cities whose urban folk drew their wealth from commerce. This trade had grown considerably, especially in the Baltic and with Spain in the 14th and 15th centuries. As a result, the Netherlands by the middle of the sixteenth century was, with northern Italy, a site of the greatest capital accumulation (Israel 1989: 12–38).

Each of the seventeen provinces, as earlier reported, enjoyed the right to consent to its own taxes. Parts of Philip's empire beside the Low Countries, unable to support the costs of Philip's wars, had, according to Braudel, "...one after another, silently refused to support the expenses of his campaigns" (1973, II: 676). Philip, fighting throughout Europe, was utterly broke. At one point, as a result of the anxieties provoked by such finances, his Secretary of War confessed, "I live in terror of something irreparable happening" (in Thompson 1976: 76). Desperate for revenues, Philip sought to tax the wealthy Netherlands. Charles had demanded a wide range of taxes in 1542–44 (Israel 1995: 132). Philip added to these in 1556 by insisting upon revenues that were said to be so great that they were an "unheard of sum" (ibid.: 136). William the Silent, a crucial Dutch leader at the time, described the effect of these exactions when he lamented, "We suffer with all our heart over the multitudinous and excessively cruel violences, the excessive burdens, taxes..." (in Rowen 1972: 40). "Excessively cruel violences" were about to realize the Secretary of War's terror: "irreparable" damage would happen.

Netherlanders began to resist efforts to expand Habsburg fiscal domination by the 1550s. Two hundred nobles from the different provinces founded a league to check Spanish influence in 1566. Philip chose at this point to maintain his authority by using violent force, which produced a revolt. This moved Philip to send his ablest general in 1567, the Duke of Alva, whose brutal repression came to be known as the Spanish Fury. The fury failed and the Union of Utrecht (1579) was promulgated, forming a Dutch Republic out of the seven northernmost of the provinces. War, however, dragged on and off until 1648, when, in the Treaty of Munster, Spain recognized Holland's independence. A small country had defeated the most powerful in Europe; how could this have happened?[6]

A number of answers to this question have been given, but that of C. R. Boxer still appears to be widely accepted. He attributed Dutch successes ultimately to "...the truly remarkable economic development of the two maritime provinces of Holland and Zealand" (1965: 4). Such economic growth involved capital accumulation. However, the mere fact of this accumulation is not an explanation of how capital came to flow to Dutch military institutions. Part of the answer to this question pertains to who controlled the Dutch state that emerged during the revolt. Government in Holland was conducted by town councils, provincial States, and the States-General. For example, in the province of Holland there were eighteen towns with town councils, each with a right to send a delegation to the provincial State. Each delegation to this State, no matter how large, had but a single vote. The nobility also sent a delegation, but it too had only a single vote. After the Union of Utrecht, each province sent a delegation to the States-General. The three levels of government in this state "were dominated by the regent class" (Haley 1972: 72).

The regents (*heeren*) were an oligarchy, a small number of persons with the right to be public officials, who were of "wealth and assured social position" (ibid.: 59), and who — at the time under consideration — were "intimately concerned with trade" (ibid.: 58). The association of government office with membership in the class of commercial capitalists meant, as one perceptive Frenchman of the time observed, that "In Holland, the interest of the state in matters of commerce serves that of the private individual..." (in Braudel 1979: 206). Holland was a "bourgeois state" (Hart 1993). Critically, this allowed those with private capital to formulate policy concerning the public utilization of the portion of capital that became government receipts. So when regents made decisions about revenues, they were deciding how to spend their own money, money which the Spanish

Fury sought to have deposited in the Madrid treasury. This concentrated the regents' attention upon the problem of devising an effective fiscal regime.

How did they solve this problem? The annual taxes required for the use of the entire republic were divided into quotas for each of the provinces and each province raised its quota if, and how, it saw fit. This was not an especially centralized system of tax-collection, as the States General lacked fiscal authority within the provinces. The major taxes were excises upon consumption in Holland, Zealand, and Utrecht, the most commercialized and prosperous of the provinces. While such excises were not fair, because poorer folk paid a larger percentage of their income than did the wealthy, they did allow the Dutch Republic to tap the wealth of those in the capitalist complex because the bourgeoisie were hefty consumers. So the Republic enjoyed a steady supply of revenues. Tilly, reporting on the research of Tracy (1985), suggests that other changes in public finance were equally important. He states: "The critical innovations had occurred between 1515 and 1565, when the States General of the Habsburg Netherlands... took steps toward issuing state backed annuities secured by specific new taxes and bearing attractive interest..." (1990: 90). These bonds payable annually, hence annuities, allowed the state to tap the private capital of its commercial capitalists by creating a public debt.

What made these so attractive to those with capital, was that they allowed merchants and others with money to *profit* from being taxed. A person invested a specific amount of money in an annuity and received greater than that amount in return. Spain had also experimented with annuities, called *juros*, but continually bankrupt, it "suspended payments" six times on its short term debts between 1557 and 1648 (Braudel 1976, I: 535). This made its *juros* risky. Capital rich Holland, though not especially centralized in its tax collection, was still prosperous enough to pay off its annuities from revenues — largely excise duties on basic domestic goods and comestibles (Tracy 1985) — specifically earmarked for this purpose. As a result, the Dutch Republic never defaulted on its public debts. This made annuities one of the safest forms of investment and, hence, a way of minimizing risk in an entrepreneur's program of private capital accumulation.

As Homer Sidney has noted, strong Dutch state credit accounted for "a good part of the military success..." (1963: 124). This was because the annuities were part of a fiscal regime that directly linked the complex of commercial capitalist institutions of Holland with those of the governmental complex, especially the *ontvanger-generaal* (receiver-general) and *thesaurier-generaal* (treasurer-general). The former of these "supervised the receipts and actually handled the money...", while the latter had "...responsibility for the expenditures of the central government" (Price 1994: 218). Monies, ultimately derived from the capitalist complex, flowed to the receiver-general, on to the treasurer-general, and finally on to Dutch "armies and navies" (Davis 1973: 90).

So the "expansion of Dutch commerce" allowed Maurice of Nassau, who took command after 1584, to build the second largest army in Europe by 1597 (Israel 1995: 253) and, perhaps more to the point, "...to pay his soldiers well, and punctually" (Dupuy and Dupuy 1986: 460) when Spain was too broke to do the same. The result was a "highly disciplined, homogeneous, responsive, professional army, at least a match for the finest Spanish troops" (ibid.: 460) that by 1600 had fought Habsburg armies to a standstill. Hostilities with Spain stopped in 1609, only to resume again in 1622 as part of the Thirty Year War. Between 1622 and 1640 the costs of the Dutch armed forces rose from 13.4 million to 18.8 million florins. Spanish military needs exceeded those of Holland, but Spain, with its bad credit history, experienced enormous troubles securing even the least revenues needed for war. The Dutch government had little problem raising these revenues through its annuities. These revenues tended to be spent disproportionately upon naval men and materials, because Holland had devised a naval strategy to stimulate its commerce. By the time of the defeat of the Spanish Armada (1588), Holland had become the strongest seapower (Davis 1973: 184). Portugal had been incorporated into Spain in 1580, and attacks upon Portuguese commercial holdings, especially in the east during the next sixty years were an important part of the Dutch anti-Spanish naval strategy. Admiral Maarten Tromp utterly devastated Spanish seapower at the Battle of the Downs (1639). By 1640 Holland had won control over the lucrative Asian trade (Boxer 1969: 106–128). Spain was ready for peace, which came in 1648.

There is irony in the events just narrated. The Habsburgs had to expand their fiscal domination to continue predatory accumulation to continue wars to which they were already committed. So Philip and his ministers tried to raise additional revenues from the Low Countries, thereby threatening Dutch capital accumulation, producing not the desired revenues but eighty years of warfare. This combat meant that the Dutch now had to have their own revenues for their own predatory accumulation. These they secured by resorting to a form of public finance, the annuity, used by the Spanish government. We have seen how earlier during Iberian expansion war was good for business, but that business was indifferent to war. Now the Dutch had made business great for war. The more capital crafty Dutch merchants had accumulated, the more annuities they could purchase, making possible more ships for Tromp's navy and soldiers for Maurice of Nassau's army. What the Spanish did to help themselves helped their foes to hurt them.

North and Thomas assert that Holland in the hundred years between 1575 and 1675 became the "first country to achieve self-sustained growth" (1973: 145). What they suggest by this is that the Dutch created an economic system that was capable of accumulating capital on a purely economic basis. Certainly, as Wallerstein notes, "no other country had achieved such a well integrated agro-industrial complex" (1980: 44). However, if the Dutch had made business good for war, they had equally — as was just noted — made war good for business; and what had been instituted in the process of doing this was a complex of a type that had never before been seen in the world.

The exercise of Dutch violent force produced after 1570 a "dramatic upsurge" of overseas trade (Boxer 1965: 7). Davis reports that Holland fought in the Indian Ocean "... to seize Portuguese bases and exclude Portugal and England from the most valuable places of trade, and... to terrorize island rulers into acquiescence to Dutch terms..." (1973: 184). He further suggests that naval operations were conducted so that Dutch merchant capital would enjoy "...the gains of monopsonistic buyers and monopolistic sellers" (ibid.: 184). Similar wars were fought in the New World and the Baltic. Holland's shipping grew tenfold between 1500 and 1700. As of 1670, the Dutch owned more than the combined shipping tonnage of England, France, Portugal, Spain, and the different German states (Wallerstein 1980: 46). This suggests that Holland achieved "self-sustained" growth during the 17th century, at least in part, because the use of violent force "for the advancement and protection of trade" allowed it to achieve "world-trade primacy" (Israel 1989: 411).

Philip's Secretary of War had been right to live "in terror" because "something irreparable" was happening. One begins to apprehend the outlines of this when one calculates the full string of linkages involving the complex of capitalist and governmental institutions in Holland. The annuities directly linked commercial enterprises in the capitalist complex to the treasury in the governmental complex. The decisions of the regents directly linked the treasury to the army and navy, and actions of these military institutions to secure and protect trade advantages linked the governmental complex back to the capitalist complex, thus completing a circle. Complexes, it will be recalled, are defined here as groups of institutions in which force is accumulated and concentrated. "Networked" complexes are complexes in which more than one form of force is accumulated and concentrated. Holland had such a networked complex because increases in capital force could be used to expand violent force, and vice versa. This networked complex might be termed a "military capitalist" complex after the two complexes that were mutually reinforcing. This networked complex was certainly capable of "self sustained" growth, but of a different variety than that imagined by North and Thomas. Predatory and capitalist accumulation were two logics of the *same* complex, helping to sustain each other. It was as if Philip had tilted at an innocent windmill that metamorphosed itself into a great Leviathan that smashed him, his armies, and any dream of "universal monarchy."

The force of these two logics led in the seventeenth century, as the title of Schama's work (1988), evoking this period puts it, to *The Embarrassment of Riches*. However, grave problems loomed for the Dutch Leviathan. Some were geographic; others were fiscal. Holland was wedged between France to the south and England, just across the channel, to the west. Both countries had studied the Dutch rise to affluence with interest. Further, though Holland had prospered through the use of public debt, it had never really centralized its taxes. In principle, each of the provinces provided taxes to the legislative States-General. In reality, each of the provinces was complete master in its own house, which meant that sometimes the provinces provided taxes to the center and sometimes they did not (Haley 1972: 69). Another country in the seventeenth century would build a better fiscal system, to Holland's detriment.

IV

"...whosoever commands the sea commands the trade, whosoever commands the trade of the world commands the riches of the world, and consequently the world itself" (Sir Walter Raleigh, 1618. In Modelski and Thompson 1988: 7).

"A country abounding with merchants and manufacturers... abounds with a set of people who have it at all times in their power to advance, if they choose to do so, a very large sum of money to government" (Adam Smith 1776, vol. II: 392).

Early on, only a hundred years or so into the Iberian expansion, when England was still on the northern fringe of stately respectability, Sir Walter Raleigh had a plan for commanding "the world itself." His plan depended upon the strengthening of naval forces to control commerce. A hundred-and-fifty years later, when England had done it, and dominated a good proportion of "the world itself," others — like Adam Smith — realized that the trick to doing this was getting the merchants and other wealthy sorts, "to advance" their money to the government. Advancing and commanding were manifestations of a better military-capitalist complex than that of the Dutch, and it is the story of the building of this complex that is told below. The British military-capitalist complex had two parts to it: a fiscal regime that linked capital to predatory accumulation and a military regime that linked predatory to capital accumulation. I treat the former linkage first.

Building a fiscal regime: The years between the reigns of Charles I (1625–49) and William and Mary (1689–1702) were dominated by confrontation between parliament and the Stuart kings over revenues. The Stuarts wanted them. Parliament was not so sure it wanted, in Smith's terms, "to advance" them (Goldstone 1991: 102). This clash provoked the English Revolution which led to Civil War (1642–1649) that resulted in Oliver Cromwell's (1649–58) Commonwealth, which ended with the Restoration of the Stuarts (1660) and, finally, culminated in the Glorious Revolution (1688), a revolution that set a Dutch monarch on the throne and established that it would be parliament that would govern England. This breathtaking sequence of British constitutional history has been interpreted by Whiggish historians as part of a stately progress towards parliamentary democracy. I differ and offer a reinterpretation of these events as ones that occurred during the centralization of early modern Atlantic stately fields as part of struggles between the crown and the upper classes as to the nature of this centralization. Struggles that in the British instance built a better fiscal regime, in part by making virtue out of necessity, roughly between 1637 and 1694. I am at pains below to describe the six virtues of this regime that gave it real advantages over its competitors in the field of centralizing Atlantic states at the time.[7] Let us begin by recognizing the first of these. To do this we need to understand something of the English upper classes.

By the early seventeenth century there were two major segments to the upper class. One segment, the peerage and gentry, was a landowning class, but one that produced crops for the market, rented its lands for profits, and invested in different trade, manufacturing, and financial enterprises. This aristocracy, then, was in Cain and Hopkins' terms (1986), a "gentlemanly capitalist" class. The second segment of the upper class was commercial in origin and was divided into a number of different sub-segments. There were merchants involved in a relatively short-distance broadcloth trade in Europe that had been active since the Middle Ages. Toward the end of the sixteenth century there emerged a group of merchants who traded in the goods of the Near and Far East. Merchants who traded with the colonies of the New World appeared at the very end of the sixteenth century and the beginning of the seventeenth. Finally, there were those of the City, persons involved in purely financial dealings. This commercial class, according to Brenner, was "maturing" and aggressively "oriented toward making the most of the growing opportunities that could be derived from the long distance trade and a colonial empire, and as well from war finance..." (1993: 713). Thus, both of England's upper classes at the end of the sixteenth century were capitalist.

During the Revolution and the Commonwealth the different merchant segments of the commercial class became significantly represented in parliament, with the colonial merchants attaining "unprecedented influence" by Cromwell's time (Brenner 1993: xiii). The Glorious Revolution was really only glorious for the gentlemanly capitalists, for it insured that they too would have their very considerable influence in Parliament (Cain and Hopkins 1986: 510). Parliament, thus, was not especially democratic. Rather, it was a class act, a distinctly capitalist class act. So by 1688 England had done what Holland had also accomplished. Persons who made governmental, including fiscal, decisions and who additionally accumulated capital were together in the same institution, parliament. This relaxed crown/upper class conflict because it allowed gentlefolk "to advance" some of their money to the crown, certain that it would be they who spent it in their interests. This, then, was the first virtue of the English fiscal regime.

It is time to consider a second virtue. Parliament during the Restoration enacted far-reaching legislation that abolished certain feudal payments to the sovereign. In effect, this did away with any remaining remnants of the medieval fiscal system. In place of feudal dues to the crown, "Parliament arranged for the sovereign to receive income in the form of taxation, which Parliament could raise or reduce in amount" (Palmer and Colton 1965: 150). This not only institutionalized Parliamentary, i.e. capitalist, control over the fiscal system; it meant that taxes flowed into the Exchequer from all parts of the realm where the Parliament exercised authority. This effectively centralized the fiscal operations, for it placed all the territories, and classes, of the state under the fiscal control of one center, Parliament, something that neither Spain nor Holland had been able to accomplish. Centralization, then, was the second virtue of the British fiscal regime.

A third virtue was the creation of a large and capable bureaucracy that could actually insure that revenues were delivered to the center. There appear to have been only 1200 officials serving the entire state in the eleven years between 1649 and 1660 (Alymer 1961: 169). However, by 1688 there were over 2500 administrators whose sole responsibility was tax collection (Brewer 1990: 65).[8] The growth of a fiscal bureaucracy conferred two major benefits. The first of these was that revenues could be collected more efficiently; there was far less spillage out of government coffers than occurred with other systems of revenue collection, such as the tax farming favored by the French. The second benefit was that it helped create a widespread perception that the system was fair. This was because such a bureaucracy allowed the government actually to calculate how much it collected from whom; something that was impossible in any other European fiscal regime at that time.

The belief that taxation was fair in England coupled with the fact that fiscal decisions were made by those with capital contributed to the fourth virtue of the fiscal regime. This was that Britain taxed itself at higher rates than did its Atlantic competitors by the end of the seventeenth century. The growth in total revenues far outstripped the French and the Dutch between 1672 and 1715. This is not surprising in the French case because their revenues stagnated, but it is surprising in the Dutch case, because their revenues doubled (Dickson and Sperling 1976: 313). It is estimated that by the beginning of the eighteenth century the English were paying about 17.6 livres per capita in annual taxes, while their French counterparts were paying only half this amount. By the end of the century a Britisher paid three times the annual taxes of a French person (Brewer 1990: 89).

The fifth and sixth virtues of the English fiscal regime have to do with the type of revenues acquired. Most revenues came from excise, customs, and hearth taxes. Excise taxes were duties on domestically produced commodities. Customs were taxes on international trade, largely imports. The hearth tax was a graduated property tax. The hearth tax, basically a land tax, burdened those with the most land, the gentlemanly capitalists. Excises and customs were felt more by merchants. Most revenues, by the eighteenth century, came from the first two taxes,[9] which were basically taxes on trade. Thus as trade expanded, so could taxes. This situation encouraged gentlemanly capitalists to support commerce, because it reduced pressures to increase the hearth tax.

The sixth, and final, virtue of the British fiscal regime was the adoption of the Dutch practice of annuities. In *The Financial Revolution in*

England (1967), P. G. M. Dickson provides an account of the history of public credit in England. The institutions that extended such credit began to be developed during the reign of the Dutch sovereign of England, William of Orange, who ruled England as William III. William's government, in order to finance the Nine Year's War, borrowed 1,200,000 pounds from a group of private investors who, in return for holding government bonds, were permitted to operate a bank. Thus, in 1694, British annuities, national debt, and the Bank of England originated at the same time.

There has been controversy as to which elements of this fiscal regime were more important: the development of public deficit finance, made possible by the annuities, or the taxes, resulting from excise and customs duties. P. G. M. Dickson (1967), for example, has downplayed the importance of the taxes and emphasized that of public borrowing. My judgement is that all six virtues conferred a total package of benefits not available to the other Atlantic states, but that Dickson is correct to emphasize public borrowing. The first of these benefits was that the fiscal regime heavily involved those with capital in decisions concerning the acquisition and utilization of revenues, legitimating the system to those with money. This advantage was shared only with Holland. The second benefit was centralization. All the revenues from all the places and peoples over which Parliament had control came to one center. This advantage was never achieved by the Spanish or Dutch. The third advantage was that it taxed more heavily than did its competitors, two to three times, for example, more than the French. Fourth, because of the large, professional fiscal bureaucracy, it taxed more efficiently than its competitors. Fifth, as did Holland, it combined public borrowing, making possible rapid bursts of increased revenues to finance the extraordinary expenses of wars, with steady increases in excises and customs, made possible by increased trade, to pay off the borrowing. Thus, only England's fiscal regime had this total package of fiscal virtues.

But I think Dickson is sensible to stress the importance of public borrowing. Deficit finance was the key to military success because it "enabled England to spend on war out of all proportion to its tax revenue, and thus to throw into the struggle with France and its allies the decisive margin of ships and men..." (1967; 9). By the end of the eighteenth century, it was no secret to some who were influential in the French government that England's fiscal regime had this "decisive margin." For example, when Jacques Necker, who was in charge of government finances for a period under Louis XVI, published his national budget, the *Compte Rendu au Roi* in 1781, he proposed to reorganize the French revenues along the lines of the English model (Harris 1979).

It needs to be understood that this English fiscal regime linked capitalist with military institutions. The three taxes — customs, excise, and hearth — in conjunction with the annuities took capital from both the gentlemanly and commercial capitalists. This capital went to government institutions where, under parliamentary control, most of it went directly to military institutions. Roughly 70 to 80 percent of the English budget was spent on the military in the years 1690 through 1790 (Mann 1986: 484–85). This allowed capital force, accumulated in the capitalist complex, to be used by the government complex to accumulate violent force. Predatory accumulation, then, was at least partially dependent upon capital accumulation. Let us regard this as a way of making virtue out of necessity. Capital accumulation is an economic necessity for capitalists. The British fiscal regime made a virtue of this necessity because its public deficit financing made possible a vigorous flow of capital to its commercial capitalists who held the annuities, and it was this virtue that gave England the "decisive" edge in war. It remains in the following section to show how predatory accumulation produced capital accumulation.

Building a military regime: The British military regime assumed its distinctive characteristics at roughly the same time that the better fiscal regime was built. These institutions bore the imprint of what commentators have termed a "blue-water" strategy, whose fundamental tenets were: 1. that most hostilities against European opponents would be conducted at sea; 2. that these actions would be conducted by the British navy, which would be constituted so that it could overwhelm its opponents; 3. that land hostilities in Europe would be avoided; and, 4. if this should prove impossible, that they be conducted by the troops of allies encouraged by English subsidies.[10] This strategy was official government policy under the Commonwealth (1649–60) and Charles II (1660–85). It made the navy the major military institution. The "secret" of British naval success at this time was the "broadside" (Dupuy and Dupuy 1986: 531).

There were three periods between 1585 and 1815 when this British military system exercised such violent force. The first of these, the "Seadog" era, 1585–1603, involved Britain against Spain and Portugal (Portugal had been incorporated into Spain in 1580). This era might be thought of as the "prehistory" of British naval dominance, when the advantages of the accumulation of violent force along the lines of a "blue-water" strategy became manifest. A second period occurred in the second half of the seventeenth century (1652–74), when

England and Holland fought a set of three, largely naval, wars. The third period was at the end of the seventeenth century and throughout the eighteenth, when England and France fought from 1689 through 1815.

Elizabethan England, for reasons made clear below, entered the Dutch Revolt on the side of Holland in 1585. However, the English navy was too small at this time to challenge directly the combined naval forces of Spain and Portugal. So Elizabeth's government encouraged its merchants to conduct naval operations. This they did either though investments in privateers or in trading houses, like the East India Company, that were authorized to have military capabilities. The Seadogs — Drake, Hawkins, and Raleigh — were the captains of the ships of such commercial enterprises.[11]

There is question as to how one should conceptualize the violence exercised by merchants through their privateering and trading companies. Merchants are agents of private institutions in civil society, so it seems plausible to classify their institutions as forms of "nonstate violence," as does J. E. Thomson (1994). However, privateers and trading company armed forces were not independent of governments, for as Thomson notes further, "All the practices of nonstate violence...were authorized by states. They were officially sanctioned" (ibid.: 21). English privateers, for example, in addition to attacking shipping, performed convoy duty, at times acted as blockaders, coast guards, and troop carriers. Privateers and trading company militaries were a bit like militias; sometimes they went about their ordinary, private lives, at other times they were authorized to perform state duties. So it seems misleading to insist that such institutions were purely nonstate. Parastatal institutions, like militias, are ones in civil society that are vested with government functions. The Seadogs were agents of parastatal institutions of violence. Further, as we shall discover, their violence was especially "intimately... connected" with commerce (Andrews 1964: 223).

English commerce in textiles expanded in the period between 1480 and 1550. Thereafter, the textile trade declined and stagnated between 1550 and 1614 (Brenner 1993: xi). Following 1550, English merchants developed new trading ventures in the Near and Far East (Davis 1973). However, much of English commerce in the sixteenth century was conducted in the Netherlands, especially Antwerp, and the Spanish/Dutch conflict disrupted this trade.[12] It did so especially seriously after Britain joined the conflict in 1585.

Privateering and trading company militaries supported English merchants threatened by these wartime losses. For example, trade in the Far East was opened in part by the naval operations of the East India Company. During the first decades of the seventeenth century the company constructed nearly eighty naval vessels, which it deployed against the Portuguese in India. The company first established a foothold at Surat (1608) and then defeated a number or Portuguese squadrons, which allowed it to control the Strait of Hormuz. This gave English merchants a commercial advantage over their Portuguese counterparts in western India and Persia.[13] Thus, England solved the problem of the blocked entrepots by going beyond them directly to the source of their imports.

When Britain entered the Spanish/Dutch dispute, its privateers began a "...predatory drive...to win by fair means or foul a share of the Atlantic wealth of the Iberian nations" (Andrews 1984: 356). This involved plundering, destroying, and extorting wealth from Spanish ships and settlements in what amounted to "state-sponsored terrorism" (Thomson 1994: 23). The predations of these privateers helped British commerce in three ways. First, by 1603 the Seadogs had achieved the "wholesale destruction" of the Spanish merchant marine (Andrews 1964: 226), a feat that clearly diminished the ability of Spanish commerce to compete with that of England. Second, though this privateering did not directly lead to major new trades, it did aid English merchants in the following ways. It provided them with goods to trade, because the cargos of prizes were taken back to England and sold. During the Elizabethan era, privateers' prizes amounted to ten to fifteen percent of England's total imports (Andrews 1964: 128). The revenues from these sales earned "super-profits" (ibid.: 229), because the costs of securing goods by plundering them were considerably less than by purchasing them. Further, privateering led to increased shipping and maritime expertise (Andrews 1964: 230), both because merchants had to build more vessels to serve as privateers and because these new vessels had to be operated in new waters, especially in the New World, where the English lacked experience. Third, the knowledge gained in these new waters, especially in the West Indies, led to the very first British attempts at commerce in the region, a region that in the next hundred years was to become commercially vital to England. Thus, parastatal naval force, either in the form of privateers or the East India Company, had contributed to merchant capital accumulation in the tough times of the late sixteenth and early seventeenth centuries; but when the Dutch finally triumphed over the Spanish, times were to become even tougher for English capital accumulation.

Holland, had risen, as Simon Schama describes it, from a "ramshackle and beleaguered confederacy...into a global empire" in only a few generations, where "Capital begot capital with astonishing ease..." (1988: 223, 323). This capital accumulation was skillfully driven by practices to preempt competition, monopolize supply, and to control all conditions of trade, ranging from the production of raw materials to the terms of international and domestic sales. England was insulated partially from commercial competition with Holland while Holland was preoccupied with its revolt from Spain (Israel 1988). However, the end of this conflict brought "commercial carnage" (Brenner 1993: 600) to British merchants. Government officials were aware of the commercial problems with the Dutch, and as one general of the time, General Monck, indelicately put it, "What matters, this or that reason? What we want is more of the trade that the Dutch now have" (in Wilson 1957: 20).

Holland's trade, of course, was conducted by ships across oceans, so a large, fully-specialized naval force had to be instituted in order to get at "more" of Dutch commerce. A strengthening of the British navy began under the Stuarts and was greatly increased under Oliver Cromwell (Ashley 1961). Two-hundred and seventeen new ships were added to the fleet in the years between 1646 and 1659. After the Restoration, 25 larger ships were added to this fleet. Naval administration improved. Officers were chosen more on ability than nobility. Tactics as prescribed in the manual *Fighting Instructions* emphasized line-of-battle operations that were designed to maximize broadsides. Thus, at precisely the time when war with Holland was approaching, the royal navy emerged with its "blue-water" qualities.

Violent force was visited upon Holland in a series of three wars (1652–54; 1665–67; and 1662–74).[14] Just who won and who lost these wars depends upon how "winning" is defined. If winning is restricted solely to the outcomes of military operations, then the first war was an English victory. However, the second war included a Dutch raid up the Thames river that was disastrous for England and so angered Sir William Batten, Surveyor of the Navy, that he confided, in the presence of Pepys's sharp ear, "I think the Devil shits Dutchmen" (in Schama 1988: 234). The Second Anglo-Dutch war was won by Holland, with the third a draw. Israel believes that overall Holland got the better of these conflicts (1989: 209–13; 255–56; 279–300). However, according to Boxer, Dutch participation in these wars increased Holland's national debt about 4.5 times, placing a crushing debt burden upon it. This ultimately made it difficult to continue building enough warships to compete with Britain (1965: 105–6). England, with its better fiscal regime, experienced fewer problems in this regard. So, in purely military terms, Holland may have won the three wars, but it came out of them with a lesser ability to accumulate violent force to oppose Britain in the future.

Further, England had fought the wars over commerce and here it experienced triumph. In the first war England took 1700 Dutch merchant ships. In the second and third wars fewer ships were taken, but the royal navy still seized more than it lost (Pemsel 1977). Carter believes that the second Anglo-Dutch war resulted in a "...downturn of the Dutch Republic's prosperity..." (1975: 6). The weight of shipping in the North Sea was thrown in England's favor (McGowan 1981). Just prior to the start of this combat, Holland lost its North American colonies to England, and as a result lost control over the trade with this prosperous region. Thus the second war was especially important in the Atlantic, for it helped to establish a "...fuller English hegemony over a whole complex network of Atlantic trades including tobacco, sugar, fur, slaves, and codfish" (Kammen 1970: 33). Further, as early as the first war, "The Dutch had failed totally in their major war aim, to secure the right of their ships to trade freely everywhere unhindered by the British navy of the Navigation Act" (Capp 1989: 89). This meant that from roughly 1660 England was able to enforce its Navigation Acts, whose measures were specifically designed to reduce Dutch commerce.

As a result, the playing fields of Anglo-Dutch commercial rivalry began to shift. In the three decades between 1660 and 1690, English foreign trade increased more than fifty percent. As G. M. Trevelyan cheerily put it, "At the end of the Stuart period," in 1688, "England was the greatest...trading country in the world, and London outstripped Amsterdam as the world's greatest emporium" (1953: 235). Unquestionably, the exercise of English violent force during the three Anglo-Dutch wars was a determinant of this situation. French military pressure also played a role, but the increase of British capitalist domination at the expense of Holland was the first great victory for blue-water military regime. It might have shat Dutchmen now and then, but England got what England wanted, "...more of the trade that the Dutch now have." However, a greater challenge than that of Holland loomed.

England fought six wars with the French between 1689 and 1815, a veritable "Second Hundred Years War" (Buffinton 1929: 3), that included the War of the League of Augsburg 1689–1697, the War of Spanish Succession 1701–13, the War of Austrian Succession 1740–48, the Seven Years War 1756–68, the American Revolution 1776–83, and the Napoleonic Wars 1794–1815. The wars were fought throughout the globe and, thus, have been called the first "World War" (ibid.: 3). Critically, as Goldstein observes, they "...centered on access to the wealth from the extra-European periphery" (1988: 319). Access to extra-European wealth, in considerable measure, derived from control over the trade of these regions.

Seventeenth century France was the largest and wealthiest country in the field of centralizing Atlantic states.[15] During the reign of Louis XIII (1610–43), many of the affairs of state were gathered in the hands of Cardinal Richlieu. He formulated a policy favoring the increase of French naval and commerical strength and the courting of Holland as an ally against England. Louis XIV (1643–1715), the Sun King, attempted to take over where Spain had left off and to make France the dominant power in Europe. As part of this strategy, his Minister for Finance and Commerce, Jean-Baptiste Colbert, continued Richlieu's policies. This Richlieu/Colbert policy, of course, committed France to a contest for capitalist domination in the Atlantic stately field. Of course, Holland and England were France's two main rivals in this competition.

One of the ways Colbert encouraged commerce was to subsidize shipbuilding. By the 1660s, France had developed a substantial merchant navy, with the result that overseas trade, especially with northern Europe, Spain, the Levant, and French colonies, greatly expanded, and France took her place alongside the great trading nations, England and Holland. France began a trade war against England in 1674 by, among other measures, raising tariff barriers against British goods (Clark 1923: 63–72). However, it was still not clear where the real war would occur. The richest source of early modern capital accumulation derived from overseas trade. At the time, although Spain had been mortally wounded, it still had an enormous empire — including the Spanish Netherlands (Belgium), parts of Italy the Franche-Comté in Burgundy, and much of the New World. So the big question that tantalized Europe in the late 1600s, as every student of modern European history is taught, was that of "...the eventual disposition of the entire Spanish empire" (Palmer and Coulton 1965: 166). The Sun King aimed to have this empire with its enormous trading opportunities.

Initially Louis struck in the War of Devolution (1677–68) in which he sought to conquer two Spanish areas in Europe, the Spanish Netherlands and Franche-Comté. Holland, threatened by the prospect of the loss of the Spanish Netherlands as a barrier against an aggrandizing France, organized an alliance with Sweden and England. This was called the Triple Alliance, and it obliged Louis to withdraw from the Netherlands and make peace. However, the Sun King had been outraged at being thwarted by the Dutch and resolved to acquire the Spanish Netherlands by directly defeating Holland. In 1672 Holland itself was invaded, provoking what has come to be known as the Dutch War (1672–78). Sonnino (1988) has emphasized Louis' personal motives as the cause of the war. However, Adam Smith, long ago (1776), had attributed the conflict to Franco-Dutch commercial competition. Israel tends to suppport Smith, showing how Colbert expected to abort the "Dutch world-trade supremacy through war..." (1989: 297). Louis may have been emotionaly ill-disposed towards Holland, but his attitude was expressed as part of a pre-existing French policy to increase French capitalist domination.

Effective control over Holland during this war was conferred by the States General upon William of Orange. He negotiated another alliance, including the Austrian and Spanish Habsburgs, Denmark, and Brandenburg. This alliance fought Louis to a standstill. William then became, ten years after the end of the Dutch War, king of England. This effectively united the two powers during his reign. Louis, who is supposed to have confided on his deathbed, "I have loved war too much," now schemed to acquire all of Spain's empire through inheritance. Such intentions were unacceptable to his foes. William III formed yet another anti-Louis alliance, that of the League of Augsburg. When the League and France opened hostilities in 1689, Britain found itself a major actor in the conflict. Louis, in hindsight, had made *the* fatal mistake of modern French history. He had ignored the Richlieu/Colbert policy of alliance with Holland and had, in fact, driven the two greatest trading nations into alliance against him. The fighting in the War of the League of Augsburg form 1692 onward involved "mutually ruinous war against trade" (Kennedy 1987: 103).[16] None of the combatants was able to achieve a decisive advantage. Louis, however, needing time to recuperate, negotiated a peace (1697) that left the central issue of who was to get what in the Spanish empire "still unsettled" (Palmer and Colton 1950: 167).

Four aspects of this war might be emphasized. The first is that Britain's better fiscal regime was beginning to pay off. The war saw a "...spectacular increase in war finance" (Root 1994: 188). The second aspect is that in considerable measure the war was fought to create overseas commercial advantages. England and France raided and seized each other's settlements in Hudson's Bay, Newfoundland, along the St Lawrence, and the inland frontiers of the North American colonies as well as in the Caribbean, West Africa, and India. A third aspect of the war was that at the naval battle of La Hougue (1692) the French had their flagship, the Royal Sun, crippled and lost fifteen more of their finest ships. Wallerstein has called this victory a "turning point" (1980: 248) because, as Ehrman had noted, "Command of the sea had passed in one blow to the allies and in particular to England" (1953: 398). England would not lose this naval dominance until World War II. Finally, even though the fighting had not been decisive, it did stop Louis. The Peace of Ryswick (1697) that ended the conflict "...gave commercial benefits" both to England and Holland "...which tended to increase their own seapower..." (Mahan 1957: 176).

However, three years later, Louis still believed he could secure the entire Spanish Empire by asserting a supposed Bourbon right to its throne. When the reigning Spanish King, Charles II, died in 1700, he stipulated that the succession to the Spanish throne should go to Louis' grandson, Philip of Anjou. From Paris the cry was heard, "The Pyrenees exist no longer." This meant war, specifically that of the War of Spanish Succession.[17] William negotiated the last of his coalitions, the Grand Alliance. Again Britain participated as the major partner. Again this was in good measure "...to guard and nurture English commerce" (Brewer 1990: 171). Hostilities began in 1702, and the royal navy was able to handle the French navy with ease. Britain's allies were equally successful against France on land. Louis had been finally stopped.

Two facets of the War of the Spanish Succession should be stressed. First, the conflict strained British government revenues to the absolute limit. England covered much of the cost of the war for its allies, as well as its own expenses (Jones 1988). Even though France was the larger, wealthier country, Louis was able to spend only about as much in his two wars between 1688 and 1713 as did his foes (Dickson and Sperling 1961). British public debt stood at about sixteen million pounds sterling at the beginning of the War of the Spanish Succession. As a result of the sale of annuities it was at about forty million pounds sterling at its end (Brewer 1990: 115). This suggests that by the end of the War of the Spanish succession, a poorer country, England, but one with a better fiscal regime, was able to frustrate Louis' intentions. France, because it lacked a fiscal regime that could generate more revenues than its foes, would not get the empire of Spain.

A second aspect of the War of the Spanish Succession that should be emphasized is that it was a commercial success for England. As one member of Parliament said, defending the Peace of Utrecht (1713) which ended the conflict: "The advantages of this peace appear in the addition made to our wealth; in the great quantities of bullion lately coined in our mint; by the vast increase in our shipping employed since peace in the fisheries and in merchandise; and by the remarkable growth of the customs upon imports and of our manufactures" (in Williams 1966: 48). Contemporary accounts of events by biased participants can be inaccurate. However, in this instance the gentleman from Parliament was correct. The war stimulated British "... trade in all its branches" (Mahan 1957: 196). Why was this the case?

There appear to be two reasons. First, at least for a time during and after the conflict, the war "ruined" French commerce (Hugill 1993: 123). This meant that French merchants were less able to compete with their English counterparts. Second, England acquired certain regions and rights that gave its merchants still further competitive advantages. For example, England acquired Gibraltar and Port Mahon in the Mediterranean,[18] which gave it control over the Mediterranean trades. England also took Cape Breton Island, with its port Louisburg, the key to the St Lawrence river and Canada. This stimulated trade based upon the rich fisheries in that region.

Britain was additionally granted the *asiento*, a monopoly right to supply slaves to Spanish colonies in the Caribbean and South America. This right in itself was of benefit, but it became even more so as the *asiento* became the basis for a flourishing smuggling trade with the Spanish colonies. France made a number of concessions in favor of Portugal. These in turn allowed England to dominate trade with Portugal and its colonies, and this commerce was especially profitable, because gold had just been discovered in Brazil. It is important to realize that these competitive advantages did not go to Holland, England's ally in the fighting, but foe in the competition over capitalist domination. Israel insists that the acquisition of these benefits at the expense of Holland "... marked a significant step towards Britain's supplanting the Dutch as the world's dominant commercial power" (1989: 375). Thus, England effectively vanquished ally and foe in the War of the Spanish Succession, gaining a considerable competitive edge for expanding its capitalist domination. Only three decades after the end of the War of Spanish Succession, "half" of the world's commerce "... was done under the British flag" (Dorn 1940: 105).

The War of the Austrian Succession, a quarter of a century later, was largely a contest between the Bourbons of France and the Habsburgs of central Europe. However, by the late 1730s, "French trade was booming at a time when trade was sluggish in England" (Brewer 1990: 173). British merchants were experiencing problems with the French, especially in the Caribbean and in India. France had captured the northern European market in sugar, driving out the

English product in the 1720s (Davis 1973: 307). Consequently, French sugar imports from the Caribbean exceeded those of the British: roughly 65,000 tons to 41,000 tons circa 1740 (Beaud 1983: 234). In addition, France seemed to be rapidly expanding its holdings in India.

In such an atmosphere, according to one source, "English merchants and manufacturers began to think it was time to halt French expansion in the world" (ibid.: 45). British politicians became "obsessed" with the fear of French competition in Spanish markets (Pares 1963: 62). Pamphleteers peddled the belief that "A rising trade may be ruined by war; a sinking trade has a chance to revive by it" (in Pares 1963: 62). William Pitt, the leading British politician of the day, put it thus in 1739: "When trade is at stake...: you must defend it or perish" (in Robertson 1962: 26). As a consequence, Prime Minister Walpole led his government into the fighting, first against a Spain allied to France (1739), and then against France.[19]

The war had a more global reach than the previous Anglo-French conflicts. Operations occurred in Europe, North America, the Caribbean, and India. It was largely a naval affair, with both French and Spanish shipping being driven from the seas. The French West Indies were blockaded. However, both sides decided to end the war before it arrived at a military resolution. So the treaty of Aix-la-Chapelle that ended it (1748), established nothing except the *status quo ante bellum*. In Carlyle's words, this was "A mere end of fighting because your powder is run out" (in Williams 1966: 67).

But fighting between the two states never really stopped. Rather, the rivalry took on an "urgency and ruthlessness" (ibid.: 1966). The French under Dupleix began a territorial expansion in India that menaced English trading settlements. They exhibited no inclination to evacuate certain Caribbean islands that they were supposed to under the terms of the Aix-la-Chapelle treaty. But, above all, it was upon the North American frontier that matters were most explosive. Here was open and bitter war. So France and Britain, only eight years after what proved to have been a false peace, returned to arms. The stakes were brutally clear: who would achieve "...supremacy in the growing world economy..." (Palmer and Colton 1965: 250).[20] The issue would be decided by who had the most revenues to transform into the most violent force; so, to use a quip of the Sun King, "...it would be the last *Louis d'or* — and the last ship — that would win..." (in Robertson 1962: 62).

In Europe military operations did not assume the magnitude of a disaster for France. Overseas they did. The Engish navy completely dominated the seas. British commanders took over Calcutta and Chandernagore (1757), Louisbourg and Fort Duquesne (1758), Quebec

(1759) and Montreal (1760). "For the first time since the Middle Ages," as one French historian, Martin, expressed it, "England had conquered solely by the superiority of her government" (in Mahan 1957: 289). It was not, however, the British government in its entirety that made the French defeat a reality. Rather, it was the better fiscal regime. Braudel puts the matter thus: "The national debt," resulting from the sale of annuities, "was the major reason for the British victory. It had placed huge sums of money at England's disposal at the very moment when she required them" (1984: 378). At the beginning of the Seven Years War, the British national debt was on the order of eighty million pounds sterling. At the end of it, the debt was approximately one-hundred and forty million pounds sterling (Brewer 1990: 114).

Most of the funds for the annuities came from English commercial capitalists. Some, however, as Neal has emphasized, came from Dutch capitalists (1977: 35). The reason those with capital were eager to invest in British annuities was, as Middleton put it, due to "...the strength of British credit..." (1985: 216). British bonds were guaranteed by Parliament. Britain had never defaulted on its debts. The French monarchy had dealt with its debt at the end of the Thirty Year War and the War of Spanish Succession by repudiation.

During the Elizabethan years, British revenues equalled those of only one province in France (Stone 1967). Britain, as earlier noted, had caught up with France by the time of the first two Anglo-French wars because of the implementation of its better fiscal regime. French government revenues "...were not enough to pay for a continuing succession of new wars" in the eighteenth century (Riley 1986: 132).[21] Thus burdened with an "antiquated" (Dorn 1940: 351) fiscal regime, France simply could not raise the sums that England could by the Seven Years War. Certain French officials of the time were aware of this. Cardinal de Berni, writing to his successor at the foreign ministry in only the second year of the war, predicted that France would be "ruined" because, "No navy, consequently no strength to resist England. The navy has no more sailors, and having no money cannot hope to procure them..." (in ibid.: 353). The year 1759 became known as an *annus mirabilis* of British arms, with decisive victories in North America, Europe, the Caribbean, Africa, and Asia. France had no hope. The Treaty of Paris (1763) formally concluded what had been decided long before. The "antiquated" fiscal regime insured that Louis would spend his last *Louis d'or* long before England spent its last pound.

How did Britain's victory effect its capital accumulation? Answers to this question have, in considerable measure, turned upon judgements as to the effects of the Seven Years War on French and British trade. There has been debate concerning French trade. Riley argues that in eighteenth century France "...the trend of commercial activity was one of impressive growth" (1986: 105). Others take a darker view. François Crouzet argues that the Seven Years War was extremely disruptive of French trade (1966: 264). Robert Foster argues that the mid-eighteenth century wars "...had a permanently debilitating effect upon French overseas trade" (1980: 12).

I believe that both sides in this exchange make helpful points. Certainly, Riley is correct to note that French trade did grow in the eighteenth century. However, much of this increase was in European markets, where French commerce rose 200 per cent between 1715 and 1783, while British commerce grew only 140 per cent (Davis 1973: 307). Nevertheless, France might have done better. It was not so much that France's commerce suffered as a result of its defeat. Rather it was that England enjoyed exceptional gains, for "...it had made advances in the West Indies and West Africa, had virtually eliminated French influence from India, and, most important of all, was now supreme in most of the North American continent" (Kennedy 1987: 114). In a sense, though there were two wars to follow, England had "...essentially defeated France in the periphery and deprived France of its right to compete outside Europe" (Goldstein 1988: 325). Thus, England had "...access to vast new wealth, which its rivals did not enjoy" (Kennedy 1987: 138). Total English trade in the Americas and India grew from roughly 2,850 to 12,626 million pounds sterling between 1699–1701 and 1772–4 (Davis 1962: 300–1), an increase of well over 400 per cent.

The Seven Years War, then, might be interpreted as the culmination of a process that had been in operation since the Anglo-Dutch Wars. The blue-water military regime linked military institutions to those of commercial capitalist complex by exercising violent naval force to produce conditions for commercial capitalists to organize their accumulation of captial. Capital accumulation, then, became at least partially dependent upon predatory accumulation in a manner that made "English commerce...foremost in the world..." (Beaud 1983: 63).

The evidence suggests that in the seventeenth century England acquired its fiscal and the blue-water military regimes. The fiscal regime provided a strong flow of revenues from capitalist institutions in the capitalist complex to the treasury and the military in the governmental complex. In turn, the military regime provided a counter-flow of capital due to the commercial advantages to the capitalist complex.

CONCLUSION

Eric Wolf, in *Europe and the People Without History*, noted that European states became more "consolidated" by the late Middle ages (1982: 101). What Wolf called consolidated I have termed centralized. He, then, observed that "...several of the consoldiated states sought out new frontiers in a collaboration between war-making rulers and the merchant class" (ibid.: 101). This insight is both obvious yet penetrating. It had long been obvious to scholars that there was a great deal of killing and profiting during the early modern period. What was so original about Wolf's insight was that nobody else had recognized these for what they were, aspects of a *common* structure. The making of modernity in the field of early modern Atlantic states was, in some measure, history of making a structure in which there was "collaboration" between governmental killing and private profiting. I have sought in this article merely to enlarge upon Wolf's original insight, elaborating upon the nature of the collaboration.

The history of Atlantic states in feudal fields followed a logic of predatory accumulation. Lords fought to acquire more land to extract greater revenues from agricultural laborers so that they might command a larger host in a later round of fighting. But this logic of medieval predatory accumulation was largely unrelated to how merchants were acquiring their profits. Spain and Portugal developed a new logic of predatory accumulation during their expansion that catalyzed capital accumulation because their rulers purchased violent force on the market from merchants. This made war good for business. Unfortunately, Iberian rulers never linked the two accumulations reciprocally, because they failed to innovate fiscal regimes that could move significant amounts of capital from capitalist to governmental complexes. So business was not good for Spanish war.

Spain attempted to use violent force to impose the fiscal regime it needed on the Low Countries. The resulting Eighty Year War was a catastrophe for Spain and led to a structural revolution in the field of centralizing Atlantic states. The Dutch, to defend themselves from the Spansih Fury, developed the fiscal regime that Philip wanted. They used the increased revenues form this fiscal regime to institute a military regime whose increased violent force crushed Spain while at the same time securing competitive advantage for Dutch merchants to increase their capital force. Here was the first military-capitalist complex where there was "collaboration" between capitalist and governmental complexes. England, of course, went on to build a better military-capitalist complex. This complex might be thought of as the motor of the "great Leviathan" of modernity, because it allowed the two reciprocating logics of predatory and capital accumulation to rachet up further violent and capital force, adding to the accumulations of these forces that were already occuring within the capitalist and governmental complexes. So the British Leviathan acquired, and exercised, more violent and capital force than had hitherto been possible, leading by the end of the eighteenth century to a degree of fiscal and capitalist domination that was global in reach.

The reinterpretation of early modern Atlantic state history that has just been offered is itself an elaboration of an older anthropological tradition. Many anthropologists came to believe in the years between the publication of Marcel Mauss' *The Gift* (1924), Lévi-Strauss' *Elementary Structures of Kinship* (1949) and Marshall Sahlin's *Stone Age Economics* (1972) that stateless peoples were structured on the basis of different forms of reciprocity. These reciprocities involved, in my terms, exchanges of roughly equal amounts of economic force betweeen institutional complexes of relatives in fields of kinship. The logic of these reciprocities was not that of an accumulation. Violent or economic force did not premanently increase and concentrate in the fields of kinship. Rather, the giving of gifts and counter-gifts followed a logic of perpetuation. Kin saw to it that they gave and received what they needed.

Anthropologists were never particularly interested in, or successful at, extending their analysis of reciprocity to modern society. However, the argument I have made situates a reciprocity at the very core of the Leviathan that had emerged by 1763. However, this reciprocity was a grim and paradoxical one, for it makes possible its opposite. It included only a tiny upper class of those who controlled government and capitalist complexes. These upper class persons collaborated with each other through reciprocal exchanges of capital and violent force to help each other expand their fields of fiscal and capitalist domination, thereby excluding all others from the acquisition of these forces. This article began in a playful mood, promising readers a whale of a story. I apologize for misleading them, because the story of what emerged by 1763 has been no joke. The Leviathan was a military capitalist complex, the force of whose reciprocating logics killed so that the rich could get richer, and got richer so that the killers might do it again, only more so.

NOTES

1. A more complete account of the new social anthropology is in progress (Reyna, ND). Readers might note that force and power are defined as follows. "Force" is that which makes power. "Power" is the ability to make things occur. This ability results from force, the combination of resources whose utilization generates power. So understood, there are many types of forces. Violent and capital force are important in this article. The key resource in "violent force" is the means of destruction. The key resource in "capital force" is money.
2. Others beside Bartlett have realized that there was a late medieval expansion in Western Europe (Jones 1987, Scammel 1981).
3. Medieval fiscal regimes are discussed in Henneman (1971), Miller (1972), Strayer and Holt (1939) and Mann (1986: 418).
4. Discussion of Spanish government and revenues during the time under consideration can be found in Hillgarth (1978), Alvarez (1966) and Thompson (1976).
5. Roberts (1967), Parker (1989), and Downing (1992) discuss the "military revolution".
6. Analysis of the rise of the early modern Dutch economy can be found in Zanden (1992); of the revolt, in Geyl (1958) and Parker (1977); and of the nature of the state, in Hart (1993) and Price (1994).
7. Accounts of the creation of England's early modern fiscal regime are in Brewer (1990) and Dickson (1967).
8. The pace at which fiscal departments expanded was not constant. The most rapid growth was during the Nine Years War and its almost immediate successor, the War of Spanish Succession (1688–1714). There were approximately 6000 persons working in some part of the fiscal bureaucracy by 1714 (Brewer 1990: 67).
9. Customs, excise, and land taxes provided 90 per cent of 18th century state revenues. Excise and customs surpass land taxes as revenue sources after 1714 (Brewer 1990: 95).
10. Bluewater is sometimes referred to in the literature as "maritime" and "navalist" strategy. I follow Kennedy's (1976) and Duffy's (1980) accounts of the founding of the British navy.
11. Corbett's (1898) account of the Tudor navy and privateering remains useful. Andrews (1964) is more recent.
12. Extensive discussion of English commerce during late Tudor and early Stuart times can be found in Brenner (1993: 3–50). During the period 1571–1640 there were only 36 years of good trade (Hinton 1955). Not all trade problems were due to the Dutch/Spanish conflict. However, a considerable problem that the conflict did pose to English trade was that it tended to cut English merchants off from their entrepots in Iberia and the Low Countries, and it was from these that they got their imports for England.

13. The Portuguese/British conflict at the turn of the seventeenth century in the Indian Ocean is described in Andrews (1984: 270–77) and Chaudhuri (1965: 80–96).
14. The Anglo-Dutch wars are discussed in Wilson (1957), Mahan (1957: 126–141), and Pincus (1994).
15. Wallerstein says of France compared to England, "France had four times the population of England and a far larger army. She was rich in natural resources with excellent ports and naval bases. Furthermore, her industrial production was growing..." (1980: 246).
16. Useful histories of War of the League of Augsburg can be found in Clark (1923), Ehrman (1953), and Powley (1972).
17. Accounts of the War of Spanish Succession can be found in Clark (1928), Crouse (1943), Thompson (1968), and Jones (1988).
18. Britain had secured naval control of the Mediterranean by 1706, forcing France "...entirely out of that sea..." and, as a result, "...we...secured our trade with the Levant, and strengthened our interests with all the Italian princes..." (Campbell, in Mahan 1957: 203).
19. Literature pertaining to the British participation in the War of the Austrian Succession is limited; see, however, Richmond (1920) and Baugh (1965).
20. The Seven Years War is analyzed in Entick (1763–64), Corbett (1907), Pares (1963), Sharrard (1975), Middleton (1985), and Riley (1986).
21. Discussion of the deficiencies of the fiscal regime of France in the eighteenth century can be found in Goldstone (1991: 196–221), Morineau (1980), and Mathias and O'Brien (1976). Its fundamental problem was that most taxes were drawn from the weakest sector of the economy, peasant agriculture (Goldstone 1991: 202).

REFERENCES

Alvarez, M. F. (1966). La España del Emperador Carlos v. Madrid.

Aylmer, G. E. (1961). The King's Servants. London: Routledge.

Anderson, Perry (1979). Lineages of the Absolutist State. London: Verso.

Andrews, Kenneth (1964). Elizabethan Privateering. Cambridge: Cambridge University Press.

——— (1984). Trade, Plunder and Settlement: Maritime Enterprise and the Genesis of the British Empire, 1480–1630. Cambridge: Cambridge University Press.

Ashley, Maurice (1961). Financial and Commercial Policy Under the Cromwellian Protectorate. New York: Augustus Kelley.

Bartlett, Robert (1993). The Making of Europe, Conquest, Colonization and Cultural Change 950–1350. Princeton, NJ: Princeton University Press.

Baugh, Daniel (1965). British Naval Administration in the Age of Walpole. Princeton: Princeton University Press.

Beaud, Michel (1983). A History of Capitalism, 1500–1980. New York: Monthly Review Press.
Boxer, C. R. (1965). The Dutch Seaborne Empire, 1600–1800. New York: Knopf.
—————— (1969). The Portuguese Seaborne Empire, 1415–1825. New York: Knopf.
Braudel, Fernand (1972[1949]). The Mediterranean and the Mediterranean World in the Age of Philip II. Vol. 1. New York: Harper Row.
—————— (1975). The Mediterranean and the Mediterranean World in the Age of Philip II. Vol. 2. New York: Harper Row.
—————— (1984). The Perspective of the World: Civilization and Capitalism, 15th–18th Centuries. Vol. 3. New York: Harper Row.
Brenner, Robert (1993). Merchants and Revolution: Commercial Change, Political Conflict, and London's Overseas Traders, 1550–1663. Princeton: Princeton University Press.
Brewer, John (1990). The Sinews of Power: War, Money and the English State, 1688–1783. Cambridge, MA: Harvard University Press.
Buffinton, A. H. (1929). The Second Hundred Years War. New York: Holt.
Cain, P. J. and A. G. Hopkins (1986). The Political Economy of British Expansion Overseas, 1750–1914. Economic History Review XXXIII(4): 463–490.
Capp, Barnard (1989). Cromwell's Navy: The Fleet and the English Revolution, 1648–1660. Oxford: Clarendon.
Carter, Alice (1975). Neutrality or Commitment: The Evolution of Dutch Foreign Policy, 1667–1795. London: Edw. Arnold.
Chaudhuri, K. N. (1965). The English East India Company. New York: Reprints of Economics Classics.
Clark, G. N. (1923). The Dutch Alliance and the War Against French Trade, 1688–1697. London: Longmans.
—————— (1928). War Trade and Trade War. Economic History Review 1(2): 277–278.
—————— (1975). The Foundation of Sociology. New York: Wiley.
Corbett, J. S. (1898). Drake and the Tudor Navy. 2 Vols. London: Longmans.
—————— (1907). England and the Seven Years War: A Study in Combined Strategy. 2 Vols. London: Longman.
Crouse, Nellis (1943). The French Struggle for the West Indies, 1665–1713. New York: Columbia University Press.
Crouzet, F. (1966). Angleterre et France au XVII siècle: Essai d'analyse comparative de deux croissances économiques. Annales, E.S.C. 21(2).
Davis, Ralph (1962). English Foreign Trade, 1700–1774. Economic History Review XV (2): 285–303.
—————— (1973). The Rise of the Atlantic Economies. Ithaca, NY: Cornell University Press.
Diaz, Bernal (1963). The Conquest of New Spain. Harmondsworth, England: Penguin.

Dickson, P. G. M. (1967). The Financial Revolution in England: A Study in the Development of Public Credit, 1688–1756. New York: St Martins.
Dickson, P. G. M. and John Sperling (1961). War Finance, 1689–1714. *In* New Cambridge Modern History. Vol. 6. Cambridge: Cambridge University Press.
Dorn, Walter (1940). Competition for an Empire. New York: Harper.
Downing, B. (1992). The Military Revolutions and Political Change. Princeton: Princeton University Press.
Duffy, Michael (1980). The Foundation of British Naval Power. *In* The Military Revolution and the State, 1500–1800. M. Duffy, ed. Exeter, UK: Exeter Studies in History. #1.
Dupuy, R. E. and T. N. Dupuy (1986). An Encyclopedia of Military History. New York: Harper.
Durkheim, Emile (1957). Professional Ethics and Civic Morals. London: Routledge.
Edmundson, G. (1911). Anglo-Dutch Rivalry During the First Half of the Seventeenth Century. Oxford: Clarendon.
Ehrman, John (1953). The Navy in the War of William III. Cambridge: Cambridge University Press.
Elliot, J. H. (1964). Imperial Spain, 1469–1716. New York: St Martins.
Engels, F. (1962). Anti-Dühring; Herr Dührings Revolution. Moscow: Foreign Languages Publishing House.
Entick, J. (1763–64). The General History of the Late War, Containing its Rise, Progress, and Events in Europe, Asia, Africa, and America, 5 Vols. London: E. & C. Dilly.
Feiling, Keith (1968). British Foreign Policy, 1660–1672. London: Frank Cass.
Foster, Robert (1980). Merchants, Landlords, Magistrates: The Dupont Family in the 18th Century. Baltimore: Johns Hopkins Press.
Geyl, Pieter (1958[1931]). The Revolt of the Netherlands. New York: Barnes and Noble.
Giddens, Anthony (1984). The Constitution of Society. Los Angeles: University of California Press.
——————— (1985). The Nation-State and Violence. Los Angeles: University of California Press.
Godinho, Vitorino (1944). A Expansao Quatrocenista Portuguesa: Problamas das Origens e da Linha de Evolucao. Lisboa:
Goldstein, Joshua (1988). Long Cycles, Prosperity and War in the Modern Age. New Haven: Yale University Press.
Goldstone, Jack (1991). Revolution and Rebellion in the Early Modern World. Los Angeles: University of California Press.
Gramsci, A. (1971). Selections from Prison Notebooks. London: Lawrence and Wishart.
Haley, K. H. D. (1972). The Dutch in the Seventeenth Century. London: Harcourt, Brace, Jovanovitch.
Hamilton, E. J. (1934). American Treasure and the Price Revolution in Spain, 1501–1650. Cambridge: Harvard University Press.

Harris, Robert (1979). Necker, Reform Statesman of the Ancien Regime. Los Angeles: University of California Press.
Hart, Marjolein C. 't. (1993). The Making of the Bourgeois State: War, Politics and Finance During the Dutch Revolution. Manchester: Manchester University Press.
Henneman, J. B. (1971). Royal Taxation in Fourteenth Century France. Princeton, NJ: Princeton University Press.
Hillgarth, J. N. (1978). The Spanish Kingdoms, 1419–1516: Castilian Hegemony. Vol 2. Oxford: Clarendon.
Hinton, R. W. K. (1955). The Mercantile System in the Times of Thomas Mun. Economic History Review VII(3): 277–90.
——— (1959). The Eastland Trade and the Commonwealth in the 17th Century. New York: Cambridge University Press.
Hobbes, T. (1958). The Leviathan. Indianapolis: Bobbs Merrill.
Homer, Sidney (1963). A History of Interest Rates. New Brunswick, NJ: Rutgers University Press.
Hugill, Peter (1993). World Trade since 1431: Geography, Technology and Capitalism. Baltimore: Johns Hopkins University Press.
Israel, Jonathan (1988). Competing Cousins: Anglo-Dutch Trade Rivalry. History Today XXXVIII: 17–22.
——— (1989). Dutch Primacy in World Trade, 1585–1740. Oxford: Oxford University Press.
——— (1995). The Dutch Republic. Oxford: Oxford University Press.
Jones, D. W. (1988). War and Economy in the Age of William III and Marlborough. New York: Blackwell.
Kamen, Henry (1991). Spain, 1469–1714. London: Longman.
Kammen, Michael (1970). Empire and Interest: The American Colonies and the Politics of Mercantilism. New York: Lippincott.
Kautsky, J. H. (1982). The Politics of Aristocratic Empires. Chapel Hill, NC: University of North Carolina Press.
Kennedy, Paul (1976). The Rise and Fall of British Naval Mastery. New York: Scribners.
——— (1987). The Rise and Fall of Great Powers. New York: Random House.
Kent, H. S. K. (1973). War and Trade in Northern Seas, Anglo-Scandinavian Economic Relations in the Mid-Eighteenth Century. New York: Cambridge University Press.
Koenigsberger, H. G. (1971). The Hapsburgs and Europe, 1516–1660. Ithaca, NY: Cornell University Press.
Lang, James (1975). Conquest and Commerce, Spain and England in the Americas. NewYork: Academic Press.
Lenin, V. I. (1939[1913]). Imperialism: The Highest Stage of Capitalism. New York: International Publishers.
Leon-Portillo, Miguel (1962). The Broken Spears, The Aztec Account of the Conquest of Mexico. Boston: Beacon.

Lévi-Strauss, C. (1969). The Elementary Structures of Kinship. Boston: Beacon.
Luxemburg, Rosa (1951[1913]). The Accumulation of Capital. New Haven: Yale University Press.
Lynch, John (1991). Spain 1516–1598, From Nation-State to World Empire. Cambridge, MA: Blackwell.
Mahan, A. T. (1957[1890]). The Influence of Seapower Upon History. New York: Sagamore Press.
Mandel, Ernest (1968). Marxist Economic Theory. London: Merlin Press.
Mann, Michael (1986). The Sources of Social Power: A History of Power from the Beginning to AD 1760. New York: Cambridge University Press.
Mathias, P. and P. O'Brien (1976). Taxation in Britain and France, 1715–1810: A Camparison of the Social and Economic Incidence of Taxes Collected for the Central Government. Journal of European History 5: 601–650.
McGowan, Alan (1981). The Ship. Tiller and Whipstaff: The Development of the Sailing Ship, 1400–1700. London: National Maritime Museum.
Middleton, Richard (1985). The Bells of Victory: The Pitt-Newcastle Ministry and the Conduct of the Seven Years War, 1757–1762. Cambridge: Cambridge University Press.
Miller, E. (1972). Government, Economic Policies and Public Finance, 1000–1500. In The Fontana Economic History of Europe, The Middle Ages. C. M. Cipolla, ed. London: Fontana.
Modelski, George and W. R. Thompson (1988). Seapower in Global Politics. Seattle: University of Washington Press.
Morineau, M. (1980). Budgets de l'état et gestion des finances royales en France au dix-huitième siècle. Revue Historique 264: 289–336.
Morgan, L. H. (1877). Ancient Society. New York: H. Holt & Co.
Neal, Larry (1977). Interpreting Power and Profit in Economic History: A Case Study of the Seven Year's War. Journal of Economic History XXXVII(1): 20–36.
Nef, J. U. (1958). Cultural Foundations of Industrial Civilization. Cambridge: Cambridge University Press.
North, D. C. and R. P. Thomas (1973). The Rise of the Western World. Cambridge: Cambridge University Press.
Oliveira Marques, A. H. de. (1972). History of Portugal, from Lusitania to Empire. New York: Oxford University Press.
Pagden, A. (1990). Spanish Imperialism and the Political Imagination. New Haven: Yale University Press.
Palmer, R. R. and Joel Colton (1965). A History of the Modern World. New York: Knopf.
Pares, Richard (1963[1936]). War and Trade in the West Indies, 1739–1763. London: Frank Cass.
Parker, Geoffrey (1977). The Dutch Revolt. Harmondsworth, UK: Penguin.
——————— (1989). The Military Revolution, Military Innovation and the Rise of the West, 1500–1800. New York: Cambridge University Press.

Pearson, M. N. (1991). Merchants and States. *In* The Political Economy of Merchant Empires. J. D. Tracy, ed. New York: Cambridge University Press.

Pemsel, Helmut (1977). A History of War at Sea. An Atlas and Chronology of Conflict at Sea from Earliest Times to the Present. Annapolis, MD: Naval Institute.

Phillips, J. R. S. (1988). The Medieval Expansion of Europe. New York: Oxford University Press.

Pincus, Steven (1994). Popery, Trade and Universal Monarchy: The Ideological Context of the Outbreak of the Second Anglo-Dutch War. English Historical Review CVIII (422): 1–30.

Powers, James (1988). A Society Organized for War, The Iberian Municipal Militias in the Central Middle Ages, 1000–1284. Los Angeles: University of California Press.

Powley, E. B. (1972). The Naval Side of King William's War, 16th/26th Nov. 1688–14th June 1697. Hamden, CT: Archon Books.

Prescott, William (1949). History of the Conquest of Mexico. London: Allan and Unwin.

Price, J. L. (1994). Holland and the Dutch Republic in the Seventeenth Century, the Politics of Particularism. Oxford: Clarendon.

Rahn-Phillips, Carla (1990). Trade in the Iberian Empires, 1450–1750. *In* The Rise of Merchant Empires: Long Distance Trade in the early Modern World, 1350–1750. J. D. Tracy, ed. New York: Cambridge University Press.

Reitzer, L. (1960). Castillian Commerce and Finance in the Sixteenth Century. Journal of Modern History XXXII (3): 213–23.

Reyna, S. P. (1990). Wars Without End, The Political Economy of a Precolonial Africa State. Hanover, NH: University Press of New England.

——————— (1994). A Mode of Domination Approach to Organized Violence. *In* Studying War, Anthropological Perspectives. S. P. Reyna and R. E. Downs, eds. pp. 29–69. London: Gordon and Breach.

——————— nd Hot Stuff, Essays in the New Social Anthropology. Manuscript.

Richmond, Herbert (1920). The Navy and the War of 1739–1748, 3 Vols. Cambridge: Cambridge University Press.

Riley, James, C. (1986). The Seven Years War and the Old Regime in France: The Economic and Financial Toll. Princeton, NJ: Princeton University Press.

Roberts, M. (1967). Essays in Swedish History. Minneapolis: University of Minnesota Press.

Robertson, C. G. (1962). Chatham and the British Empire. New York: Collier.

Root, H. L. (1994). The Fountain of Privilege. Los Angeles: University of California Press.

Rowen, H. H. (1972). The Low Countries in Early Modern Times. New York: Walker.

Sahlins, M. (1976). Culture and Practical Reason. Chicago: University of Chicago Press.

Scammell, G. V. (1989). The First Imperial Age: European Overseas Expansion, c. 1400–1715. London: Unwin Hyman.
Schama, Simon (1988). The Embarrassment of Riches: An Interpretation of Dutch Culture in the Golden Age. Los Angeles: University of California Press.
Sharrard, O. A. (1975). Lord Catham, Pitt and the Seven Year's War. Westport, CN: Greenwood Press.
Sidney, Homer (1963). A History of Interest Rates. New Brunswick, NJ: Rutgers University Press.
Smith, Adam (1776). The Wealth of Nations. Dublin: Whiteston.
Sombart, Werner (1913). Studien Zur Entwecklungsgeschichte des Modernen Kapitalismus. Krieg und Kapitalismus. Munchen: Duncker & Hombot.
Sonnino, Paul (1988). Louis XIV and the Origins of the Dutch War. Cambridge: Cambridge University Press.
Stein, S. J. and B. H. Stein (1970). The Colonial Heritage of Latin America. New York: Oxford University Press.
Spencer, Herbert (1896). The Principles of Sociology. New York: Appleton and Co.
Stone, Lawrence (1967). The Crisis of the Aristocracy, 1558–1641. New York: Oxford.
Strayer, J. R. (1982). Western Europe in the Middle Ages, 3rd. ed. Glenview, IL: Scott, Foresman and Co.
Strayer, J. R. and C. H. Holt (1939). *Studies in Early French Taxation.* Cambridge, MA: Harvard University Press.
Tallett, Frank (1992). War and Society in Early Modern Europe. New York: Routledge.
Thompson, I. A. A. (1976). War and Government in Habsburg, Spain. London: Althone.
Thompson, J. F. and E. A. Johnson (1937). An Introduction to Medieval Europe, 300–1500. New York: Norton.
Thompson, M. A. (1968). Louis XIV and the Origins of the War of Spanish Succession. *In* William III and Louis XIV. R. Hatton and J. S. Bromley, eds. Liverpool: Liverpool University Press.
Thomson, David (1950). England in the Nineteenth Century. Harmondsworth: Penguin.
Thomson, J. E. (1994). Mercenaries, Pirates and Sovereigns: State Building and Extraterritorial Violence in Early Modern Europe. Princeton: Princeton University Press.
Tilly, Charles (1975). Reflections on the History of European State Making. *In* The Formation of National States in Western Europe. C. Tilly, ed. Princeton, NJ: Princeton University Press.
────────── (1990). Coercion, Capital, and European States, AD 990–1992. Cambridge, MA: Blackwell.
Tracy, J. D. (1985). A Financial Revolution in the Habsburg Netherlands, *Renten and Renteniers* in the County of Holland, 1515–1565. Los Angeles: University of California Press.

——— (1991). Introduction. *In* The Political Economy of Merchant Empires. J. D. Tracy, ed. New York: Cambridge University Press.
Trevelyan, G. M. (1953). History of England, The Tudor and Stuart Era. Vol 2. Garden City, NY: Anchor.
Vilar, Pierre (1974). The Age of Don Quixote. *In* Essays in European Economic History, 1500–1800. Peter Earle, ed. Oxford: Clarendon Press.
Vives, Jaime (1972). The Economics of Catalonia and Castile. *In* Spain in the 15th Century, 1369–516. R. Highfield, ed. New York: Harper and Row.
Wallerstein, Immanuel (1976). The Modern World System. Vol. 1. New York: Academic Press.
——— (1980). The Modern World System, Vol. 2. New York: Academic Press.
Williams, Glyndwr (1966). The Expansion of Europe in the 18th Century: Overseas Rivalry, Discovery and Exploration. New York: Walker and Co.
Wilson, C. H. (1941). Anglo-Dutch Commerce and Finance in the Eighteenth Century. Cambridge, UK: Cambridge University Press.
——— (1957). Profit and Power: A Study of England and the Dutch Wars. London: Longmans.
Wolf, Eric (1982). Europe and the People Without History. Los Angeles: University of California Press.
Zanden, J. L. van (1992). The Rise and Decline of Holland's Economy: Merchant Capitalism and Labour Markets. Manchester: Manchester University Press.

Chapter TWO

Colonialism and the Efflorescence of warfare: The New Ireland Case

Abraham Rosman and Paula G. Rubel
Barnard College, Columbia University

> Rosman and Rubel ask their readers to consider what seems, at first glance, to be just another case of "primitive" tribal war in the south Pacific at the end of the nineteenth century. Their keen insight, however, shows that this outburst of fighting among New Irelanders was precipitated by a growth of agrarian capitalism in the Pacific that served to supply raw materials to industry in capitalist states.

The role of warfare in prestate or "tribal" societies was of interest to anthropologists even before the advent of fieldwork at the end of the nineteenth century. In general, in the early stages, anthropologists interested in warfare investigated the ways in which it functioned in so-called pristine societies unaffected by culture change. Not finding any such societies, they acted as if the societies they did study were unaffected by direct or indirect contact with Europeans and not subject to other foreign influences. This tradition is continued today in Knauft's recent encyclopedic theoretical history of Melanesian warfare (1990). Later, different kinds of causal explanations for warfare, its effects on social systems, as well as the factors that "maintained warfare" were of primary concern (see Haas 1990).

More recently, discussion has shifted to a rephrasing of the problem as warfare in the "tribal" zone, which is defined as "The area continuously affected by the proximity of a state, but not under state administration..." (Ferguson and Whitehead 1992: 3). We now recognize that European contact with indigenous peoples in the many areas of the world where the World System and its empire builders penetrated had a whole series of consequences, technological, economic, political, social, environmental, and pathological with the introduction of new diseases, etc. New patterns of warfare in the tribal zone were also a result of the territorial expansion of states (Ferguson and Whitehead 1992: 18ff). In their discussion, Ferguson and Whitehead put forth several analytical categories, including wars of resistance and rebellion against the state itself, the enlistment of indigenous people as an armed force by state agents, and war between indigenous peoples themselves as they respond to their changing circumstances. The discussion that we will present in this paper concerns the third category. This kind of warfare might be over control of newly developed trade in European items of all kinds, including guns, trade in captive laborers, or wars of plunder (Ferguson and Whitehead 1992: 23–4).

In our recent research on the regional history of New Ireland, we have noted that there was an efflorescence of warfare coincident with the first intensive contact of the New Irelanders with Europeans in the 1880s. By efflorescence, we mean an increase in the frequency of occurrence of violent conflicts and in the intensity of fighting that was brought about by the introduction of guns and iron axes used as tomahawks. The way in which warfare was carried out also changed to some extent. Up until intensive European contact, warfare between politically autonomous villages was endemic, but since no group had a long-term advantage, either as a consequence of more resources, weaponry, or manpower, there was a balance of power between warring groups.

The first description of the indigenous pattern of New Ireland warfare before it was transformed by intensive contact with Europeans is that provided by John Coulter, the surgeon aboard the English ship *Hound*, who came to New Ireland in 1835. During this period, many ships stopped in New Ireland to reprovision, but hardly any Europeans went ashore. Coulter visited a village that was at war with people from another district. He made a trip to their "outpost," which was guarded by "....thirty grim-looking warriors all armed with lances, clubs, bow and arrows, and their bodies streaked with red ochre" (Coulter 1973 [1847], Vol.1: 269). Coulter describes the bodies of slain enemies with legs cut off at the knees and hands cut off at the wrists, preparatory to cooking, and he deduced that the New Irelanders were cannibals. He took part in a raid in which the villagers he was with were attempting to retrieve men who had been captured. On this occasion he used his gun, since his party was outnumbered, noting, "This new instrument of warfare, both in effect and sound, at once staggered them" (Coulter 1973 [1847], Vol.1: 287). In order to return to their home village from an allied village after the prisoners had been rescued, it was necessary to go past a bay belonging to still another hostile group where they were attacked by canoes. From Coulter's longer description it would appear that contiguous groups were "traditional enemies" to one another and usually at war. On the other side of one's enemies were one's allies, forming a checkerboard pattern of allies and enemies. This same pattern of organization of enemies and allies was reported by Bell in the 1930s for the island of Tanga off New Ireland (Bell 1935).

More intensive contact with Europeans began in 1875 with the arrival of missionaries. During the early 1880s labor recruitment began and a network of European trading stations was established as part of the expansion of the copra trade. This network of trading stations was superimposed upon the earlier New Ireland checkerboard pattern of allies and enemies. The establishment of trading stations by Eduard Hernsheim, a German copra trader, in places like Nusa and Kapsu along the northeast coast made the groups that lived there much more important nodes of exchange. When trading stations were established at two villages that were traditional enemies to one another, the intersection of the two patterns produced interesting results. For example, Hernsheim was able to call on the Nusa people to help him put down the "uprising" of the people of Lavongai village when they attacked his station there, since the Lavongai were the traditional enemies of the people at Nusa (Hernsheim 1983: 135). In this case the Nusa people considered the Europeans allies; in other instances,

Europeans seem to have been put into the category of enemies and their stations attacked.

The introduction of guns through trade or via labor recruiters resulted in significant changes in the balance of power if one side had guns and the other did not. Guns also affected the way in which warfare was organized. In pre-contact times, besides raiding, warfare also involved two sides massing on a battlefield, with displays and mocking of the enemy. But the devasting long-range effects of guns no longer permitted such displays, and brought about changes in how these kinds of wars were fought. Guns began to be dispensed in increasing numbers, and by 1884 the Australian government reiterated its prohibition against the trading of firearms by labor recruiters. That year the Captain of the *Ariel*, a labor recruiting ship, was barred from the labor trade for having supplied rifles to the people of Nusa (Corris 1968: 92). Groups that had acquired one or two guns had advantages over those that had none. Earlier in the nineteenth century, as was the case in other parts of the Pacific, iron axe heads began to be traded to New Irelanders by whalers and other visitors in return for fresh supplies. These were hafted onto three-foot hardwood handles, becoming what Europeans called "tomahawks." In the 1800s, these iron war axes were much more widely distributed than guns. Oral history accounts concerning the latter part of the nineteenth century indicate that the introduction of iron axes resulted in an increase in hostilities and an efflorescence of warfare. New Irelanders describe a period of intensified warfare (called *rom* in Patpatar) that developed after European contact. It is reported that the clan warrior, who held a special position different from the Big Man, led the clan into war. Clan warriors always had such axes, but other warriors in the clan might also have them (Rosman and Rubel, field notes, 1987).

The first description we have of the New Irelanders' use of guns in their own inter-village warfare comes from Jean Baptiste Octave Mouton, a trader and planter, who had come to New Ireland to recruit workers for his plantation in New Britain. While in Labur in 1892, recruiting labor for his plantation in New Britain, Mouton observed the way warfare was being conducted at that time. The people at Labur took Mouton to their allies in the next district, who were engaged in fighting a third party. According to Mouton, "They wanted the protection of our firearms to protect them in their raid they were making in the next district to revenge themselves of a similar raid. One of the enemies [sic] has a shneider rifle and they were afraid of him and thought of using us as protection" (Mouton 1974: 95). When one's traditional enemy has even a single gun, the balance of power is disrupted. In this case, the other side, without any guns, enlisted a white man and his guns to redress the balance. Though the latter was present, he did not fire a single shot.

Germany had annexed New Ireland in 1884 as part of its colony of German New Guinea. Though the German Government first ran it as a commercial enterprise by the Neu Guinea Kompagnie, it began to take administrative control of the colony in the early 1890s and appointed Albert Hahl as the new Imperial Judge in 1895. One of the first actions of the Neu Guinea Kompagnie had been to form a police force recruited from "among the natives of Neu Mecklenburg or from the Solomon Islands" (Neu Guinea Kompagnie, Annual Report for 1886–87: 12). In 1895, Hahl had twenty-four Police Boys under his command, with seventy-five men in reserve. Most of his activities in New Ireland (at that point called Neu Mecklenberg) seem to have involved undertaking punitive expeditions in reprisal for raids by the local people on European trading stations.

By this time guns had become an extremely important factor in inter-village warfare. In September of 1896, a sentry, who was from Madina on the east coast of New Ireland, broke into the armory at Herbertshohe (later renamed Rabaul), the capital of the colony in New Britain. He and fourteen of his fellow villagers from Madina stole five rifles and five hundred cartridges. They made their escape in a stolen cutter pursued by Hahl, who was unable to catch them. Hahl noted in his memoirs that they "....had absconded to help their home village which was reported to have engaged in a fight with a neighbouring district" (Hahl 1980: 18). However, Hahl reports that with the help of the five stolen rifles, by the middle of October, they were "....carrying out extensive raids of pillage and vengeance, bringing recruitment, trade and communications to a complete standstill" (1980: 18). Hahl launched a retaliatory raid, and a band of warriors armed with spears from a village that was enemy to Madina joined Hahl's party of Police Boys. At Leineru, another traditional enemy of Madina's, Hahl commandered canoes and launched an auxiliary force of men from Leineru to block off Madina from the sea while he took his land force into the hills behind Madina to attack them the next morning. The Madina people were taken by surprise and resisted in "bitter fighting," but then fled to the south. Hahl recaptured some ammunition, but not the stolen rifles. Though Hahl tried to prevent it, his local allies took the bodies of their slain enemies back to their villages to be consumed.

The men of Madina had stolen the rifles in order to use them to take vengeance against their traditional enemies. Hahl, the European, was employing the existing pattern of traditional enemies and allies to his own advantage, as Hernsheim had. However, this incident had repercussions, in that subsequently the people of Madina raided a trading station that had recently been established by Hernsheim at Leineru village. According to Hahl, "...this station was robbed and destroyed by natives from the village of Madine (Madina) when they avenged themselves on the natives of Leineru, their hereditary enemies, for their assistance they had rendered to me" (Hahl 1980: 30). As Firth notes, "In the fights between the Madina people and their enemies on the opposite coast line in New Ireland both sides were led by men who had served with the German police" (1978: 33).

Somewhat later, Hahl received a deputation from the district of Bom, a west coast village in the Namatanai area, who complained to him that they and their neighbors were being menaced by people from the east coast village of Sohun. According to Hahl, "There had been fighting before between themselves and these people with whom they had a long-standing blood feud. But since they themselves had joined the Wesleyan Mission and therefore now refrained from all hostilities, peace had reigned in recent times. But now some of their members who had been working in the mountains had been killed, their bodies taken off as booty and devoured. They appealed to me for help to prevent further bloodshed" (Hahl 1980: 45). The troop that Hahl brought with him to Bom was joined by local people "from all sides." After crossing the mountains to the east coast, they encountered the well-armed enemy (who did not appear to have guns) in a clearing.

In Hahl's account, "They sprang up shouting their war-cries and brandishing their weapons. I did not need to give any orders to my men. They saw before them an open field of fire and formed up to the right and left of me with lightening speed. Some of our allies also rushed forward inciting the men to shoot and fight. With difficulty, I restrained my troops and called on the enemy to quit the field. It was a tense moment. But the other side realized that their only hope was to flee which they then did with astonishing speed in the direction of the sea. Now there was no holding the warriors, who rushed screaming and shouting after the escaping enemy. I kept back my troops except for five men... for I was anxious to take the village belonging to the other side in order to try to mediate peacefully between the warring factions. But my plans were frustrated — from the forward line I heard shots and the savage war cries of hand to hand fighting.... The fugitives...took flight immediately some of their number were felled by the bullets of the soldiers. The corpses of these unfortunates were most terribly mutilated by their hereditary enemies, every one of whom had to plunge his spear once into the blood of the enemy. By this time I had gathered my forces together again and marched to the village, followed by the natives with spears. The village itself [Sohun] was well-tended and clean and made a good impression. But all attempts to make contact with the fugitives failed. Blood had been spilt and this destroyed the possibility of negotiation.... The next day we marched over the mountains.... As seven of the enemy had fallen, in the eyes of the natives we had won a great victory. The result of the battle was announced as we approached the village on the ridge by wild chanting.... I put to sea that same evening, leaving instructions with the chiefs of the various districts to refrain from all hostilities on their side and to inform me immediately of any recurrence of hostilities from the west. I had intervened in this case principally because any increase in blood feud activity would not only destroy the modest coastal trade and recruitment, but also, more importantly, cripple the work of the mission for a long period" (Hahl 1980: 45–47).

It is clear in this example that Hahl and his troops were called in by one side in an ongoing situation of enmity between traditional enemies. One side, professing to be members of the Wesleyan Mission and now commited to peace, rather than warfare, called upon Hahl and his troops for help. However, the villagers of Bom and their allies participated in the fighting in a traditional manner, killing seven of the enemy, mutilating their bodies, and dipping their spears into the blood of the enemy. These were hardly the actions of devout Christian converts who claimed now to be peace-loving. No doubt earlier conceptualizations about enemies and allies were still operative. It would appear that one side used their conversion to Christianity as an excuse to bring Hahl with his squad of Police Boys armed with rifles in on their side, thus creating an imbalance of forces between groups that were traditional enemies.

Hahl's stated intentions were to mediate and make peace between the two sides, but this was certainly not the outcome of this incident, nor of others in which Hahl intervened. The European way of making peace was very different from the New Ireland way. Hahl seemed to be using a European frame of reference when he thought that he could subdue a village and then force it to make peace with its enemies. Time after time, blood was shed, after which he entered a village to find no one to negotiate with. One can speculate that when he talked about attacking a village with the avowed intention of mediating a dispute, he was merely putting a more reasonable cast on his description of his actions, since in all previous instances his attacks brought about bloodshed and the dispersal of the villages, rather than mediation of the dispute. It would seem that Hahl did not understand the nature of the ongoing relationship between traditional enemies in New Ireland, nor that peace could only be established between them, though only for an uncertain length of time, by the exchange of shell money and pigs, and later feasts.

Although warfare had been endemic in the area, from the establishment of the trading stations in 1880 until the Germans set up a District Office on New Ireland at Kavieng in 1900 the number of violent conflicts and concomitant punitive expeditions had increased considerably. As noted above, this increase in violence was recognized in the oral history accounts, although its cause was attributed to the greater numbers of weapons like war axes with iron heads that had been introduced earlier through European contact. Though this was certainly a factor, the main cause of the increase in warfare in our opinion was the imbalance caused by Europeans being drawn into the relations between traditional enemies.

Before intensive contact with Europeans, villages were autonomous political groups and each village had its enemies and allies. No one village, district, or clan, was much more powerful than any other and a rough balance of power existed. While one clan might, through good fortune, grow larger in population than its surrounding enemies, it never had the resources to turn short-term advantages into long-term conquest and domination of its enemies. When intensive contact with Europeans began, some clans and villages were more involved with Europeans than others. This could take a variety of forms. Establishment of a trading station in a village would give that village a distinct advantage in acquiring trade goods and sometimes guns. It might occur when a Wesleyan Methodist mission was established in a village, placing that village under the protective arm of the church (and the gun of Rev. George Brown), or when a worker returned to his village with some knowledge of Pidgin English and thus was able to serve as a translator for the labor recruiters, giving his village special access to trade goods and guns. The groups that became stronger as a result of European contact would try to act on their newly acquired advantage and attack their traditional enemies. Those enemies could also try to acquire guns, trade goods, or a mission station to become at least as powerful as their enemies. When a village was weakened because many of its able-bodied young men were away as a result of labor recruitment, it became vulnerable and was often attacked by its traditional enemies.

The involvement of the Europeans took several forms, as we have described above. Sometimes a side that felt itself very weak would complain to the European authorities about attacks from its traditional enemies in order to bring the Europeans into the fighting to increase the power of their side and defeat their enemies (as in the case of the village of Bom). A New Ireland man might become a police boy serving elsewhere in the colony, get guns, and lead his group against its traditional enemy, as in the example of Madina and Leineru. Not only were the Europeans drawn into the pattern of traditional enmity between groups, as Hahl was drawn into the conflict between Leineru and Madina, but when a European trader like Hernsheim wanted to retaliate against a New Ireland group for the killing of one of his traders or the wrecking of a trading station, he made use of his knowledge of the pattern of enemies and allies and would draw the traditional enemies of the culprits into action on his side.

With intensive European contact, the previous balance of relations between groups was seriously tipped in favor of certain villages and clans. Differences in power between villages as a result of these various kinds of contacts with Europeans might have been turned into long term advantages, resulting in those villages increasing in size and scale and coming to control other villages and perhaps developing confederacies as, we shall see, happened elsewhere. However, intensive European contact, the catalyst in this process, all too quickly spelled the end of New Ireland political autonomy with the establishment of a colonial government.

Information on the Solomon Islands reveals significant similarities to the New Ireland case. Zelenietz relates that long-standing hostilities existed between local groups in New Georgia. The first traders came there in the 1830s, trading European goods including iron axes for bêche-de-mer and tortoise shell. Villages close to the sources of bêche-de-mer had an advantage. Zelenietz notes, "Those armed with the new weapons were superior militarily, which probably resulted in increased headhunting and, later, in the formation of large scale alliances" (1979: 94). There was a great increase in the political stature of a small number of leaders who controlled the production of shell money, the flow of goods in inter-island trade, and the distribution of rifles (Zelenietz 1979: 103). These leaders also launched headhunting raids, which increased in intensity at this time. Successful raids enhanced the leader's renown and led to the formation of larger alliances. While such an increase in the political stature and power of village leaders also occurred in New Ireland, an expansion in the scale of political units as seems to have occurred in New Georgia did not.

Events on Santa Isabel, another island in the Solomons, were much the same. Raiding and killing were said to be endemic in the precontact past, and relationships between regions were dependent upon the nature of relations between their dominant Big Men. When labor recruiters and traders began to come to Santa Isabel, they dealt with the recognized leaders, who profited from this by acquiring iron axes and guns, which they used to increase their political influence and raiding activities. White notes, "The increased pace of raiding and headhunting forays from 1860 to the end of the century put enormous pressure on central Santa Isabel which, together with the raids from the western Solomons, exacerbated internecine fighting" (White 1979: 120).

These cases from the Solomon Islands document an efflorescence of warfare after contact, which is attributed to the introduction of new forms of weaponry like iron axes and guns. However, the Solomon Islands cases seem to indicate that in this area, in contrast to New Ireland, there was also an expansion in the scale of political units in the form of large-scale alliances as well as an increase in the power of political leaders.

The history of the expanding fur trade in northern North America seems to reveal an analogous efflorescence of warfare as this trade expanded westward, and the traditional balance of power between groups was disrupted. In discussing the warfare between the Huron and the Iroquois, Trigger notes, "Thus, towards the end of the 16th century, there was severe conflict between the Iroquois and the groups living along and north of the St. Lawrence, presumably both Laurentian and Algonquian. This conflict was of a different sort from the blood feuds and prestige-seeking of ordinary warfare in the region and was in fact a contest for control of the St. Lawrence valley" (Trigger 1962: 249). The control of the valley would then enable the Iroquois to deal directly with the French traders at the Tadoussac trading post rather than having to deal with tribal middlemen. After dispatching the Laurentians, the Iroquois conducted warfare against the Huron, apparently for the same reason. By this time the Huron and the Iroquois were organized into leagues "...as an indirect result of European trade" (Tooker 1963: 120). The Iroquois defeated the Huron in 1647–1649 because they had more guns and a shorter supply line to the European traders to the south (Tooker 1963: 117). This case has parallels to our Pacific material, but there are also differences. The "blood feuds" that Trigger refers to as the precontact state seem very similar to the pattern of hostilities in New Ireland. However, in the efflorescence of warfare in the immediate post-contact period in North America, the pattern of warfare changed as it increased in scale. The increase in scale in both political organization and in warfare in the Iroquois-Huron case seems much greater even than the changes that occurred in the Solomon Islands. In the Iroquois case, traditional enemies were fighting over control of trade with the Europeans. This was not the case in New Ireland.

Wolf, in his history of the contact between Europeans and what he refers to as "the people without history," notes, "The fur trade thus changed the character of warfare among Amerind populations and increased its intensity and scope" (Wolf 1982: 161). For example, as the fur trade moved west to the forests of Ontario and Manitoba, there was an increase in warfare between the Dakota Sioux and the Assiniboine and their allies, the Cree (Ray and Freeman 1978: 43). In 1682, during the first decade of the Hudson Bay Company's establishment of trading posts in the Hudson Bay area, the Assiniboine and the Cree, using English guns, attempted to prevent the Dakota Sioux, who had had no contact with Europeans up to this point, from directly trading with the Hudson Bay Company (Ray and Freeman 1978: 44). The French and English were very much involved in this conflict, each attempting to gain a monopoly, or at least an advantage, in the fur trade. The French at first tried to arrange a peace between the warring sides, and, failing in this, "...the French *coureurs de bois* attempted to use these hostilities to their own advantage. In an effort to discourage the Assiniboine from trading with the English the *coureurs de bois* threatened to lead Siouan war parties against the former groups if they did not cease trading with the Hudson's Bay Company... in the 1720s French *coureurs* sent Siouan war parties into what is now northern Ontario and central Manitoba" (Ray and Freeman 1978: 44).

An efflorescence of warfare occurred here on the northern Plains, as it did in New Ireland, because the Europeans and their activities upset the balance of power. This case is similar to the Iroquois-Huron case described above, where traditional enemies expanded their earlier conflicts to include competition over trade with Europeans. These cases exemplify the warfare over trade discussed in Ferguson and Whitehead (1992: 24–26). The reasons for warfare in the northern Plains became primarily economic as some groups tried to monopolize the trade with Europeans, attempting to force others to use them as middlemen. The Europeans themselves tried to entice or to force groups to deal exclusively with them, even to the point of becoming the allies of one side in an indigenous conflict.

It had earlier been assumed that with European contact in the form of missionary activity and trade there would be a decline in hostilities and warfare. However, more recent studies are beginning to reveal that the immediate post-contact period in many places was one characterized by an efflorescence of warfare.

There was also a significant change in the kind of warfare that was taking place, as exemplified by the wars between Iroquois and Huron, and between Assiniboine and Dakota Sioux. In pre-contact times, warfare in these Native American societies was like that which had been described as endemic in New Ireland — independent communities were engaged in an unending state of conflict with neighboring groups, their "enemies," to defend their autonomy. In this endeavor they were assisted by allies with whom they had a common enemy, forming a checker-board pattern of enemies and allies. There was a general balance of power in this type of warfare, with no one group being able to attain a long term advantage over a number of others.

With extended European contact, the type of warfare conducted before contact changed into warfare of a different sort. The purpose of the new type was the control of strategic resources. Warfare now could result in one group completely dominating another, even decimating them, as the Iroquois did to the Huron. Warfare in New Ireland never reached the level where one group dominated or decimated another. The intrusion of Europeans and their guns into the ongoing network of enemy and ally relationships between New Ireland villages only produced an upsurge of violence and a significant increase of warfare in the early colonial period.

In many parts of Melanesia and New Guinea, as well as elsewhere in the world, endemic warfare existed, yet no one society was able to take advantage of the situation by overrunning and conquering its neighbors to set up conquest states. A state of equilibrium, more or less, existed between the warring politics. This equilibrium was brought to an end with European intrusion and the introduction of more effective and deadlier arms.

This ethnohistorical study of the causes of the efflorescence of warfare as a consequence of intensive European contact in New Ireland and elsewhere has contemporary relevance. Modern day Somalia is an instance where parallels seem to be present. The Somali population was culturally and linguistically homogeneous, with a tradition of nomadic pastoralism subsumed within an overarching segmentary lineage organization (Ian Lewis 1961). All Somali are descendants from Somaal, their eponymous ancestor, and the founder of their lineage organization. There are six clan-families, subdivided into clans, primary lineages, etc. The effective unit that could be mobilized into action was the sub-lineage, the *dia*-paying group, which paid and received blood money when feuding occurred. Agriculturalists concentrated around two southern Somali river valleys, who are the descendants of ex-slaves, were adopted into the existing segmentary lineage organization. Before the colonial period, a general state of equilibrium existed between segments of the segmentary lineage system. Lewis describes how weaker segments made "contracts" with outside lineages to defend themselves against closely related, but stronger segments, thus maintaining the equilibrium.

During the colonial period, which began in the last three decades of the nineteenth century, Somalia was divided into British, Italian, and French imperial zones of influence and ultimately into the British and Italian Protectorates. The segmentary lineage system was incorporated into the colonial governments and "...titular clan leaders and elders of lineages were in many cases officially recognized by the Administration and granted small stipends" (Lewis 1965: 105). As a consequence, some clans and lineages had more influence than others. After Somali independence in 1960, when British and Italian Somalilands were merged into an independent state, political parties developed. The country was organized into a democracy. However, "The curse of pastoral egalitarian anarchy loomed on the horizon.... For example, in the March 1969 parliamentary elections, 64 parties, in a population of barely four million contested the elections. The 65 parties represented the 64 or so important lineages and sub-lineages in the genealogical system" (Samatar 1991: 17). When individuals were elected to high positions of leadership, such as the presidency or the office of prime minister, patronage was distributed to their clansmen. The assassination of the president that took place in 1969 was in revenge for the harassment of the assassin's sub-clan before the election. Clan politics were still operative, but by this time, the balance of power between the social structural entities on the several hierarchical levels of the segmentary lineage system had been completely disrupted and equality remained only as an ideology.

On October 21, 1969 General Siyaad Barre, commandant of the army, seized power in a coup d'état. His clan, the Marehan clan and those related to it in the Daarood clan-family, became dominant in the country. During the Barre period, clans and clan-families for the first time in the modern period became the basis for political parties as well as armed militias (Adam 1992: 12). Opposition to Barre was framed in clan terms.

Large amounts of modern weaponry had been introduced into Somalia by both the U.S. and the Soviet Union as part of the competition between the two during the Cold War. The USSR had provided military as well as economic assistance from the time Somalia became independent and this continued during Barre's dictatorship. The US had provided only economic aid, but began to provide military aid as well when the USSR switched its support to Ethiopia during the Somali-Ethiopia war of 1977–78. Barre "....turned all his energies to impose a clan hegemony – believing that the huge amounts of military power the cold war had placed in his hands would be sufficient to destroy the natural historical balance of power between Somali clans as well as the burning desire for recognition and equality" (Adam 1992: 25).

The growing opposition to Barre's hegemony took the form of liberation fronts organized by clans and clan families in different parts of the country, and Barre was finally overthrown in January 1991. At that point a new government could not be formed, and a state of anarchy, in which different groups fought one another, ensued. Some eight militias based on clans and clan-families are now in possession of the massive armaments that flowed into the country from the US and the USSR and control their respective areas. Even gangs in urban areas such as Mogadishu "...are closely linked to various clans and work from well-defended bases in the city" (Adam 1992: 21). The only effective political institutions present in Somalia today are armed clan militias, based upon clans and clan-families within the segmentary lineage structure. These militias are led by men characterized as "warlords," despite the fact that even the most prominent "...do not exercise effective governmental control nor do they head efficient military organizations" (Adam 1992: 21). In an ironic way, these clan militias are in balance, since none of them "...is likely to prevail over the others" (Samatar 1991: 22).

In Somalia, as was also the case in New Ireland before the colonial period, a balance of power between autonomous political units more or less existed and there was no indigenous centralized authority or state organization. Several factors operated in both cases, but at different times. In New Ireland, the disruption in the balance of power and the efflorescence of warfare occurred when Europeans introduced guns and when they supported one village or its traditional enemy village in a particular situation. In Somalia, the colonial period brought an inbalance between units in the segmentary structure when some clans were favored over others. The democratic period following independence was an attempt to reassert a balance of power in which political parties represented lineages and sublineages, and this was what undercut the possibility of establishing a viable centralized state. Under Barre's dictatorship, the dominance of his clan and clan-family led to the greatest destabilization of the balance of power between units of the segmentary lineage system, though he was ultimately toppled from power because of the segmentary lineage system. The influx of weaponry that began shortly after independence also contributed greatly to this destabilization. The present-day situation in Somalia is characterized by a return once again to a precarious balance between clan militias, which are fighting one another ultimately for control over the entire country. Though none has the power to establish absolute power over all the others, each settles for blocking any other clan from doing so. This, in a sense, represents a continuation of the ideology of equality between clans and a return to a kind of warring balance of power between them. The major parallel between the New Ireland and Somalia cases is in the fact that when external political agents and forces, and, in particular, modern weaponry are introduced into political systems based on rough balance of power, the results are an increase and efflorescence in the scale and intensity of warfare. Though present-day Somalia and New Ireland in the early colonial period would seem to be totally different, the causes of the efflorescence of warfare in both instances seem to be similar.

NOTE

This paper was originally delivered at the annual meetings of the American Anthropological Association in Chicago in 1991. We would like to thank the National Science Foundation (Grant number BNS-8605676, "The Structure of Exchange Networks in New Ireland") and the John Simon Guggenheim Foundation for fellowship support of our field research on New Ireland.

REFERENCES

Adam, Hussein M. (1992). Somalia: Militarism, Warlordism or Democracy? Review of African Political Economy No. 54: 11–26.
Bell, F. L. S. (1935). Warfare among the Tanga. Oceania 5: 255–76.
Corris, Peter (1968). Blackbirding in New Guinea Waters. Journal of Pacific History 3: 85–105.

Coulter, John (1973[1847]). Adventures on the Western Coast of South America and the Interior of California: including a narrative of the incidents at the Kingsmill Islands, New Ireland, New Guinea and other islands in the Pacific Ocean. 2 Vols. Boston: Milford House, Inc.

Ferguson, R. Brian and Neal L. Whitehead, eds. (1992). War in the Tribal Zone: Expanding States and Indigenous Warfare. Santa Fe: School of American Research Press.

Firth, S. G. (1978). Albert Hahl: Governor of German New Guinea. In Papua New Guinea Portraits: The Expatriate Experiences. James Griffin, ed. pp. 28–47. Canberra: Australian National University Press.

Haas, Jonathan, ed. (1990 The Anthropology of War. New York: Cambridge University Press.

Hahl, Albert (1980). Governor in New Guinea. Canberra: Australian National University Press.

Hernsheim, Eduard (1983). South Sea Merchant. Boroko: Institute of Papua New Guinea Studies.

Knauft, Bruce N. (1990). Melanesian Warfare, a Theoretical History. Oceania 60 (4): 250–311.

Lewis, I. M. (1961). A Pastoral Democracy: A Study of Pastoralism and Politics among the Northern Somali of the Horn of Africa. London: Oxford University Press.

——— (1965). The Modern History of Somaliland: from Nation to State. New York: Frederick A. Praeger.

Mouton, Jean Baptiste Octave (1974). The New Guinea Memoirs of Jean Baptiste Octave Mouton. ed. Peter Biskup. Canberra: Australian National University Press.

Neu Guinea Kompagnie. (1979). Annual Reports 1886–1899. In German New Guinea: the Annual Reports. ed. and trans. by Peter Sack and Dymphna Clark. Canberra: Australian University Press.

Ray, Arthur J. and Donald B. Freeman (1978). Give Us Good Measure: An Economic Analysis of the Relations Between the Indians and the Hudson's Bay Company Before 1763. Toronto: University of Toronto Press.

Rosman, Abraham and Paula G. Rubel (1987). New Ireland field notes.

Samatar, Said S. (1991). Somalia: A Nation in Turmoil. London: Minority Rights Group Report.

Tooker, Elizabeth (1963). The Iroquois Defeat of the Huron: A Review of Causes. Pennsylvania Archaeologist 33: 115–23.

Trigger, Bruce (1962). Trade and Tribal Warfare on the St. Lawrence in the Sixteenth Century. Ethnohistory 9: 240–56.

White, Geoffrey (1979). War, Peace, and Piety in Santa Isabel, Solomon Islands. In The Pacification of Melanesia, Margaret Rodman and Mathew Cooper, eds. ASAO Monograph Series, No. 7. New York: University Press of America.

Wolf, Eric (1982). Europe and the People Without History. Berkeley: The University of California Press.

Zelenietz, Martin (1979). The End of Headhunting in New Georgia. *In* The Pacification of Melanesia. Margaret Rodman and Mathew Cooper, eds. ASAO Monograph Series No. 7. New York: University Press of America.

Chapter THREE

Insurrection in the Texas Mexican Borderlands: The Plan of San Diego

Candelario Sàenz

Have you ever wondered, what *were* gunfights in the "wild west" really about? Sáenz helps to answer this question. He describes a case of ethnic conflict in South Texas in which a gunflight was part of what might be termed an "ethnic cleansing." Anglos shot up *Tejanos* (Mexican-Americans) to degrade them economically and politically when the *Tejanos*' position in a global capitalist system deteriorated.

INTRODUCTION

Studies of colonialism in such diverse places as Algeria, South Africa, India, and Ireland, as well as modern experience in such crisis locations as Rwanda, Bosnia, and Palestine have highlighted the processes of population replacement and the impoverishment of conquered populations under the hegemony of the colonial elite and the transformation of these populations into degraded and abject sources of cheap labor in the service of that elite. These processes took place in Texas after the Mexican War of 1848, known in Mexico as "The American Invasion," and they constituted a form of internal colonialism.

This paper examines what happened in South Texas along the Rio Grande in the first half-century after the conquest of 1848. Here there was continuing economic prosperity under the political/military power of the Mexican-American population. This prosperity was based on the wool Tariff Act of 1867, which made wool production extremely profitable in South Texas due to favorable labor conditions and the ownership of grazing land by the Mexican population. Thus the cost of any downward transformation in the division of labor was perceived as too expensive by the Anglo elite. This resulted in what historian David Montejano has called a "structure of peace" (1987), that ended just before the beginning of World War I with the final collapse of the wool trade in South Texas, triggering a renewed offensive by the Anglo elite to effect the complete disenfranchisement of the Mexican population. This collapse of the structure of peace following the end of the wool production led Anglos to attempt a veritable ethnic cleansing, which in turn led to a Mexican insurrection known to historians as *The Plan of San Diego Revolt*.

This article is written from the perspective of a Mexican-American from the border area whose ancestors were direct participants in the events described.

THE PLAN OF SAN DIEGO EXPLAINED

On the 18th of May, 1912, three Mexican-Amercian officials were gunned down in front of the Duval County Courthouse in San Diego, Texas. The killers were a group of Anglo-Americans led by former Duval County Sheriff Charles K. Gravis (Anders 1982: 175, 177–78; Caro 1982: 721). In October 7, 1912 article in *La Libertad*, the Spanish language newspaper of San Diego, editor Francisco Gonzales lamented the collapse of the once excellent social relations between Anglos and Mexicans into ones of "grieving and hate."

After many delays and a change of venue to the distant East Texas town of Richmond, the defendants were found not guilty for lack of evidence, not withstanding the testimony of several Mexican-

American eye-witnesses to the murders. These acquittals were made in April 1914, more than two years after the killing of the three Mexican-American officials (Anders 1982: 178). These killings were to provoke a violent reaction in the following year — the outbreak of the Plan of San Diego revolt.

On February 1, 1918, the headlines of the *Brownsville Herald* screamed, "Atrocious Plot Unearthed: Widespread Conspiracy to Rob, Murder and Pillage Revealed." Only days earlier, on the twenty-fourth of January, a document called the *Plan de San Diego* (Texas) had been found in the possession of a young man named Basilio Ramos, a former resident of San Diego, Texas.

The original *Plan de San Diego* called for a violent revolt in which all Anglos of age sixteen and over would be executed and the whole region of the southwest would be reconquered from the United States and then turned over to the populations of Mexican, Indian, Japanese, and African-American origin to be governed under a decentralized and democratic form of government in which each ethnic group would be given parts of the conquered territory to govern on their own. Although nothing at all happened on February 20, the date on which the uprising was called for, by the summer of 1915 South Texas was plunged into violent revolt by groups of armed Mexican-Americans flying the red standard of the *Plan de San Diego* with the words "Equality and Fraternity" spelled out in white letters. This armed revolt by Mexican-Americans led to an even more lethal response by armed posses and Texas Rangers acting to quell the revolt.

Eventually, Federal troops were sent in, mainly to protect Mexican-Americans from the violent depredations of the South Texas Anglo minority. Although the *Plan de San Diego* is recognized by the small number of American historians who have studied it as the only irredentist revolt in United States history, its significance was largely misinterpreted by historians until the recent publication of *Rebellion in the Borderlands*, by James Sandos (1992). In this essay I enrich Sandos' analysis by adding new information on the social background of this revolt in San Diego, Texas, and its hinterlands.

MEXICANS, WOOL, AND THE HISTORY OF SAN DIEGO

San Diego, Texas, a town of some 4500 people, mostly of Mexican ancestry, is the administrative seat of Duval County. In the nineteen-fifties it briefly gained national attention and notoriety in connection with alleged irregularities in the election of Lyndon B. Johnson to the U.S. Sentate by a margin of only 87 votes (Caro 1990: 389–391). As Robert Caro notes in his biography of Lyndon B. Johnson, *Means of Ascent*, the South Texas political machine that facilitated Johnson's rise to power in 1948 rose out of Mexican-American outrage over the murder of three Mexicans by Anglo Americans in 1912 (Caro 1990: 184). It was, ironically, outrage over these same murders that motivated the *Plan de San Diego* revolt.

While the buildings visible along Highway 44 through San Diego are in the architectural idiom of rural Texas — prefabricated gasoline stations with attached mini-marts and dilapidated washeterias — a detour through the side streets reveals evidence of the town's rich multi-ethnic 19th century history. In the old town center, along the route of the old Camino Real from Mier, Mexico, is a Mexican-style plaza with an impressive whitewashed masonry kiosk with a red Spanish tile roof. Older residents say that the radical reformer and revolutionary, Catarino Erasmo Garza, once gathered large crowds in his orations from that same kiosk. Sidewalks radiating from this structure are lined with benches shaded by a canopy of live-oak and elm trees.

On the streets surrounding this plaza are an impressive brick Catholic church and a number of large houses made of cut limestone *Sillar* blocks in the Spanish colonial style of the old Nuevo Leon. Also facing the main plaza are two larg buildings that once served as trading houses, with the logos *Levi and Sons, 1910* and *Meek and Croft* written into their brick facades. Nearby are other large commercial buildings that once belonged to the Hoffman, Guerra, Tover, Rios, and Cohen families. Gone is the old Martinet hotel — once the Best hotel in South Texas and a preferred dining spot for day trippers on the Texas Mexican Railroad from Corpus Christi. All of the trading houses had large underground storerooms with steel gratings opening onto the sidewalks such as one sees in New York. These storerooms were useful in hoarding commodities and supplies that could be sold for a substantial profit in times of scarcity.

In the 1890s, San Diego was a multi-national and multi-ethnic commercial trading center and a major stop on the Texas Mexican Railway between Corpus Christi and Laredo. Its majority population was of Mexican ancestry, led by a well-educated, prosperous land-owning elite specializing in sheep ranching, wool production, and retail trade. The membership in San Diego's Scottish Rite Masonic lodge was completely Mexican and constituted the commercial and ranching elite of the community.

There was also a prosperous Jewish community, the Cohen, Henry, Levi, and Moses families, among others, who celebrated Rosh Hashana in the Hebrew year 5649 in San Diego (*Corpus Christi Weekly Caller* Sept. 3, 1888). In addition, there were French residents, some of whom had fled Mexico after the collape of Maximilian's Mexican Empire in 1865.

The Anglo settlers constituted a small minority, but they already dominated the political arena. Some of these, including James O. Luby and John Buckley (grandfather of journalist William F. Buckely), were of Irish Catholic descent and were largely sympathetic to the Mexican population, particularly the ranching and commercial trading elite. There were also Anglo Protestants, who were largely hostile to Mexicans.

In 1888, the Mexican elite, in coalition with a few sympathetic Anglos, attempted to wrest control of the county from the dominant Anglo political machine. John Buckley ran for sheriff under this coalition, which was known as the *Botas* (the boots). In that election Buckely and Catarino Erasmo Garza, the firebrand editor of the Spanish language newspaper *El Libre Pensador (The Free Thinker)* stumped the county, gathering support for this reform ticket. Although Buckley and the Mexican candidates won in the initial count (*San Antonio Express* Nov. 9, 1888) the election was thrown out by the Anglo-dominated commissioners court on flimsy grounds, alleging voting irregularities (*Corpus Christi Weekly Caller* Nov. 17, 1888).

In the waning months of 1891, Catarino E. Garza, disappointed in his attempt at electoral reform is South Texas, led a revolution against the Mexican dictator Profirio Diaz with an army of 600 well-armed and mounted men recruited from San Diego and nearby communities. This event, practically forgotten by history, was covered by a team of reporters from *Harper's Weekly* (January 23 & 30, 1892). The vaunted Texas Rangers had made the first attack on the Garza forces, but they were completely routed and the incident ultimately required the depolyment of the Third U.S. Cavalry to defeat the Garza forces.

The short period of time within which Catarino E. Garza was able to muster his army and the ferocity with which Mexican-Americans took up his cause surprised most observers. This revolt should have been interpreted as an indicator of the anger felt by the Mexican-American community at their declining political influence and political power in Texas at the turn of the century.

The ability of the Mexican-Americans to mount such an impressive military force in the 1890s was due to prosperity based on wool production. The major work on this subject, David Montejano's *Anglos and Mexicans in the Making of Texas* (1987), notes the importance of wool production to the Mexicans of South Texas, but implies that the prosperity of the Mexican population declined after the 1880s. Montejano writes that, "In the 1880s the sheep industry began a long decline, and with it went many Mexican fortunes; by 1890 only the counties bordering the Rio Grande had significant numbers of sheep; by 1910 the industry had almost vanished completely from South Texas" (1987). The decline noted by Montejano involved mainly Anglo producers with higher capital and personnel costs, while it was precisely the Mexican wool producers along the Rio Grande who continued to prosper and who were able to sustain armed insurrection.

A U.S. Department of Agriculture report, *Sheep Industry of the United States* (Carman, Heath, and Minto 1892), provides hard data for the wool industry in the United States in the period between 1870 and 1890. This report notes the significant role of the Wool Tariff Act of 1867 in the dramatic increase in wool production in Texas after 1870 (Carman et al. 1892: 897). This tariff act, which was followed by further tariff increases over the years, was intended to protect the wool producers of the northeastern states. In fact it had little effect in restoring the wool industry in New England, but it provided an economic incentive for production in south Texas, where cheap and available land and low labor costs allowed substantial gains to wool producers. This was because the high tariff knocked the Mexican side of the Rio Grande out of the market, so that on the American side — with reduced competition and an inexpensive labor force — there was immense profit. Additionally, the economic opportunity provided by the Wool Tariff Act of 1867 stimulated the improvement of the common Mexican sheep of South Texas by breeding with improved Merino sires. The original Mexican sheep produced only one pound of wool per shearing, while the improved stock produced five to six pounds (Carman et al. 1892: 897).

As of 1890, at a time when Montejano's sources indicate a decline in Texas wool production, the number of sheep in Texas was at an all-time high of over five million head and the annual wool clip was thirty million pounds — making the state among the largest producers in the United States (Carman et al. 1892: 898). Among the highest producing counties in the state were the three south Texas counties with a high Mexican producer population, Webb, Duval, and Starr, each with over one hundred thousand sheep and an annual wool clip of over 650,000 pounds. Nearby Zapata county had over fifty thousand head and produced over 325,000 pounds per year (Carman et al. 1892: 896).

In these four counties, Duval, Starr, Zapata, and Webb, wool production led to the prosperity of the Mexican elite living in San Diego, Laredo, and Rio Grande City, the major towns of this area. Members of the landowning elite sent their children to college at the Catholic St. Edward's College in Austin, Texas. They were able to field political candidates, hire good Anglo lawyers to defend their land and livelihood, and to outfit horsemen with arms and ammunition to support movements like the Catarino Garza revolt of 1891 and 1892.

The prosperity of the Mexican population of the border counties made ethnic cleansing, such as had already occurred in other parts of Texas and in California, a difficult and dangerous proposition. So instead, there came to be, according to Montejano, a "structure of peace" between Anglos and Mexicans in which Anglos generally controlled the political system but in which Mexicans were allowed spheres of local political influence and a good measure of respect. Montejano argues that it was the political power and prosperity of this Mexican population which prevented the implementation of the Jim Crow system of racism against Mexicans that prevailed in other parts of the newly conquered southwestern regions of the United States (1987: 34–49).

However, The turn of the century brought crisis to the wool industry. According to the *Annual Wool Review* for 1902, the number of head of sheep was down to 1,440,000 from 2,786,000 the previous year and over five million in 1890 (*Annual Wool Review* 1902: 10). By 1908 a panic had occurred in the United States wool industry, and in Texas production fell even further (*Annual Wool Review* 1908: 5).

This decline resulted from a changing organization of competition in the world capitalist system. The rise of cheap steamship transportation and the availability of cheap wool produced by exploited, native labor in Australia, New Zealand, and Argentina, along with reductions in the wool tariffs, priced Texas wool out of the market. In the United States, what remained of the industry moved to New Mexico, Arizona, and Colorado, where cheap Mexican labor could still herd sheep profitably on arid lands.

Catarino Garza's friend John Buckely liquidated his remaining herd of 5,000 sheep in 1901 (*Corpus Christi Weekly Caller* March 12, 1901). But in 1908, my grandfather, Candelario Sàenz, still had several thousand head of sheep. In that year Candelario was visiting with two shepherds guarding one of his flocks near the hamlet of Palito Blanco when he was arrested by the Texas Rangers on suspicion having murdered the Anglo democratic leader of Duval County, John-Clearly — a charge that was later dropped for lack of evidence. One of the shepherds, still living in 1960, recalled the event and my grandfather's comment, "If any of us makes a false move they will kill us like dogs."

While Candelario was still raising sheep in 1908, by 1912, when he was murdered at the polls on election day, he had left wool production and was working as a cotton buyer and broker for Don Manuel Rogers' San Diego cotton gin. He was one of many Mexican producers in South Texas who had survived the downturn in prices at the turn of the century but were wiped out in the wool panic of 1908.

THE PLAN OF SAN DIEGO

The document known as the *Plan de San Diego* called for a rebellion by the Mexican-American population on February 20, 1915 and the creation of an independent state in the former Mexican regions of the United States southwest, including Texas, New Mexico, Arizona, Colorado, Nevada, and California. In expansive terms this document called for the formation of a liberating army of all races and peoples that was to be made up of Mexican-Americans, African-Americans, Indians, and Japanese immigrants in California. Proclaiming *Uno como todos y todos como uno* (All for one and one for all), the *Plan de San Diego* promised to liberate African-Americans from the "tyranny of the Yankees," and to return to the Apaches and all other Indians, "the territories stolen from them," in exchange for their military support. Provisions were also made for the liberation of Japanese-Americans living in California.

Augustin S. Garza, originally of Monterey and a former school teacher in San Diego, a slight and dapper man with a glass eye who wore gold-rimmed glasses and sported a fancy cane, was to be the commander-in-chief. Followers of the plan were to carry a red flag with a white diagonal fringe and with the slogan *Igualdad y Independencia* in white on the red field. As each region of the U.S. southwest was liberated, resident African-Americans, Indians, and Japanese were to be given their own autonomous territories and their own unique flags (*El Plan de san Diego*, January 6, 1915).

Although there was no uprising on February 20, by midsummer the revolt began in earnest and plunged South Texas into a bloodbath of raiding by partisans of the *Plan de San Diego* and violent reprisals by Texas Rangers and Anglo-American vigilante groups. Ranchers Aniceto Pizaña and Luis de la Rosa emerged as leaders of the *Plan de San Diego* insurrectionist army. Flying the red flag of the *Plan de San*

Diego, they led separate attacks against such targets as the Norris King Ranch section headquarters and the Fresno pumping station in the Rio Grande Valley. In an attack that suggests the Anarchist program of Mikhail Bakunin, they blew-up the railroad bridge at Tandy's Station just north of Brownsville as the train was passing over it, derailing the train and rolling it into a ravine.

The bomb attack on the Corpus Christi to Brownsville train and the murder of an Anglo passenger caused pandemonium among Anglo Americans in South Texas. Lonn W. Taylor, a curator at the National Museum of American History, recalls the account given by his great-aunt who lived in Kingsville, about 50 miles northwest of Brownsville, at that time. She was attending Sunday evening service at the local Methodist Church when an armed deputy entered and walked up to the pulpit, spoke to the preacher briefly, and then turned and said to the crowd, "The Mexicans have revolted and are murdering people all over South Texas. I have arranged for the owner of the hardware store to open-up presently so that all of you can buy arms and ammunition to defend yourselves against these bandits."

As the Anglos took-up arms, bloody reprisals and atrocities followed, including the summary execution of four Mexican-American men who had been captured in the vicinity of Tandy's Station by Texas Rangers and the still unsolved murder of 15 Mexican-Americans at Ebenezer, a rail depot along th Rio Grande. The bodies at the Ebenezer depot lay there for many hours because friends of the murdered individuals were afraid of being murdered themselves if they approached the place.

In the panic following the raids by Aniceto Pizaña and Luis de la Rosa and the partisans of the *Plan de San Diego*, Anglos began shooting Mexicans on sight, as in the case reported by Sandos in which an Anglo woman "walked out on her porch to see two Mexicans passing by. She drew a pistol and fired three times before they returned her fire, wounding her slightly in her forearm" (Sandos 1992: 98). According to Sandos, at least twenty border raids were conducted by de la Rosa and Pizaña and the raiders killed thirty-three Americans, wounded twenty-four, and destroyed several thousand dollars worth of property. While the raiders lost thirty-two men, many other Mexican noncombatants were slain by Rangers and vigilantes (Sandos 1972: 23). The situation came to resemble that of Northern Ireland in 1973, when the dominant Protestants, operating through the vested legitimacy of the civil government, began a reign of terror against the despised Catholic minority, which finally required the intervention of the British army, initially, to protect the Catholic minority. In the South Texas case, in September 8, 1915 the U.S. Army intervened, sending the Third U.S. Cavalry to end the slaughter of Mexicans by local authorities and vigilante groups.

Details of the *Plan de San Diego* have been documented in historical studies by William M. Hager (1963), Juan Gomez-Quiñonez (1970), James A. Sandos (1972) and by Charles H. Harris and Louis Sadler (1978). The findings of all these professional historians agree on the general chronological sequence of arrests and raids and on the fact of violent reprisals against Mexican-American civilians. All of the above-noted articles, including Sandos (1972), but not Gomez-Quiñonez, conclude that the raids led by Luis de la Rosa and Aniceto Pizaña were *not* directly related to the *Plan de San Diego* uprising. Gomez-Quiñonez argued that scholars should seek the genesis of the plan and the subsequent border raids by de la Rosa and Pizaña in political and social conditions in San Diego at that time. The other scholars argued that the *Plan de San Diego* had nothing to do with San Diego, Texas, in spite of its name. They suggest instead that 1) the plan was formulated by partisans of the Mexican revolutionary leader Victoriano Huerta or by German plotters seeking to destabilize U.S. / Mexican relations and 2) de la Rosa's and Pizaña's raiders were either partisans of one of the Mexican revolutionary armies attempting to incite American intervention in the Mexican Revolution or else independently acting bandidos seeking booty.

William Hager seemed incredulous that Mexicans in San Diego could have formulated such a sophisticated plan. Among the historians of the *Plan de San Diego*, Hager was the only one actually to visit San Diego, Texas in search of information. Apparently the only person willing to talk to him was "judge" John Sutherland, an elderly man (in the 1950s) with a long white beard stained from chewing tobacco. John Sutherland told Harger that the plan had indeed been hatched in San Diego in a house visible from his porch.

Sutherland further contended that he had observed the plotters entering and leaving that house for a considerable period of time and that he had warned the U.S. government about the conspiracy in a letter to the U.S. Justice Department, thus making him the "original discoverer of the *Plan de San Diego.*"

Hager, however, rejected Sutherland's claim that he had observed the conspirators in action, noting that he had sent a letter of inquiry to the National Archives and that no Sutherland letter was in their files. One can question Hager's confidence in a mailed inquiry to the archivists in Washington. Finding material in the U.S. National

Archives is an art that almost always requires a personal visit to the collection. In the end, Hager's rejection of Sutherland's claim seemed to be based on his judgement that the Mexicans of San Diego, Texas were not capable of producing such a sophisticated document and he concluded that the authors must have been German conspirators.

Hager concluded that the authorship of the plan "was still a mystery." Harris and Sadler (1978) attempted to solve this mystery by showing that it was the work of followers of the revolutionary leader Victoranio Huerta. Sandos in his early study accepted this solution, but added that it perhaps was led by partisans of the new Mexican president Venustiano Carranza.

It seems astonishing that professional historians writing about events in South Texas were either unaware of the various socialist, communist, and anarchist ideologies that influenced political movements in Europe and the United States in the first decades of the Twentieth Century, or that they are unwilling to concede that Mexican-Americans in South Texas were sophisticated enough to be motivated by these potent political currents. But as Sandos was later to find, anarchism was indeed abroad in San Diego, Texas in the years leading up to the *Plan de San Diego* revolt.

Sandos later (1992) revised his original position radically. His revised position, based on newly available information sources, argued that: 1) the *Plan de San Diego* was part of an anarchist conspiracy hatched in San Diego, Texas by a group meeting at a bar on Victoria Street in that town; 2) that Luis de la Rosa had attended meetings of the anarchist Partido Liberal Mexicano (the PLM) at that bar on Victoria Street; and 3) that his later raids with his friend and associate Aniceto Pizaña were directly tied to the original conspiracy in San Diego, Texas (Sandos 1992). This revisionist interpretation is so surprisingly at variance with earlier positions that it has yet to be assimilated and evaluated by scholars dealing with the history of race and ethnic relations in South Texas.

A complicating fact concerning the *Plan de San Diego* is the fact that it was signed in the Monterey Mexico prison where "supreme commander" Augustin S. Garza and Basilio Ramos were imprisoned on January 6, 1915. It is this that makes the argument that the plan had nothing to do with San Diego seem plausible and seems to refute Gomez-Quiñonez' notion that the plan must be understood in terms of social conditions and events in San Diego, Texas. But the new information in Sandos' revisionist work (1992) clarifies the role of Mexicans in San Diego, Texas in the genesis of the *Plan de San Diego*.

SOCIAL AND POLITICAL CONDITIONS IN SAN DIEGO

I grew up in San Diego and, on reading the various early articles by Hager, Sadler and Harris, Sandos, and Gomez-Quiñonez, was puzzled that the role of San Diego was either minimized or denied. Through my childhood and youth I had heard the *Plan de San Diego* discussed by my parents and their acquaintances.

One day when I was about ten, I noticed a beautiful and unfamiliar looking pearl-leaf petal lamp in the stone *sillar* block house of our next door neighbors, the Garcia sisters, by the main plaza in San Diego. Inquiring, I was told that their brother, Dr. Jose G. Garcia, a local physician, had bought the lamp in Cuba where he had traveled around World War I. "And what was he doing in Cuba?" I asked. I was told that he was trying to avoid possible arrest in the investigations following the discovery of the *Plan de San Diego*.

Pedro G. Sàenz, my father, had a photograph that depicted *El Profesor*, Augustin Garza, the supreme commander of the *Plan de San Diego*, surrounded by a group of young men — the members of the Anarchist Partido Liberal Mexicano (PLM) group in San Diego. All of them are earnest and well dressed Mexican-American men except for one nervous looking individual in the front row, identified on the back of the picture as "M. Kaplan Russo." Mr. M. Kaplan Russo was apparently the speaker for the day, possibly an International Workers of the World (IWW) organizer. Also in the photograph is Luis (Lulo) Garcia Rogers, who was to figure importantly in the *Plan de San Diego*.

Many of the members of the PLM group that was responsible for the *Plan de San Diego* lived within a short distance of the main plaza and Victoria Street, which runs along one side of the main plaza in front of the impressive brick Catholic church in Dan Diego. Going two blocks north on Victoria Street one finds the site of the bar where Sandos says the conspirators met. A block west of that location on Mier Street was the house of old John Sutherland, whose porch faced in the direction of the bar. One block south of the main plaza on Victoria street was the *sillar* block home of Luis Garcia Rogers, making his attendance at PLM meetings a matter of a short walk.

Luis was a descendant of both the Anglo pioneer Rogers family and the original Garcia families from Mier in Nuevo Leon, Mexico, who had inherited the old Spanish San Diego Land Grant, the major source of prosperity for the wool producing Mexicans of San Diego. As David Montejano has written in *Anglos and Mexicans in the making of Texas*, the structure of peace that obtained in the countries immediately bordering the Rio Grande was socially mediated through intermarriages between members of the Mexican and Anglo elites, and through *compadrazgo*, or co-godparenthood, relationships between members of the two elites. This structure of peace depended on the continued economic prosperity of the Mexican elite and was to collapse in the wake of the Wool Panic of 1908 in the years preceding the *Plan de San Diego*.

My late father, Pedro G. Sàenz, had spoken with Luis Garcia Rogers on several occasions concerning his memories of the *Plan de San Diego*. Luis had told my father in these conversations that *El Profesor*, Augustin S. Garza, was Luis' friend and that he was sent a copy of the *Plan de San Diego*, to be delivered by Basilio Ramos, for Luis' approval. Basilio Ramos, of course, was caught by customs officials while crossing the border in possession of the plan, giving it away.

I interviewed Blanca G. Perez, the surviving daughter of the late Luis Garcia Rogers, to see if she could shed more light on her father's participation in the conspiracy. She recalled her father's interest in politics and his possession of political tracts and newspapers but she had thrown them away and she really didn't know if her father was involved in the conspiracy. What she did know was that her father had been in the midst of the gunfight and carnage in the murder of the three Mexican-American officials and she said that her father had travelled to distant Richmond, Texas to testify at the trial of the Anglo murderers. Blanca said that her father had never gotten over the disappointment of seeing the defendants in that trial go free for lack of evidence.

Remember, San Diego was a place where a Mexican-American elite of approximately 300 prosperous ranchers lived in relative harmony with the Anglos. Evidence for the prosperity of the Mexican elite can be found in the 1990 St. Edward's College Catalogue, which shows eight Mexican-Americans and only one Anglo from Duval and nearby Starr counties attending that year (*Saint Edward's College: Seventh Annual Catalogue* 1891: 32–35). My grandfather Candelario Sàenz was one of those eight boys and I know from family tradition that it was money from the wool clip that sent him to college.

The murders, however, destroyed this "structure of peace." They took place on May 18, 1912, when Duval County Commissioner Don Pedro Eznal, Deputy Sheriff Antonio Anguiano, and my grandfather Candelario Sàenz, town constable and announced candidate for Sheriff, were shot by a group of Anglos led by Charles K. Gravis. Sàenz and Eznal were both unarmed, as required by Texas election law, because they were involved in the official preparations for local elections to be held on that day. This fact was noted in the May 25 issue of *La Libertad*, San Diego's Spanish language newspaper, which noted that neither of the men had so much as a pocket knife in their jackets with which to defend themselves.

According to my 1992 interview with a living witness to the events of May 18, 1912, Gregoria Benavides de Garcia, who was Candelario Sàenz' sister-in-law, the day began early, with Candelario going to the courthouse at dawn to begin setting up the ropes to mark off the limits for electioneering. As town constable, Candelario was usually armed, but on this day he left his weapons at home, as was required by Texas law for election officials. Gregoria Benavides had slept over with her half-sister Teresa at Candelario's house and helped her with early breakfast. They were about to leave with her other sisters to visit a ranch in the prosperous Benavides' family's *caretela* (six-seater carriage). The oldest and strongest sister, Zulema, was at the reins. As they were about to leave they heard shots ring out, and quickly after, the awful news of the murders.

C. K. Gravis, backed up by three men armed with high-powered rifles, loaded with filed bullets (for more lethal spin), had waited in ambush at the courthouse in a Buick touring car. Then they walked up to challenge Don Pedro Eznal, a rancher, merchant, and Freemason and a major leader of the Mexican-Americans in Duval County, of which San Diego was the county seat. It was Don Pedro Eznal, an older man, who was the intended victim of Gravis and his friends. Seeing his friend in trouble, Candelario Sàenz rushed to Eznal's aid. Gravis had already drawn his gun on the two unarmed men and Candelario lunged at him, attempting to knock the gun out of his hand. He was shot in his side and as he fell he was hit again in the spine, killing him instantly.

Eznal was shot by Gravis' back-up men from the Buick touring car, as was Antonio Anguiano, a young deputy sheriff who rushed to the two older political leader's aid. He was shot in the back by a bullet that emerged in his bowels so that as he lay in his death agony his intestines heaved in and out with each breath. As this tragedy unfolded, a young man stood amidst the flying bullets and the dying men, saw everything and was traumatized by what he saw. This young man was Luis Garcia Rogers. This was a "gunfight" in the Old West.

Hearing the ghastly news, the 12 year old Gregoria, taking her five year-old sister Petra in hand, ran to tell her sister of the unfolding tragedy. When they got there, Teresa had already heard the news. She handed her infant son Pedro over to Gregoria and ran towards the courthouse, her just-washed hair streaming in the breeze. According to Gregoria, a local amateur artist saw her run by and later drew her from memory, with her waving hair.

The trial venue was changed to the distant and strongly Protestant town of Richmond in East Texas near the Louisiana border, and the trial dragged on until mid-April 1914. It resulted in an acquittal for all the defendants for "lack of evidence." Luis Garcia Rogers had travelled to distant Richardson, Texas at his own expense to testify as a witness for the prosecution, and after the acquittals of Gravis and the other defendants, he told and retold his version of the events to anyone who would listen — until his death in the 1960s. However, what Luis said did not matter in a world controlled by Anglos.

During the trial testimony, it was claimed that Antonio Anguiano, who was a sheriff's deputy, had been shot first, after threatening Gravis and an Anglo doctor named Roberts. Eyewitnesses, mostly Mexican, said that Anguiano had been shot last, and at some distance from the main altercation as he ran towards the disputants in accordance with his official duty to intervene and restore peace. This claim, that Anguiano was shot first, seems to have been an attempt by the defense to bolster an argument for "self-defense" by Gravis and his friends, by drawing attention from the fact that Eznal and Sàenz were both unarmed and defenseless. When unarmed and defenseless men are killed in an argument it is murder, not self-defense.

Many people attributed the verdict to a hostile jury, and emotion ran high among San Diego residents of Mexican ancestry. There had been high hopes for justice through the courts and great resentment when the verdict that the defendants were "innocent for lack of evidence," was reached by the all-Anglo Richardson County jury. Perhaps we might compare the feelings of the Mexican-Americans to those of African-Americans in Los Angeles after the announcement of the Rodney King verdict, which led to the Los Angeles insurrection of 1992.

The murder of the three San Diego men, I propose, was the event that demolished the structure of peace and accommodation in San Diego and surrounding Duval county. I would argue that the Anglos were emboldened by the loss of Mexican economic power after the collapse of the wool market in 1908 and were moving to effect a final solution — the complete disenfranchisement of the Mexican population. By murdering the leading political leaders of the Mexican-Americans in an open and public way, they expected to scare the Mexicans out of politics. The intent of these murders wasn't lost on the Mexican-Americans of San Diego, and there was massive public demonstration of this resentment, particularly on the day of the murder, when the Texas Rangers had to be called in to rescue the suspected killers from a Mexican mob.

According to Sandos' information, the PLM group of San Diego had been meeting since 1905. Luis Garcia Rogers was a member of that group and one can only wonder at the effect that the murders in 1912 and the acquittals in mid-1914 would have had on discussions at the PLM meetings. One could easily surmise that after the acquittals, talk at the PLM meetings might have shifted into raging plans for vengeance that included murdering all Anglos over the age of sixteen which, of course, was at the heart of the *Plan de San Diego*. The fact that Luis Garcia Rogers believed and told pedro Sàenz that Augustin S. Garza was sending him a copy of the plan for his approval strongly suggests that the plan, although actually written in the Monterey prison, was actually the result of discussion and debate following the murders of the three Mexican-American officials in San Diego. It is also significant that the date of the ratification of the *Plan de San Diego* by its signers on Feb. 12, 1915 was only a few months after the acquittal of the Anglo defendants in mid-April of 1914.

ANARCHIST SYNDICALIST ROOTS OF THE PLAN DE SAN DIEGO

It might have occurred to the historians Harris and Sadler, Hager, and the earlier Sandos that an insurrectionist plan that invoked a *liberating army of all races and peoples*, might have had something to do with some of the internationalist socialist, communist, or anarchist movements that had been developing in Europe and the United States between the 1870s and World War I. The red flag with the slogan *Equality and Fraternity* and the proposal to divide their imagined state into autonomous democratic entities might have even specifically identified the plotters as Anarcho Syndicalists to an historian well informed on 19th Century European political history. That all of this went unnoticed is evidence, in my estimation, that most historians who have researched this incident were unwilling to allow that Mexican-Americans were capable of philosophical reflection and of being influenced by complex ideological movements.

As it happened, Sandos was able to demonstrate beyond a reasonable doubt that there was an Anarchist political organization in

San Diego Texas. The *Partido Liberal Mexicano* (the PLM), which had been formed by the brothers Ricardo and Enrique Flores Magon, Praxedis Guerrero, and others, was indeed an Anarchist organization based on the principles and teachings of Peter Kropotkin, Mikhail Bakunin, and Errico Malatesta (Sandos 1992: 3–23). Their Anarchist newspaper, *Regeneracion,* which featured images of Kropotkin, Bakunin, Malato, Malatesta, and even the playwright Henrik Ibsen (1992: 19), was subscribed to by members of the San Diego Texas PLM group, including *Plan de San Diego* raiders Luis de la Rosa and Aniceto Pizaña (1992: 72–24). In 1914 a group of Freemasons from Mexico, including Basilio Ramos and Professor Garza, opened a bar on Victoria street across from old John Sutherland's porch on Mier Street. To open this bar they obtained a surety bond through the credit of the San Diego chapter of the Scottish Rite masons. This bar was to function as a place of recruitment and plotting for the *Plan de San Diego,* and it was visited on a number of occasions by raider Luis de la Rosa (1992: 79–100).

As James Sandos perceptively noted, *El Profesor* and Supreme Commander of the *Army of All Nations and Races,* Augustin S. Garza, a one-eyed general with a lack of depth perception, might not have been particularly effective as a military commander. However Garza had already proselytized and converted Luis de la Rosa, a former deputy sheriff from Brownsville, to the revolutionary cause. Already converted, because he had met the founder of the PLM, Ricardo Flores Magon, and had read *Regeneracion,* was rancher Aniceto Pizaña. He, however, was originally reluctant to join the *Plan de San Diego* but was later radicalized, and joined the conspirators after the Texas Rangers raided his ranch searching for evidence of his participation in the revolt (Sandos 1992: 88).

While the violence and killing went on in the lower Rio Grand Valley, San Diego remained quiet for the duration of the uprising. A number of citizens, including Dr. José Garcia, fled to Cuba for the duration of the crisis, but as the insurrection quieted down, they returned. C. K. Gravis stayed in San Diego until his death, but he found it necessary to hang heavy blinds and curtains over his windows. Candelario Sàenz' sister, my *tia* Maria Sàenz, a good horsewoman and an excellent shot, publicly declared her intention to shoot Gravis for murdering her brother and she used to stand in front of his windows at night looking into his house, to remind him of this threat.

By the time I was growing-up in San Diego in the 1950s there were only a few Anglos in San Diego. I went to Catholic Parochial

School with the daughters of the Anglo owner of the local Chevrolet Dealership and Doctor E. E. Dunlap. By the time they went to High School the Anglo girls were sent off to boarding school in San Antonio so that they wouldn't make undesirable marital alliances. After all, there was no longer a "structure of peace" in San Diego.

CONCLUSION

What is surprising is that such a richly documented, major violent uprising by the Mexican-Americans of South Texas remains unknown. It is completely unmentioned in the standard U.S. history curriculum taught in schools. Perhaps the reason this is the case lies in the bias of U.S. historians, who fall over themselves to present American history as effortless and unproblematic in the area of assimilation of minority populations. The events that I have just described tell another story, one of the violent resistance of an ethnic minority to its economic degradation and political disenfranchisement following an equally violent act, an ambush that sought to "ethnically cleanse" this minority of its leaders. And this violence was played out against the rhythms of a global capitalism. When the ethnic minority was prosperous due to its wool production, marry them; when the bottom had dropped out of wool, and prosperity was gone, kill them.

REFERENCES

Anders, Evan (1982). Boss Rule in South Texas: The Progressive Era. Austin: The University of Texas Press.
Annual Wool Review (1902). A Bulletin of the National Association of Wool Manufacturers, 683 Atlantic Ave., Boston, MA.
——————— (1908). A Bulletin of the National Association of Wool Manufacturers, 683 Atlantic Ave., Boston, MA.
Carman, Ezra A., H. A. Heath, and John Minto (1892). Sheep Industry of the United States. U.S. Department of Agriculture, Washington, DC.
Caro, Robert (1982). The Path to Power. New York: Vintage Books.
——————— (1990). Means of Ascent. New York: Vintage Books.
El Plan de San Diego (1915). January 6.
Gomez-Quiñones, Juan (1970). The Plan of San Diego Reviewed. Aztlan 14: 5–24.

Hager, William A. (1963). The Plan of San Diego: Unrest on the Texas Frontier in 1915. Arizona and the West 5: 327–36.
Harris, Charles and Louis Sadler (1978). The Plan of San Diego and the Mexican War Crisis of 1916: A Reexamination. Hispanic-American Historical Review 57: 381–408.
Montejano, David (1987). Anglos and Mexicans in the Making of Texas, 1836–1986. Austin: University of Texas Press.
Sandos, James A. (1972). The Plan of San Diego: War and Diplomacy on the Texas Border, 1915–1916. Arizona and the West 14: 5–24.
————— (1992). Rebellion in the Borderlands: Anarchism and the Plan of San Diego, 1904–1923. Norman, OK: University of Oklahoma Press.

Chapter FOUR

War in Uganda: North and South

Joan Vincent

There has been frequent civil war in post-colonial Uganda. One of the puzzles of this fighting is that it has been more vicious in certain areas than in others. Vincent, one of the world's most distinguished political anthropologists, unravels this puzzle. She explains variations in the ferocity of violence in terms of the existence of a scheme of cultural classification, a cultural hegemony, that differently evaluates Ugandans' degree of civilization. Some Ugandans, those to the north, were classified as less civilized and were warred against with greater ferocity. Vincent argues that this cultural hegemony was introduced during the colonial period by the British as part and parcel of their introduction of agrarian capitalism. People in the north, where there was less capitalist agriculture, were seen as "savages."

"A whole history remains to be written of *spaces*...from the great strategies of geopolitics to the little tactics of the habit" (Foucault 1980: 149).

This essay addresses the silenced spatiality of war.[1] It has become contemporary to argue the neglect of geography in favor of history, the implicit subordination of space to time, as the geographer Edward Soja (1989) puts it, but clearly both spatial and temporal factors have to be taken into account in the analysis of war.

It will not be possible here to do more than suggest that the social production of space in Uganda throughout the colonial period — the implantation, delimitation, and demarcation of the spatial dimensions of power — underlies the large inventory of 'small wars' inscribed on the map of postcolonial Uganda. The palimpsest of political resistance and counter-insurgency, of tyranny and terror, is a cross-hatched document that will take more than a lifetime of interpretation. Here one aspect alone of its spatial dimensioning is considered: the apparently perduring cultural divide between North and South.[2] I draw attention to the distinctive geographies of war within the two regions.

In this essay I review critically structural representations of the Uganda military in terms of ethnicity ("tribalism") and uneven development. I argue that explanatory value should be attached to the political economy of engaging in war and its historicity rather than to the colonial construction of ethnicity and uneven capitalist development. It is useful, I argue, to distinguish both critically and empirically between contextual and textured warfare; in postcolonial Uganda the War of Liberation in the south (1978–1979) and the as yet unnamed insurgency and counter-insurgency in Teso in the north (1985–1992) serve to illuminate the distinction.

Finally, in a postscript, I attempt to document the impact of the war on Teso through the use of census figures. I suggest an explanation for the severity of this impact that derives from the themes addressed in the body of the essay. Thus, I suggest not ethnicity but cultural nationalism and the stereotyping of 'enemies,' not uneven development but a specific agricultural production system and a particular geographical terrain, contributed to a mode of conducting war in Teso that led to what some have considered state repression akin to genocide. I do not go so far; my postscript presents preliminary population statistics published in a census that was taken as the Teso war was drawing to an end.

THE CONSTRUCTION OF COLONIAL UGANDA

The establishment of the first British administration in what became the Uganda Protectorate in 1890 — a military administration — rested on the combined resources of the British crown (using troops drawn from imperial outposts outside of Africa) and the Buganda kingdom. Jointly they enclosed a territory that stretched as far as the pre-existing imperial boundaries of other European nations would allow. Colonial state formation centered on Mengo, the royal capital of Buganda, and extended north, east, and west for up to two hundred and fifty miles in each direction. The colonial power appointed Baganda Agents to advise conquered monarchs and administer directly, and forcefully if need be, acephalous regions. Colonial sovereignty rested on Baganda sub-imperialism (Roberts 1962; Twaddle 1993; Vincent 1983b). Small colonial wars were fought intermittently on the soil of peoples peripheralized by colonial state formation, and these continued more intensively in postcolonial Uganda (Vincent forthcoming).

Colonial pacification was completed — more or less — by 1920. Thereafter, apart from border skirmishes with groups hoping either to raid or to secede, administrative order was maintained. Colonial histories of peripheral wars, such as these, represent them as "tribal" in nature, "ethnic" affiliations having been severed by the new international boundaries. Today, recognizing the degree to which agrarian populations are located in complex power relations that vary over space and time, their organization is better portrayed as a fluid, localized activity, initiating and responding to changing political circumstances.

Identifications and the production of identities as well as material and symbolic bonding define populations historically in movement. Imperial times bred colonial places and the hegemonic moment[3] reified languages and cultures, tribes and bounded districts, and codified them. In Uganda this lasted for the first sixty years of the twentieth century. Not pre-colonial animosities but modern state formation bred ethnic and regional conflict.[4]

In the academic culture produced by the colonial encounter two representations of war and the military predominated. The first derived from analyses of uneven economic development under colonial capitalism and was best represented in the work of Marxist Asian Ugandans Mukherjee (1985) and Mamdani (1976). The second reflected social science understandings of 'tribalism' or 'ethnicity.' This culminated in Nelson Kasfir's (1976) study of ethnicity in a shrinking political arena, and Helgar Bernt Hansen's (1977) study of ethnicity and military rule in Uganda up to an including the beginning of Amin's presidency. As colonial constructs, both uneven development and ethnicity are subjected in this essay to a re-visioning that looks instead at the conditions under which each was culturally produced.

THE CONSTRUCTION OF UNEVEN DEVELOPMENT

Political scientists and economists had no problem in identifying the 'more developed' nature of the south. The introduction of colonial capitalism had, indeed, led to the political and economic advancement of southern Uganda at the expense of the north and east. Thus, as the planned, colonially administered economy matured, by the eve of independence in 1962, the uneven development of Uganda was writ large on the landscape. Postcolonial Uganda thus inherited a privileged economic hub in the plantations and urban industries of the south, particularly within Buganda, but reaching along the shores of Lake Victoria along the line of rail to the ports and depots of the East African coast. Around the capital, Kampala, a market garden and dairy industry had developed to sustain the industrial and commercial growth of the city. A cashcrop (cotton and coffee) export economy had been introduced in the east and northeast (Busoga, Bukedi, and Teso). The north (West Nile and Acholi) provided the labor pool required by the 'modernizing' economic sector in the south.

In the colonial protectorate the site of government was Mengo, the capital of Buganda, which became incorporated within the municipal boundaries of modern Uganda. But historically the physical location of any center-place of government invariably creates problems for modern territorial sovereignty. Colonial policy required that the troops stationed in Kampala (in the south) be from distant peripheral regions (Omara-Otunno 1990). Because of minimum height stipulations (common throughout the British Isles and the British Empire) recruitment favored Nilotic northerners, particularly Acholi.

These then were the inherited terrains on which histories of representations, divisiveness, and political discrimination were acted in postcolonial Uganda.

THE CONSTRUCTION OF ETHNICITY

Political scientists used the concept of ethnic identity to account for the composition of the Ugandan army and military recruitment throughout the colonial and early postcolonial era. This may be subjected to at least two criticisms. First, structural discourse often descended into unproven assertions that a political leader favored 'his own.' The British, it was said, favored the Acholi; Obote, the Langi; Amin, Nubians; Lule the Baganda; and Museveni, the Banyankole and the Baganda. In the event, intra- military relations, coups d'état and Army mutinies could all be explained away as expressions of ethnic interest. All of which, as Tarsis Kabwegyere (1974) and A. Omara-Otunno (1990) have shown, perpetuated colonial cultural hegemony. Both Obote and Museveni, as populist leaders in postcolonial Uganda, articulated alternative modes of classification and evaluation in both the 1967 and 1982 constitutions, but there has been no sustained effort among intellectuals (political scientists, economists, historians, sociologists, and anthropologists) to valorize non-ethnic identities.

More importantly, while we learn much about the structural complexion of the troops from the type of occupational ethnic breakdown that Hansen (1977) engages in so brilliantly, we know nothing about where any of these troops were deployed or what they were actually called upon to *do* — and how they did it — at any time in the country's tumultuous history. And, of course, the actual difficulty of gaining access to military documentation, or of interviewing military personnel past or present, makes such research all but impossible.[5]

In Uganda, the idiom of ethnicity, both as identity and agency, has been used repeatedly to account for economic development or backwardness (as naturalized landscape) and war (as natural antagonism). This dual usage appears to have its origin in the established practice of nineteenth century European explorers and missionaries who viewed the Buganda kingdom as the pinnacle of 'native' political evolution. Buganda was, indeed, an aggressive empire-building monarchy at the moment when the British entered the region; other African peoples paled into insignificance when compared with the Baganda.

In the turn of the century flush of enthusiasm for capitalism, expansion, and development, the Baganda were singled out for their initiative in seeking out markets, getting an education, and, above all, for their money-consciousness. Other Ugandan peoples were then viewed as being in a 'pre-monetary' stage (Powesland 1957: 9, Vincent 1982). In line with this species of Enlightenment discourse, relations between the Baganda in the south and the Africans of the north were as Culture (Civilization) to Nature. Those in the northeast were ethnically categorized as 'Bakedi' — the naked ones. Nomadic, savage, and warlike, they were contrasted sharply with the Baganda, who were clothed, sedentary, civilized, and — martial. In the eyes of the military British administrators, the Baganda had a fine military tradition even as they themselves did. In certain ways, then, for the British, the Baganda were 'people more like us.'[6] The 'like us-ness' that the British accorded the Buganda monarchy was developed further when historians began to work in postcolonial Uganda. Inscribed histories were to hand within the southern kingdoms, whereas the indigenous modes of historical discourse in the north were less familiar to them.

In the first days of empire, explorers and missionaries entered Uganda from the Sudanic north before travelling southwards along the Nile into what they perceived to be the heartland of black Africa. Very quickly there grew up a felt Christian need for a bulwark against 'Muhammedanism' and the North-South divide began to receive theological as well as evolutionary rationalization. This situation was soon to be complicated by divisions within the missionary churches north and south of the Nile. In the south Roman Catholics predominated and Catholic missionaries favored Luganda as the language of instruction. The largely Anglican north favored the use of more parochial indigenous languages or the lingua franca, Swahili, which, not incidentally, was the language of the army.

The colonial power demarcated 'tribal' administrative districts on the basis of common language, naming each after the 'tribe' that spoke it. Later, as linguists began distinguishing, classifying, and categorizing the languages spoken within the colonial territory, they made a tripartite distinction between southern Bantu, northern Nilotic, and northeastern Nilo-Hamitic languages. The one feature of the terrain that the Europeans 'knew' more definitively than any other — the River Nile — became an anomalous secondary point of reference at the same time that the simpler North-South dualism was embraced.

Anthropological discourse gave scientific legitimacy to the Nilotic divide. The structuralist paradigm established in *African Political Systems* (Fortes and Evans-Pritchard 1940) contrasted centralized and non-centralized states, convincing the Ugandan colonial administration and university students alike of the positive virtues of the southern Ugandan kingdoms and the problematic nature of ahierarchical, acephalous northern 'tribes.' Stability and order were attributed to the former; segmentary feuding and disorder to the latter. On the eve of independence, encouraged by clear manifestations of the monarchical British favoring centralized kingdoms, several peripheral districts began to select and appoint figureheads so that they might share the dignities, privileges and political spoils accorded the lacustrine kingdoms of the south.

During the colonial era these divisions — geographical, religious, linguistic, administrative, scholarly — were employed by local administrators to create political and economic competitiveness between the districts and counties (Vincent 1982; 1983b). The ethnic divisions entrenched on the eve of independence deepened in the years immediately following, largely due to the increasing value attributed by the national government and the global banking industry to the country's 'development.'[7] Ironically, Buganda's position was even further aggrandized during the socialist regime of Milton Obote, a northerner. Obote produced a Five Year Plan aimed at bringing new prosperity to the north, but not through the redistribution of southern wealth in spite of a popular northern view of southerners as 'the enemy.'

To summarize the argument thus far: Throughout the colonial period, short as it was, these two social science discourses — of ethnicity and uneven development — had become so clearly imbricated that for Ugandans certain identities appeared more desirable than others. Many of these were embedded in legal categories and framed unequal access to freedom of movement and economic advancement (Vincent 1983a, 1993a). To say that all identity is relational, formed through relations of power, is a truism. Nevertheless, the extent to which these various discourses lent themselves to a serial aggrandizement of the Buganda kingdom and the Baganda people is, I suggest, fundamental to any understanding of the structure of conflict and civil war in postcolonial Uganda. They were foundational in Ugandans' own sense of identity, transmitted through the educational system, and deployed with considerable success in the nationalisms that developed on the eve of independence. 'The Buganda Question' supplied the master discourse at the constitutional conference that preceded independence in 1962. It then fuelled four years later the first military engagement of Uganda's postcolonial army.

VIOLENCE IN POSTCOLONIAL UGANDA

Throughout the colonial period (1900–1962), the military strength of the Uganda Protectorate rested on one military battalion and a small unarmed police force. Only on two occasions in the 1940s was the Army brought into service to quell civilian disturbances. On both occasions nascent trade union activity and anti-Asian violence were involved.

In July 1966 President Milton Obote despatched the Ugandan Army, under the command of Idi Amin, to sack the palace of Mutesa, the *kabaka* (king) of Buganda after the monarch and his cabinet had announced their intention of seceding from the new state.[8] The proposed secession, it is said, was covertly encouraged by Britain. Uganda's earlier embeddedness within the British empire had marginalized it from world trade in arms. Ties to Britain were broken when it became evident that Britain's interests lay in toppling rather than upholding the socialist Obote (UPC) regime. After the defeat of Mutesa, Uganda entered the global marketplace. Obote's reliance on the army in the years that followed and his part in building up Amin's career cannot be part of this narrative. Suffice to say that the overthrow of Obote's government in a coup d'état orchestrated by Amin prefigured the destruction of the colonial legacy.

The subsequent importance of Amin's military regime (1970–79) in instigating a reign of terror cannot be over-stated. Yet the infrastructural changes he wrought in the Ugandan state were equally significant for what ensued thereafter. His division of the country into provinces under rapacious military governors and his dismantling of the colonial economy through the expulsion of Asian traders contributed to the collapse of export crop agriculture. Considerable illicit enterprise and extractive power became concentrated in the hands of businessmen, the so-called *mafutamingi* (literally, 'those with much fat'), often relatives or clients of army commanders (warlords) who hoarded and overcharged on essential goods. The rapid impoverishment of the rural population followed.

In a remarkably short space of time following the overthrow of Obote by Amin in 1973 (*a coup d'état*), the Ugandan armies became involved in the overthrow of Amin and the restoration of Obote by a military invasion from Tanzania supported by Ugandan national liberation forces (*conventional war*). This is the War of Liberation (1978–79) to be discussed in this essay. This was followed by the overthrow of Obote by the National Revolutionary Army (NRA) of Museveni in 1985 (*guerilla warfare*). Finally, the present regime, the National Revolutionary Movement (NRM) headed by Museveni, has been engaged in constant military efforts to suppress rebels in the outlying regions of the country (*civil war*). Insurgency in Teso and the NRA's measures to suppress it (1985–1992) are also to be discussed in this essay. This succession of military activity from 1973 to 1992 ranges categorically from conventional wars that have involved the troops of other nations fighting on Ugandan soil, through the indirect participation of national governments and foreign nationals in the supply of arms for paramilitary activity, through secessionist wars that have been going on for generations, to the guerrilla warfare and counter-insurgency tactics of the current NRM regime.

Declarations of 'war' have become intrinsic to the rhetoric of repression in Uganda. When the Army suppressed secession in 1966, politicians and the popular press announced that war had been declared against the Baganda. When Amin found that a large proportion of the army disapproved of his coup d'état a few years later, his newly established Military Council 'declared war' on the Acholi element within its ranks. In both cases the rebellious opposition was attributed to an ethnic group. In both these engagements, military and paramilitary, the Ugandan state proceeded to deploy its forces against a civilian population.[9] Tarsis Kabwegyere's description of "the state [as] an increasingly anti-people machine involved in the creation of untold human misery" (1987: 24) became tragically accurate.

THE CONSTRUCTION OF VIOLENCE

It is useful, I suggest, to distinguish between violence that is impersonal in operation, contingent, anonymous, and professional, from that which is indwelling, personal, parochial, and pervaded by human relations, cultures, knowledges, and inescapable histories.

The Ugandan state, through all its postcolonial regimes, has hardly acted alone. There has been no instance of systemic violence at a moment of revolutionary change in Uganda when 'foreign' interests did not frame, shape, or stimulate military action. Between 1962 and 1992 systemic violence in Uganda escalated. It did so within the context of global confrontations, the most critical of which, for Uganda, were the Cold War and the Israeli-Arab conflict.[10]

Trickle-down global military economies equipped the Ugandan Army as it expanded from one battalion in 1962 to five battalions by 1992. Paramilitary technologies increased in number, size, and sophistication. Uganda itself has no armaments industry, the army's technological growth from side arms to tanks, mortars, and rockets has been solely dependent on external production, the purchase of arms, and Uganda's entry into the global arms market. The state's military growth, along with its deployment of surveillance techniques and the instruments of State terrorism, owe much to Israel, Britain, Libya, USSR, France, and the USA. These countries in turn became the main suppliers of military and paramilitary technology to successive Ugandan regimes (Mamdani 1983).

Apart from the short War of Liberation of 1978–1979, this build-up of the military was directed solely against the state's own citizens. As Mudoola notes (1988: 291):

> Part of the Ugandan tragedy is that the post-colonial Ugandan army was built up and expanded in response to the secessionist Rwenzuru movement, disturbances in the 'Lost Counties,' the cattle raids in Karamoja, and spillover effects of the disturbances in the Congo (now Zaire) and the Sudan, and the Buganda 'Question', at the time of independence...battalions were established in the epicentres of domestic trouble spots...and the Ugandan post-colonial leadership came to regard the military as an instrument for maintenance of law and order within the state, and later as an instrument of domestic policy.

Conventional war is the strategy whereby large formations of regular armies confront each other in a series of well defined battles, advancing and retreating as a clear, usually spatially defined, goal is achieved or lost. Conventional warfare was pursued on Ugandan soil in the War of Liberation (1978–1979) to bring about the overthrow of Amin. This entailed the use of modern equipment including tanks, artillery, aircraft, and rockets. The tanks may still be seen embedded like giant dinosaurs in Buganda's roadside swamps; the telegraph poles are scarred with shrapnel from rockets. Foreign troops were involved, Ugandans and Libyans on one side and Tanzanians on the other. Two exiled Ugandan politicians, Obote and Museveni, were both engaged, the one diplomatically, the other militarily. With the Liberation Army victorious, Museveni became Minister of Defence in what has familiarly become known as the Obote Two [i.e. the restored] government.

The restoration was short lived. The National Resistance Army (NRA) embarked on a campaign to oust the Obote regime in February 1981. The war lasted until July 1985. It was first known as *The Protracted Peoples' War* and later, after political victory, as *The Uganda Resistance War*. The protracted war was "a strategy whereby popular forces — i.e. those forces supported by the masses — wage a protracted war against unpopular elements in power...The popular forces, though popular, start off with weak military units in terms of numbers, weaponry and organization. By using a protracted war strategy, they aim at turning their potential strength into actual strength, thus overcoming their weakness vis-à-vis the enemy forces" (Museveni 1985: 11).

Protracted war is said to pass through three phases: (1) guerrilla warfare; (2) mobile warfare; and (3) conventional warfare.[11] The guerrilla phase entails operations carried out by small units operating almost independently, launching short, sharp attacks, ambushes, and executions of notoriously 'anti-people elements.' To counter these attacks, the enemy (in this case, Obote's government) spreads out its forces among the localities where it is being challenged, since it cannot afford to lose control of pockets of national territory and clusters of population. Thinned out in this manner, the government's troops become more vulnerable to attack. Meanwhile the guerrillas concentrate on the disruption of communications, the economy, and the military command and intelligence networks. They focus their attacks on weak units such as the police, militia, and less elite troops. They avoid casualties, gain experience and, above all, concentrate on attacking the military on the move, not in encampments. Gaining weapons in these hit and run encounters, the guerrillas then organize companies, battalions, and brigades and embark on the second phase, mobile warfare.

Mobile warfare is a continuing phase of fluid battles. The guerrillas are not concerned by losses of territory or population control should they occur; their one concern is to preserve and expand their own forces by avoiding casualties, and destroying the enemy's means of making war — weaponry, troops, fighting morale, the economy, infrastructure, international credibility. This has been viewed as *a critical phase* in the scholarly paradigm that has emerged out of the studies of guerrilla warfare in Zimbabwe by anthropologist David Lan, political scientist Norma Kriger, and historian Terence Ranger (Kriger forthcoming). It raises questions not only of identity and alignment, but of the very legitimacy of both government and guerrilla.[12] In an account of this phase in the NRA's struggle against Obote's troops, Museveni lists thirty-three 'battle victories' (1985: 39). All are place names. *But,* unlike the roll call of battalion honors in conventional war, the names cannot be strung out in a straight line, testifying to a headlong move to capture the capital but, instead, spot the Ugandan landscape.

THE GEOGRAPHY OF WAR IN UGANDA

Two Ugandan landscapes, in particular, reveal a vantage point from which the country's postcolonial wars may be surveyed: the rolling hills of Buganda in the southwest and the arid plains of Teso in the northeast.[13] Accepting for the moment the master discourse of the cultural divide between North and South (in order subsequently that it may be problematized) this essay contrasts the impact of war in a treecrop (plantain) environment in the southwest with a grain (millet) environment in the northeast. The problematic at its heart is the savagery and viciousness with which war was apparently conducted in the one terrain in contrast with the other. Why was it that the war in the south was comparatively short-lived, confined, and controlled, whereas that in the north was protracted, topographically unsettled, and bloody to the extent that charges of genocide have been made. Initially — but only initially, as we shall see — a contrast between conventional war and guerilla war stands out as a possible explanation.

Buganda is a dissected plateau lying to the north and west of Lake Victoria. Its landscape is composed of flat-topped hills and wide, swampy valleys. The rich soil favors a diversified and productive pastoral and arable agriculture. Rainfall is reliable throughout the year, allowing plantains to be grown as a year-round staple. Banana plantations require little labor and stands remain productive for many years. Robusta coffee, sugar-cane, and cocoa are also grown. Buganda's plantain-and-coffee zone forms an arc around the northern shores of Lake Kyoga stretching inland for about 30 miles. It is often referred to as Uganda's 'fertile crescent.'

In southwest Buganda in 1978–9, the war between Amin's troops and those of Tanzania and the Liberation Army had been fought at headlong speed, largely with mechanized vehicles and sophisticated weaponry. Towns had been shelled and enemies dislodged, but the fighting had been from town to town, capture and recapture. As the armies approached, the people fled from roadside villages and settlements, retreating further and further into the bush, hiding in the protective groves of dispersed family members. Some, it was said, fled from their homes and hid for as long as a year in the bush, returning stealthily at night only to harvest their plantains. The fertile Buganda countryside, supporting a dense population on its banana plantations, was relatively untouched by the war.

Teso, by contrast, lies to the northeast of the Nile and to the north of Lake Kyoga. Its landscape is composed of short grass savanna, eaten into by the wide swampy papyrus waterways of the lake and the Mpologoma river. Rainfall is bimodal with a major dry season from December to March; the average rainfall is about 40 inches per year. The soil consists of clay loams and loams in the south and sandier, more infertile, lands in the north. Scrub vegetation extends over wide areas of low hill country.

Population is thinly dispersed. Finger millet and sorghum are the staples; critically (and unlike plantains) both are *annual* crops. Groundnuts, cassava, and sweet potatoes, *also planted annually*, contribute to the diet. Cotton was introduced as a cash crop and generally precedes millet in Teso's crop rotation. Both millet and sorghum cultivation are labor intensive: ox-ploughing, harrowing, and rolling may precede broadcast or drill sowing; thinning and weeding are required; harvesting is extremely laborious. Cattle are highly valued culturally, and until 1982 there were more cattle in Teso than in any other region of Uganda.

Two aspects of Teso's agricultural regime were particularly vulnerable to the hazards of war: first, its dependence on *timely* seasonal planting; second, its call for communal labor. Clearly both conventional and guerrilla warfare might disrupt agricultural performance. More devastating in both the short and long run was, first, the impact of guerrilla bands relying on villagers to provide them with food. Secondly, and even more devastating because of its greater scale, were the counter insurgency measures of the government troops.

In the northeast the present regime was engaged in military efforts to suppress rebels for five years from 1987 through 1992. The war between the rebel guerrilla bands of the Uganda Peoples Army and Museveni's National Revolutionary Army (NRA) was a series of running battles fought throughout the Teso countryside. Standing crops were destroyed, cattle looted, and fishing prohibited. Dispersed in their homes across the countryside, the population was subjected to intermittent harassment and ultimate violence by guerrillas and government troops alike.[14]

The very nature of the terrain and the subsistence crops in each region — long-lived banana trees in the southwest and annually planted grain crops in the northeast — made for very different wars with very different impacts on the local populations. A narration of events will make this clear.

WAR IN THE SOUTHWEST (1978-79)

The war in the southwest lasted for eight months between 1978 and 1979. My focus here is on Amin's cross-border invasion of the Kagera salient; Tanzania's counter invasion; fighting in the southwest (in what are now Rakai and Masaka); and the headlong race to Kampala.

International involvement in the war was partly a legacy of presidential statebuilding practices in Uganda and Tanzania and partly the result of the international ties of exiled Ugandan politicians. These aligned Libya militarily and Israel diplomatically with Uganda, and China, Britain, and the Organization of African Unity with

Tanzania. In May 1978 Uganda began to move troops and military hardware to the Tanzanian border and some small incursions were made into the neighboring territory. In October Uganda invaded and the Kagera salient became a war zone.[15] Mig aircraft attacked Bukoba in western Tanzania and a week later over 2,000 Ugandan troops crossed the border, meeting with little resistance.[16] Withdrawing in November, the Ugandan army blew up the Kagera River bridge at Kyaka to prevent a counterattack.

The Tanzanian army began to mass south of the Kagera river in the second week of November. Crossing to the north, widespread evidence was found of looting, destruction, and slaughter carried out by Amin's troops. Several minor clashes occurred in the two months that followed, culminating in an assault on Mutukula town, where Ugandan guns commanded the salient. Capturing the town, the barbarism of the Tanzanian army was so horrific, it was said, that the Tanzanian army high command began to leash in its troops and change its strategy, recognizing that the destruction of the civilian population was counter-productive.[17] Thereafter its headlong movement towards Kampala was fast and furious, its objective: capturing the capital and setting up a new government. Resistance from Amin's troops and the Libyans was minimal and the war was over in a matter of months.

To avoid costly loss of life in the capital itself (and in keeping with Chinese military philosophy) Museveni left Amin's troops with a loophole at the east end of the city through which many fled first east and then north. Some discarded their weapons as they went, others formed groups of discontented fighting men determined to challenge the legitimacy of the new regime. The foreign arms that were discarded later, ironically, played no small part in sustaining textured war in Teso.

WAR IN THE NORTHEAST (1987–1992)

When Museveni's National Revolutionary Movement (NRM) first came into power in 1986, among its first tasks was the 'reconstruction' of the economy and the rehabilitation of the south and southwest from whence most of Museveni's supporters came. The NRM's failure to elaborate a political and economic program for the north led rather quickly to the mobilization of several guerrilla movements across a wide span of the country, including the Uganda Peoples Army in Teso (Vincent forthcoming). This was a region that had widely supported Obote's Uganda Peoples Party, and a sense of dislocation followed the ousting of Obote for a second time in 1985. The NRM made little attempt to fill the political vacuum.[18]

Immediately after Museveni's accession to power, Teso's rural populations settled back peaceably to receive the economic reconstruction promised by the internationally favored NRM regime, accepting — even welcoming — the idea of popularly elected local resistance committees (RCs) working alongside the district administrator and his team.[19] This is, perhaps, somewhat surprising, given their checkered histories under previous regimes. Men from Teso had been extensively recruited for the colonial police force, and the population's postcolonial electoral support for Obote's UPC was legendary. But, in 1986, 'democracy' mattered less than 'development.'

Within eighteen months, however, the region was aflame. Throughout Uganda the blackmarket *magendo* economy of the Amin years had restructured social and political relations drastically. Individualistic and capitalist as Teso had been during the cotton-exporting colonial era and in the development decade of the 1960s, local entrepreneurs responded avidly: land was enclosed and businesses grew, especially transportation. And, as throughout Teso's history, newly acquired wealth was invested in cattle; everywhere herds increased in size.

Inevitably almost, as throughout Teso's recorded history, massive cattle raiding by neighboring Karimojong increased proportionately. As early as 1978 military misrule in Karamoja had led to a diffusion of guns to replace spears, leading to warfare between rival groups. Then, in 1979, the Moroto armory was looted. When in 1981 drought and famine brought international aid agencies to work with the rural population of Karamoja, Teso cattle rustling organized by Ugandan army officers stationed there began to break out (O'Connor 1988). By 1986 the Karimojong were reported fully armed with machine guns, criss-crossing eastern Uganda on abandoned military vehicles.

Villagers in Teso formed local militia to protect their cattle from the raiders and violence escalated. For reasons that remain unclear, the NRM's response was to disarm the Teso villagers. Further, when the Karimojong renewed their attacks with even greater force, the state that claimed the monopoly of the legitimate use of force did not intervene. Thus, as one historian has put it, "The NRA was unable, and possibly also unwilling, to protect the Teso in early 1986, and the Teso suffered terribly as a result" (Pirouet 1991: 201).

Within months former resistance fighters from several regions of the north and east were fighting against Museveni's NRA on Teso soil. That the Uganda Peoples Army was the umbrella organization the government and press took it to be is unlikely: the forces of law and order have a tendency to magnify rebel opposition in order to account for their own inability to suppress it. Some of the combatants were survivors of the Holy Spirit movement of Alice Lakwena, others of the Uganda National Liberation Army from Acholi and Lango. There appears to have been no central command, such as in Museveni's guerrilla campaigns against Obote, nor were the Teso guerrillas led in the field by men like Museveni himself, schooled in military philosophy and practised in unconventional war. There were apparently links among the several bands, but this guerrilla fighting was no 'protracted war' executed along Maoist lines.

The scorched earth policy of Museveni's NRA as they suppressed the insurgency in the northeast was in sharp contrast to the controlled guerrilla struggle it had waged to overthrow Obote. In the guerrilla war in Teso, a subsistence economy that rested on cattle and fishing was desolated. Cattle stolen by machine-gun armed Karimojong raiders were bought from them openly by high ranking Army officers, and exported to markets in Kampala and ranches in Ankole and the southwest. No seasonal planting of millet and sorghum could be undertaken. Above all, no collective mobilization of labor such as a grain crop economy requires (Guyer 1984) was possible for years on end.

In guerilla warfare, security forces frequently impose arbitrary and terrible sufferings on villagers caught between sides in the military campaign. It is commonplace that peasants find excuses for guerrilla violence, blaming it on youthwings, deviant elements, and so on. Both contribute to the continuation of violence. In Teso, only two measures — both measures of desperation, perhaps — broke the military impasse. First (as in colonial South Africa, Malaysia, or Kenya) the resettlement of the rural population in camps, surrounded by the military and protected from the 'rebels,' removed them from the violence. Secondly, the offering of amnesty to guerrilla leaders in 1991 and the incorporation of their armed followers into the NRA was successfully, according to their own lights, pursued by the NRM. The rebels indeed came out of the bush.[20]

The first measure backfired dreadfully and tragically; disease spread in the resettlement camps, mortality was high, and only international medical and food aid prevented more suffering.[21] The second measure may well prove notoriously short-sighted since one of the few points of NRM propaganda conceded by opponents is that the NRA's protracted war against the Obote regime was a disciplined affair. Thereafter, in victory, his 'new' army has been anything but that.[22]

CONCLUSION

The contradictions evident in the conduct of the war in the northeast become simply the most recent conjuncture in what has been a potential civil war — or a potential nation-building issue — ever since the British colonial state was carved out among the peoples north and south of the Nile.

For the Teso rebels conducting a guerrilla war, the constitutional legitimacy of Museveni's regime was at issue.[23]

The army they were fighting was made up mainly of southerners, and for both sets of combatants there were old scores to settle. There was also the old Baganda southern hegemony (albeit in new southwestern guise) to come to terms with. Men of the NRA, schooled in the long-standing disparagement of northerners as barbarians, also held more recent political prejudices against the Teso supporters of Obote's second regime. The south and southwest, and particularly the Baganda, had benefitted from Amin's economic cronyism, which Obote's return had brought to an end. The Obote regime that followed was maintained in power largely by a northern army and a police force dominated by men from Teso.[24]

The guerrilla war in Teso and the counter-force that suppressed it were thus but one of the latest manifestations of the omnipresent potential for civil war in Uganda that has existed ever since the cross-Nile borders of the country were carved out of the African terrain. The savagery of that structured violence has yet to be fully explained.

POSTSCRIPT

I have referred several times to the difficulty of finding or trusting either written or oral sources relating to war in postcolonial Uganda. Experience has taught the people of Uganda that the powerholders of today may be overthrown by the powerholders of yesteryear, and, without the dangerous courage of an ideological commitment to speak out, journalists and those interviewed carefully and deliberately fashion their words, I would suggest, with double tongues. One may read what one will into their messages. It is therefore for want of anything better at the moment that I draw on certain statistics (issued recently in Uganda) to provide documentation of the 'unnatural' severity of the war in the northeast.

It seems reasonable to suggest that Teso's postcolonial war history is in some way reflected in the latest census of the population (Uganda Government 1991). From these statistics war's impact on the arid millet and sorghum growing region of Teso's two districts would appear to be documented in a way that no words alone can convey.

The provisional census records the population of Kumi district rising from 190,000 in 1969 to 239,000 in 1980 but falling to 237,000 by 1991. Soroti district had a population of nearly 380,000 in 1969 but this shrank from 476,000 to a little under 431,000 between 1980 and 1991. The severe impact of guerrilla warfare and counter insurgency activities is suggested. *These were the only two districts in the whole of Uganda to experience a negative intercensal annual growth rate between 1980 and 1991.*[25]

Much of this population loss may well have come about during the war through displacement (i.e. the flight of refugees from the war zone) as well as mortality. While some deaths were of combatants in the guerrilla fighting, even more, probably, were of civilians caught in the crossfire between the NRA and the rebels. Mortality was also high in the resettlement camps, where the people were malnourished and disease spread rapidly (TDT 1992).

Statistics on population distribution by gender also suggest the war's impact on the two northeastern districts.[26] In all but one of the counties an excess of females over males is marked; the greatest imbalance occurs in those counties that suffered the most prolonged fighting.[27]

The January 1991 census figures revealed the existence of a large refugee population in Soroti Town. The surrounding countryside had been and was being looted by both the NRA and rebel troops. The urban population rose from 15,000 in 1980 to 42,841 in 1991. In August 1991 I found extensive poverty, hunger and overcrowding among the refugees from the countryside;[28] the town itself offered little except abandoned shops and empty streets. The presence of the Army was everywhere. Throughout a countryside that had once supported a cotton-growing, cattle-owning, millet-eating rural population, no cotton was being grown, cattle were no longer kept,[29] and millet had been replaced by cassava.

To sum up: the impact of warfare on a locality may be read like a shadow on the lung of an otherwise healthy person. Kumi and Soroti were the only districts in Uganda to have suffered population decline between 1980 and 1991. I am suggesting that this can be attributed largely to the nature and impact in those districts of guerrilla warfare and counter insurgency measures.

The census figures raise the question of *why* war in the northeast of Uganda was so devastating. An initial explanation based upon the nature of guerrilla warfare compared with conventional warfare went some way towards accounting for this. The intervening variable in the Uganda case is the agricultural system, specifically, the food supply in the northeast and southwest respectively. A further explanation suggests that historical constructions of place and cultural identity worked themselves out in the present in the form of the NRA's counter-insurgency operations. The people of Teso were cast in ethnic terms as Obote's people — an obstacle to be finally removed from the path of the new order. Ugandans hegemonically encultured to perceive southerners and northerners as somehow 'natural' antagonists and (in extension of sub-imperialist evolutionary ideology) to view the latter as 'savages', were well prepared culturally to make war on the civilian population and thus render Teso one of Africa's and the postcolonial world's 'killing fields.'

NOTES

1. Research was first carried out in Teso in 1966–67. Throughout much of this period a State of Emergency had been declared in Uganda following President Obote's sacking of the *kabaka* (king) of Buganda's palace. This did not affect my up-country fieldwork. I returned to Teso for a period of further fieldwork in 1973 shortly after President Amin seized power. After a long interval, I returned very briefly to Uganda in 1989 to conduct AIDS related research in the southwest of the country. On that occasion I was advised not to go to Teso because of the fighting there. In 1991 after attending a conference on the constitution jointly organized by the Law School of Makerere University and the Institute of Human Rights of Columbia University, I was able to visit Teso. My research on that occasion was restricted to Soroti and its environs. I was advised not to travel to Serere or Gondo since there was still a great deal of military activity in that area.
2. Elsewhere (Vincent 1993b) I set this constructed dualism between North and South, so frequently given expression in nineteenth and twentieth century wars — as in the United States, Ireland, India, Korea, Vietnam — alongside the center-periphery model favored by many state analysts. For a general critique of post-Enlightenment oppositional thinking, see Dirks 1992, O'Brien and Roseberry 1991, Prakash 1992.
3. I developed this concept in a critique of Gramsci's inclusive, unified model of class and state hegemony in order to address problems arising in my historical analysis of legal transformation in Uganda. Gramsci's theory of the hegemonic apparatus is complemented, dialectically, by a theory of the crisis of hegemony. According to Gramsci, the dialectic of

the hegemonic moment (of leadership, consent, master discourses, or law) and the more restrictive moment of domination (state coercion) coexist. Further discussion of the concept of the hegemonic moment is to be found in Vincent 1994.
4. This, it will be appreciated, is somewhat contrary to Geertz's (1963) perception of segments of the periphery undergoing an "integrative revolution" which, in effect, renders primordial discontents modern or normal.
5. It is yet but one more Ugandan tragedy that Dan Mudoola (Director of Makerere Institute of Social Research and Vice-Chairman of the Constitutional Commission) who contributed (1988, 1991) to the study of the military as an institution under the current NRM regime, was accidentally killed by bomb blast in 1993.
6. British admiration for the Baganda went only so far. See, for example, their treatment of the Muganda Agent, Kakungulu (Vincent 1982, Twaddle 1993) and the restrictions they placed on enterprising Baganda who sought to enter into cotton ginning (Vincent 1983a).
7. I follow Ferguson (1990) in viewing "development" as an important site of cultural and critical intervention.
8. Inasmuch as the Buganda kingdom was the most economically advanced region of Uganda, the war of 1966 appears analogous with secession wars in Katanga and Biafra.
9. The colonial government's creation in 1960 of a paramilitary General Service Unit to provide intelligence about nationalist politicians provided a precedent and a foretaste of Uganda's postcolonial engagement with systemic anti-people violence.
10. Two examples may be given: (1) the effect of Obote's 'Move to the Left' in 1969, which increasingly alienated British support and (2) Israel's interventions in 1970 after Obote's increasing alignment with Sudanese President Nimeri. Low writes of the January 1971 coup, in which Amin and the army overthrew Obote, "There is some evidence that the chief Israel representative in the country... bolstered Amin's resolution at the critical moment, and that British firms and the British Government...were party to what was soon afoot" (1991: 317). East African leaders, such as President Nyerere of Tanzania, have frequently spoken out against their countries being pawns in the "big wars" of the western nations and their surrogates.
11. Museveni's many statements on the waging of a guerilla war clearly derive from the writings of Mao. It is perhaps less well appreciated the extent to which Mao's ideas belong within a body of warrior-philosophy widespread throughout Asia. I am grateful to Gregory Ruf and David Rosenthal for guiding me towards this literature.

Several ideas in the following discussion of Museveni's views on guerrilla warfare are to be found in the writings of the 6th century philosopher Tzu Sun. For example: to win without fighting is best; tire the enemy by flight; make a lot of surprise attacks. When they come out, you go home; when they go home, you go out. Cause division among them. Attack when they are unprepared, make your move when they do not expect it. If a military operation goes on for a long time without accomplishing anything, your rivals will begin to get ideas. Those who win every battle are not really skilful — those who render others' armies helpless without fighting are the best of all. And, most critical, surely, in the course of Uganda's military history, as we shall see: *A surrounded army must be given a way out* (Tzu Sun 1988).

12. Of these questions, the most critical for an understanding of later events in Uganda is whether Museveni waited too long 'in the bush,' thus allowing other military commanders to claim credit for the overthrow of Obote's government.

13. With the abolition of 'tribally' named districts, Teso District (inhabited mainly by Iteso) was divided into the two new districts of Kumi and Soroti. I found the people of both continuing to refer to Teso district in 1993 and retain this usage here, in part to provide referential continuity with my own earlier field locale. The local Ateso newspaper provides excellent coverage of events in the two districts.

14. Although this essay focuses particularly on Kumi and Soroti districts, the patterning of military counter insurgency appears to have been common to much of northern and eastern Uganda. Thus the historian Omara-Otunno (1991: 44), citing the Uganda Human Rights Activist Association's report for July–December 1986, details NRA activity in the north as follows:
"In some areas soldiers had completely destroyed houses, grain stores and the bore-holes. As a result many people faced starvation. In addition, thousands of civilians in Acholi were interned in concentration camps by NRA troops; according to one estimate these were: 10,000 in Gulu camps, 8,000 in Kitgum camps, and 6–8,000 in Karuma camps....Such accounts were not disputed by the government. Indeed, President Museveni admitted that NRA troops had burned food stores in the north."

15. A textured account of the war from the vantage point of a Tanzanian from Bukoba is to be found in a long epic poem by Henry R. Muhanika (1981). In a discussion of epic poetry in Kiswahili dealing with war, Zawawi (forthcoming) summarizes in some detail the events narrated in Muhanika's 1,271 verse poem.

16. Tanzanian sources (Avirgan and Honey 1982 and Muhanika (1981) refer to an orgy of looting, raping, and killing; young women being taken to a forced labor camp at Kalasizo; over 1,500 Tanzanian civilians being killed; 13,000 head of cattle at a state ranch looted, taken to Mbarara and distributed to soldiers.

17. "Then the Tanzanians began levelling the town [Mutukula]. No distinction was made between military and non-military objects. Everything was destroyed and every living thing killed. Bulldozers came in and plowed down mud huts. People too old to have fled were shot. By

midday Mutukula no longer existed except on maps. The Tanzanians had begun to take their revenge and to take it in a manner not dissimilar to the behavior of Amin's troops in the Kagera salient.

"When news of the Mutukula victory reached Nyerere, the Tanzania president was predictably pleased, but he was appalled by the army's boastful report of the death and destruction they had wrought. Nyerere issued an immediate order that from that moment on a sharp distinction must be drawn between civilian and military lives and property...

"Thus Mutukula began to teach the Tanzanian army two great lessons... The second was that protection of civilian lives and property was of both humanitarian as well as military interest and that a friendly civilian population could be a greater weapon than anything in the arsenal of either army" (Avirgan and Honey 1982: 70).

There is, as far as I know, still no authoritative, bipartisan account of this war. My understanding of it is colored, no doubt, by the Tanzanian-oriented accounts I have read and informal unsolicited accounts of the war received in Rakai district in 1988.

18. Mamdani (1988) suggests that this was due to Museveni's lack of control over his own forces. This was particularly acute with the adoption of a policy of incorporating elements of the troops it defeated into its own ranks.

19. There is, indeed, evidence that business-as-usual was a feature of the NRM's local resistance committee (RC) elections throughout Uganda. In Teso, former UPC local district councillors were elected to RCs in many instances.

20. By September 1991, 1,211 rebels had surrendered in Kumi alone, the first of Teso's two districts to be pacified. Their commanders led them out of the bush laden with mortars and machine guns. Their return to civilian life was organized expeditiously: with a few months a Kumi Progressive Association was formed of former 'rebels and ex-lodgers' (i.e. former prisoners).

21. By the late 1980s, despair, resignation, and what has been called donor fatigue had set in among the readers of the international press with respect to much of Africa and, certainly, to Uganda. The Teso experience had failed to reach the world press in 1989 and efforts to inform Labour Party politicians in Britain were, apparently, unsuccessful. A few doctors, former missionaries and administrators who had worked in Teso during the colonial era formed a charitable organization, the Teso Development Trust, which they eventually linked with the Development Department of the Church of Uganda in Soroti.

22. It has been suggested that Museveni's incorporation of defeated troops into the NRA, many of them poorly disciplined, was an effort to avert further bloodshed. In the early days it was probably also necessary for the NRA to recruit the more specialized of the enemy troops, trained in more advanced military hardware than the NRA itself had acquired (Mudoola 1991).

23. The other side of the coin, of course, is the crisis of guerilla legitimacy in Teso. Since the war in Teso 'ended' (officially) only in August 1992, I cannot explore this in the manner of Ranger, Kriger, and Lan in Zimbabwe, nor present a thick ethnographic delineation of Teso's 'resistance war' as I encountered it in summer 1991.
24. It is said in Teso that immediately after gaining power Museveni gave orders for men from several divisions of the police to report to southern barracks. It is said that they were never seen again.
25. In Kumi negative growth was −0.1 and in Soroti −0.9. Density per square kilometer remained steady in Kumi at 97.0 but in Soroti it fell from 56.0 to 51.0. This reflected, I would suggest, the NRM's earlier pacification of Kumi district, particularly the countryside just to the north of Mbale, and the failure to pacify parts of Soroti by January 1991 when the census was carried out. In Bugondo sub-county, for example, census-taking had to be suspended temporarily because of rebel harassment and was finally undertaken by Army personnel.
26. Thus:

Population by Gender

	County	Male	Female	Total
Kumi	Bukedea	35800	39200	75000
	Kumi	48600	54100	102700
	Ngora	28100	31200	59300
	TOTAL	112400	124500	237000
Soroti	Amuria	22600	22900	45600
	Kaberamaido	19300	21000	40300
	Kalaki	19900	21700	41500
	Kapelebyong	12500	11300	23700
	Kasilo	14600	15100	29700
	Serere	29200	32000	61200
	Soroti	35600	38000	73600
	Usuku	35800	38800	74600
	Soroti Town	18900	21800	40600
	TOTAL	208300	222600	430900

27. Mortality may well have been higher in Soroti, Serere, and Usuku than in the rest of Soroti district. The higher proportion of females in Kumi county may have been due to the presence there of a military camp around which many refugees settled. I have yet to explore the full implication of these figures for AIDS distribution and intervention. According to a respondent at the Soroti Catholic Mission, HIV positivity figures for Soroti and Kumi districts were as follows: Soroti District 26 per cent; Kumi District 46 per cent. That for Atutur, now a refugee

village clustered around a very large army camp located between Mbale town and Kumi was 86 per cent. It was estimated at the time that HIV positivity in the Ugandan Army was about 60 percent.
28. In August 1991 these were squatting in derelict government offices including the former Government Rest House. Those I interviewed were mainly families of women and children supported, in a few cases, by one male job holder, most of the menfolk having been killed or obliged to leave the district.
29. The scrawny beasts I saw in August 1991, grazing the open space between the district headquarters and the army camp on the Serere road, were owned by military personnel and a solitary Asian trader who had recently returned to the district.

REFERENCES

Avirgan, T. and M. Honey (1982). *War in Uganda: The Legacy of Idi Amin.* Westport, Ct.: Lawrence Hill.

Dirks, Nicholas (1992). Introduction. *In* Nicholas B. Dirks, ed. *Colonialism and Culture.* Ann Arbor: University of Michigan Press. pp. 1–25.

Ferguson, James (1990). *The Anti-Politics Machine: "Development", depoliticization and bureaucratic power in Lesotho.* Cambridge: University of Cambridge Press.

Fortes, Meyer and E. E. Evans-Pritchard (1940). *African Political Systems.* London: Oxford University Press.

Foucault, Michel (1980 [1977]). "The Eye of Power". Reprinted in C. Gordon (ed.) *Power/Knowledge: Selected Interviews and Other Writings 1972—1977.* New York: Pantheon.

Geertz, Clifford (1983). *Local Knowledge: Further Essays in Interpretive Anthropology.* New York: Basic Books.

Geertz, Clifford (ed.) (1963). *Old Societies and New States: The Quest for Modernity in Asia and Africa.* New York: The Free Press.

Guyer, Jane (1984). "Naturalism in Models of African Production," *Man,* n.s. 19: 371–88.

Hansen, H.B. (1977). *Ethnicity and Military Rule in Uganda: A Study of Ethnicity as a political factor in Uganda, based on a discussion of political anthropology and the application of its results.* Uppsala: Scandinavian Institute of African Studies (Research Report No. 43).

Kabwegyere, Tarsis (1987). *The Politics of State Formation: The Nature and Effects of Colonialism in Uganda.* Nairobi: East African Literature Bureau.

Kasfir, Nelson (1976). *The Shrinking Political Arena: Participation and Ethnicity in African Politics with a Case Study of Uganda.* Berkeley: University of California Press.

Kriger, Norma Forthcoming. "Values and the Interpretation of Guerrilla Violence: ZANLA Guerrillas Mobilization of Rural Civilians." In *Paths of Violence: Destruction and Deconstruction in African States.*

Lan, David (1985). *Guns and Rain: Guerrillas and Spirit Mediums in Zimbabwe.* London: James Currey.
Low, D. A. (1991). *Eclipse of Empire.* Cambridge: Cambridge University Press.
Mamdani, Mahmood (1976 *Politics and Class Formation in Uganda.* New York: Monthly Review Press.
——— (1983). *Imperialism and Fascism in Uganda.* London: Heinemann.
——— (1988). "Uganda in transition: two years of the NRA/NRM", *Third World Quarterly* 10 (3): 1155–1181.
Mudoola, Dan M. (1988). "Political transitions since Idi Amin: a study in political pathology." *In* Holger Bernt Hansen and Muchael Twaddle (eds,) *Uganda Now: Between Decay and Development.* London: James Currey. pp. 280–298.
——— (1991). "Institution-building: the case of the NRM and the military in Uganda 1986–9". *In* Holger Bernt Hansen and Michael Twaddle (eds.) *Changing Uganda: The Dilemmas of Structural Adjustment and revolutionary Change.* London: James Currey.
Muhanika, Henry R. (1981). *Utenzi wa Vita vya Kagera,* Dar es Salaam: University Press.
Mukherjee, Ramkrishna (1985 [1956]). *Uganda: An Historical Accident? Class, Nation, State Formation.* Foreword by Immanuel Wallerstein. With a new introduction by the Author. Trenton, New Jersey: Africa World Press.
Museveni, Yoweri (1985). *Selected Articles on the Uganda Resistance War.* Kampala: NRM Publication.
O'Brien, Jay and William Roseberry (1991). *Golden Ages, Dark Ages: Imagining the Past in Anthropology and History.* Berkeley: University of California Press.
O'Connor, Anthony (1988). "Uganda: the spatial dimension." *In* Holger Bernt Hansen and Michael Twaddle (eds.) *Uganda Now: Between Decay and Development.* London: James Currey. pp. 83–94.
Omara-Otunno, A. (1990). "African States and Domestic Conflict Resolution in Africa: An Historical Case of Uganda". Paper presented at the Thirty-Third Annual Meeting of the African Studies Association, Baltimore, Maryland, 1–4 November.
——— (1991). "The challenge of democratic pluralism in Uganda." *Issue: A Journal of Opinion* 20 (1): 41–49.
Pirouet, Louise (1991). "Human Rights Issues in Museveni's Uganda". *In* Holger Bernt Hansen and Michael Twaddle (eds.) *Changing Uganda: The Dilemmas of Structural Adjustment and Revolutionary Change.* London: James Currey.
Powesland, Philip G. (1957). *Economic Policy and Labour.* Kampala: East African Institute of Social Research.
Prakash, Gyan (1992). "Writing Post-Orientalist Histories of the Third World: Indian Historiography is Good to Think". *In* Nicholas Dirks (ed.) *Culture and Colonialism.* Ann Arbor: University of Michigan Press.
Ranger, Terence (1985). *Peasant Consciousness and Guerrilla War in Zimbabwe.* London: James Currey.

Roberts, A. D. (1962). "The Sub-Imperialism of the Baganda." *Journal of African History* 3 (3): 435–450.

Soja, Edward (1989). *Postmodern Geographies: The Reassertion of Space in Critical Social Theory.* London: Verso.

TDT [Teso Development Trust] (1992). *Teso Newsletter*, No. 2.

Twaddle, Michael (1993). *Kakungulu and the Creation of Uganda.* London: James Currey.

Tzu Sun (1988). *The Art of War.* Translated by Thomas Cleary. Boston and London: Shambhala Dragon Editions.

Uganda Government. Ministry of Planning and Development, Statistics Department.
—————— (1991). *Provisional Results of the (1991 Population and Housing census.*

Vincent, Joan (1971). *African Elite: The Big Men of a Small Town.* New York: Columbia University Press.

—————— (1979). "Teso." In *Uganda District Government and Politics.* W. Crawford Young (ed.) pp. 306–327. Madison, Wisconsin: African Studies Program.

—————— (1982). *Teso in Transformation: The Political Economy of Peasant and Class in Eastern Africa.* Berkeley: University of California Press.

—————— (1983a). "Equality and Enterprise: the cooperative movement in the development economy of Uganda." *Who Shares? Cooperatives and Rural Development.* D. W. Attwood and B. S. Baviskar (eds.), pp. 188–210.

—————— (1983b). "Sovereignty, legitimacy and power: prolegomena to the study of the colonial state in early modern Uganda." In *State Formation and Political Legitimacy.* Ronald Cohen and Judith Toland (eds.). New Brunswick: Transaction Publishers, pp. 137–154.

—————— (1990). *Anthropology and Politics: Visions, Traditions and Trends.* Tucson: University of Arizona Press.

—————— (1993a). "Trading Places: Recognizing and Recreating Legal Pluralism in Colonial Uganda", *Journal of Legal Pluralism*

—————— (1993b). "War in Uganda: Context and Texture." Paper prepared for the Symposium *Issues Surrounding Violence in Africa*, Institute of African Studies, Columbia University, April 1993.

—————— (1994). "On Law and Hegemonic Moments: Looking Behind Law in early modern Uganda." *Contested States: Law, Hegemony, and Resistance.* M. Lazarus-Black and Susan Hirsch (eds.) London: Routledge. Forthcoming: "Guerrilla Warfare in Northeast Uganda: Explorations in Textured Violence". In *Paths of Violence: Destruction and Deconstruction in African States.*

Zawawi Sharifa M. Forthcoming. "The Voice of Battles and Suffering: Swahili Utenzi Poetry, 17th–20th Centuries." In *Paths of Violence: Destruction and Deconstruction in African States*, edited by George C. Bond and Joan Vincent.

Chapter FIVE

Warfare in the Lower Omo Valley, Southwestern Ethiopia: Reconciling Materialist and Political Explanations

David Turton

Turton analyzes a post-colonial eruption of "traditional" warfare among the Mursi in Ethiopia. This outbreak in certain ways resembled that described by Rosman and Rubel, because in both instances an isolated "primitive" folk suddenly started massacring itself. Rosman and Rubel accounted for this fighting in terms of nineteenth century, capitalist growth. Turton's article equally implicates capitalist developments, but in his case these developments are those involving capitalist states' policies to defeat their opponents politically. Capitalist states throughout most of the twentieth century were opposed by communist states. This confrontation after World War II was called the Cold War. During it, throughout the world, capitalists armed their allies while communists did the same with theirs, so that even the Mursi — in the far southwest of Ethiopia — acquired automatic weapons with which to intensify enormously their "traditional" violences. Cold war provoked hot war.

To consider the anthropological literature on warfare is to be confronted with a paradox. Here are scholarly comparative surveys, meticulous descriptions, and ingenious arguments leading to conclusions that are amongst the most obvious (such as that most wars result in one group gaining access to resources claimed by another) and even banal (such as that wars occur in the absence of institutions capable of preventing them) to be found in the whole anthropological corpus. Such conclusions are unsatisfactory as explanations of warfare (rather than of particular wars) because they confirm our taken for granted cultural assumption that violence in the pursuit of individual self interest is a fact of human nature which it is the purpose of social institutions to keep in check. They confirm, in other words, what we knew, or thought we knew, already, rather than give us the shock of surprise that is the source of any new understanding.

My aim in this chapter is to reach, or at least point toward, such a new understanding of warfare by considering the case of the Mursi, a small group of agro-pastoralists living in the Lower Omo valley of southwestern Ethiopia. I shall attempt to bring together, in a single explanation, two 'theories' that have come to represent entrenched positions in an extended anthropological slogging match about the 'causes' of 'traditional' or 'primitive' warfare: the materialist and the political. My contention will be not simply that both types of explanation apply to warfare between the Mursi and their neighbors, but also that the validity of each depends upon it's being seen as the complement of the other. They are, or should be considered, two sides of the same coin.

I shall first show how measures taken to ensure the physical survival of people and cattle in the face of external attack help to make the Mursi economy more vulnerable to climatic uncertainty. I shall then ask why, given the obviously negative consequences of warfare for both individuals and groups, it is such a pervasive feature of relations between the Mursi and their neighbors. Taking a materialist tack first, I shall examine, in the second part of the chapter, the part played by warfare in Mursi territorial expansion against their northern neighbors, the Bodi (Figure 5.1). It will emerge that while this expansion has certainly been caused by land shortage amongst the Mursi and while warfare has certainly been an integral part of it, the Mursi fought their last two wars with the Bodi to ratify, by ritual means, their *de facto* occupation of territory that they had taken over, peacefully, long before.

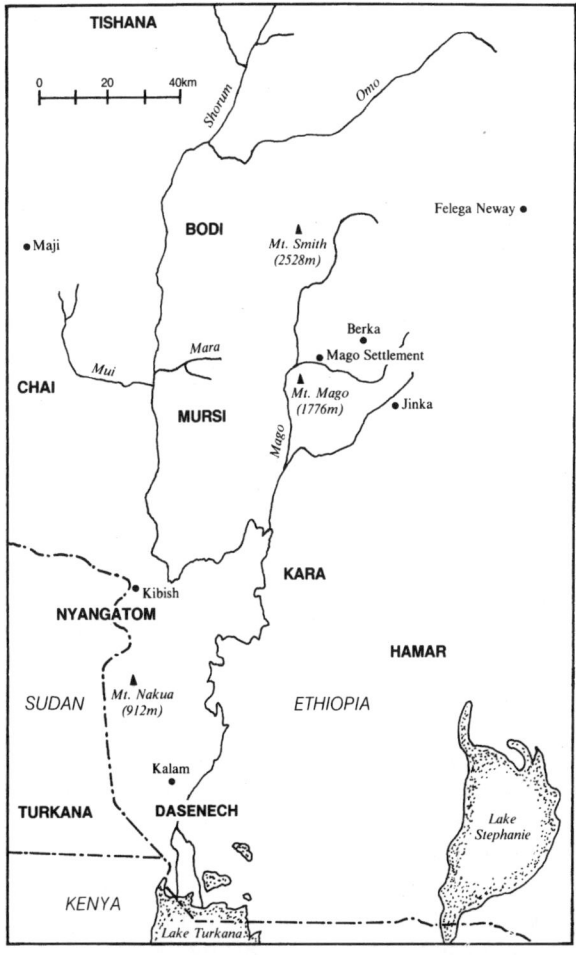

Figure 5.1. The Mursi and their neighbors.

In the third and final part of the chapter, I shall focus on the relation between warfare and political identity. The argument will be that warfare is not so much a means by which an already constituted political group seeks to extend and/or defend its territory as a means by which the very notion of its separate political identity is created *in the first place* (Harrison 1993; Turton 1978 and 1993): warfare becomes, in this light, a cause rather than a consequence of political identity. This point could be illustrated well enough by the recent history of Mursi-Bodi warfare. I shall concentrate instead on a new and devastating expansion in the scale of local warfare in the Lower Omo Valley brought about by the introduction, in the mid-1980s, of automatic weapons and by their increasingly easy availability. One group, the Nyangatom, who are southern neighbors of the Mursi, have been particularly well placed to acquire these weapons (from their friends and allies in Sudan, the Toposa) and have become, since the late 1980s, the most powerful military force in the area.

WARFARE AND VULNERABILITY

The cultural values and ethnic identity of the Mursi are firmly centered around cattle and herding, but with only about three head of cattle per head of human population, they depend for well over half of their subsistence needs on the cultivation of sorghum. Two harvests are obtained, or at least attempted, each year, one by flood retreat cultivation along the banks of the Omo (January–December) and the other by shifting cultivation in cleared woodland along the Omo's westward-flowing tributaries (June–July). Flood retreat cultivation is relatively reliable, since it depends on the heavy "summer" rains which fall over the highland catchment area of the Omo, but the cultivable area is small, being limited to land actually inundated by the flood. Shifting cultivation is highly unreliable, because of the low and erratic local rainfall.

Although cattle provide directly no more than 30 per cent of daily subsistence, they are a vital means of insurance against crop failure, when they can be exchanged for grain with the neighboring groups or in highland markets. Because the riverain forest and bushbelt of the Omo are infested with tsetse flies, cattle have to be confined, for most of the year, to the wooded grassland that rises eastward to the Omo-Mago watershed (Figure 5.2). During the dry season (October–February) they are to be found furthest to the east, the herders (mainly men and boys) then living in rough and temporary camps in the Elma

Valley and subsisting on milk, blood, and meat. The remainder of the population, meanwhile, is at the Omo, where flood retreat cultivation is in progress. With the onset of the main rains (March–April) the cattle are moved westward to more permanent settlements no more than an hour's walk from the wet season cultivation areas. The population as a whole can then benefit from the increased milk supply that is brought on by the rains, and the herders can enjoy a mixed diet of milk and sorghum porridge.

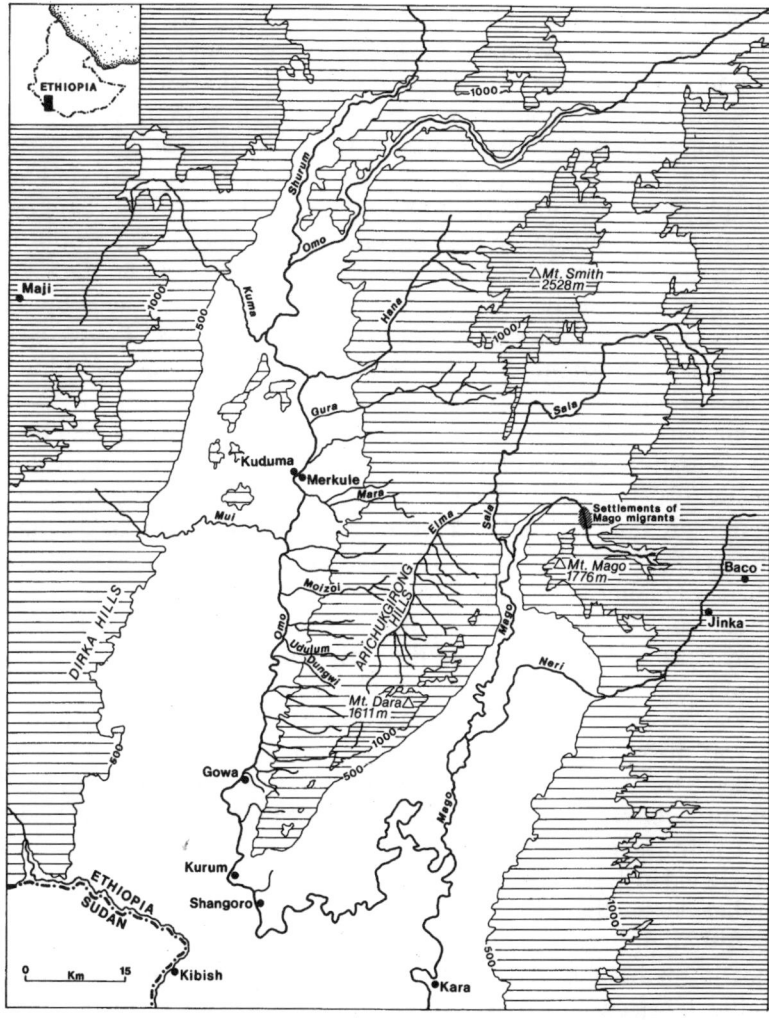

Figure 5.2. Mursiland: drainage and physical features.

The Mursi have fundamentally hostile relations with all their herding neighbors save the Chai (or Surma), who live west of the Omo and south of Maji and with whom they intermarry and share a common language. Enemy groups may be divided into two categories: those with whom the Mursi have no peaceful contacts at all and those with whom they are periodically at war but with whom they otherwise have relations of peaceful cooperation and economic exchange. The Hammar, Banna, and Bashada (Lydall 1976), to whom the Mursi refer (as I shall) by the collective term 'Hamari,' belong to the first category, and the Bodi and Nyangatom to the second. There is a paradox here, since warfare with those who are out-and-out enemies (i.e., the Hamari) is less disruptive of economic life, less destructive of human life, and less threatening to group survival than with those who are, for long periods, friends and allies. Attacks by the Hamari normally take the form of cattle raids. They are expected every year and are simply one more source of uncertainty in a highly uncertain environment that must be taken into account by individuals and groups in their subsistence calculations. Conflict with the Bodi, on the other hand, and especially in recent years, the Nyangatom, is seen by the Mursi as conflict over the occupation of territory and therefore as potentially threatening to their continued existence as an autonomous group.

Hamari raids occur in the dry season, when the Mursi take their cattle eastward to the Elma Valley and the Mago is low enough to be easily fordable. Because of the shortage of water and grazing, cattle camps are dotted widely across the countryside, which makes them an inviting target for small parties of raiders who hope to be well on their way home before the alarm has been raised and a pursuit party mobilized. A raid on one camp that took place on December 25, 1969, may be considered typical. In the early hours of the morning, a rifle shot was heard by the people living nearby, but it was assumed that the stock of this camp were being worried by hyenas. Later in the day it was discovered that the camp has been raided and three people killed—the herd owner, who had been shot, and his two sons, aged about seven and thirteen, who were lying where they had been sleeping with their throats cut. All the cattle had been taken, and their tracks led in the direction of the Mago Valley. The tracks of the raiders indicated that there were no more than four of them.

Although disastrous for individuals and families, such raids do not in themselves necessarily reduce per capita stockwealth, since cattle losses sustained in raids can, in the long run, be made up by counter raids. Other things being equal, the give and take of mutual raiding on this scale should, over time, leave neither group with net gains. Paradoxically, it is not actual raids but measures taken to cope with threatened raids that have a long term negative impact on the community's stockwealth. These are, principally, the withdrawal of cattle from the best, tsetse-free grazing areas and their concentration into large communal settlements near or within the tsetse-infested Omo bushbelt.

The advantage of concentration is that it makes more men and weapons available for the protection of the herds. It is clearly a more difficult task for a small group of raiders to approach undetected and steal cattle from a well populated and securely built settlement than from an isolated cattle camp occupied, perhaps, by three or four men and boys. Even if they succeed in getting away with cattle, the alarm can be given with such speed that they are unlikely to get far before they are overtaken by a superior force of pursuers. The disadvantage of concentration is that it makes demands on grazing and, especially, water that cannot be easily met in the eastern pastures at the height of the dry season, when the threat from raiders is greatest. A regular strategy at this time, therefore, is to take all the cattle to the Omo, the only permanent and plentiful source of water in the country, but where the risk from tsetse flies is particularly high and the limited grazing is quickly exhausted. In some years it is considered necessary for the concentration of people and stock to continue into the wet season, large settlements then being built along the eastern margins of the Omo bushbelt where, once again, the cattle are in constant danger from tsetse flies.

The threat of external attack also helps to reduce the productivity of Mursi agriculture. In some years the 'small rains' in October–November would be sufficient to allow flood retreat cultivation along streams and rivers in the dry season pastures. But planting is normally not attempted, because of the expectation that the plots would have to be abandoned in the face of raids before they could be harvested in December–January. When raiders are active in the wet season, furthermore, people do not feel safe sleeping in their rainfed cultivation areas, preferring the security of the nearby cattle settlements. This increases the likelihood that crops will be trampled by buffaloes and other game animals and eaten by baboons. It is clear, then, that measures taken to increase the physical security of people and cattle in the face of regular and expected external attack reduce the effectiveness of both pastoral and agricultural production and increase the long term vulnerability of the economy to climatic uncertainty.

Since the beginning of this century, the Mursi have become, for reasons to be outlined later, increasingly dependent on their least reliable means of subsistence, shifting cultivation. The consequent need to find new areas of untouched woodland that could be cleared for cultivation led them to push northward into an unoccupied buffer zone separating them from their northern neighbors, the Bodi. By the late 1930s they had reached their present northern boundary, the River Mara, and were 'face to face' with the Bodi. Thirty years later, with crop yields falling rapidly and further expansion northward blocked by the Bodi, the stage was being set for a disaster of classic proportions, involving drought, famine, war, and migration. Between 1971 and 1973, immediately after my first period of fieldwork amongst them (1968–70), the Mursi experienced a famine of such severity that, for the first time in living memory, people were acknowledged to have died of starvation (Turton 1977). Its precipitating cause was a failure of the main rains for three years in succession, but it was greatly exacerbated by an intensification of armed conflict that affected all the herding peoples of the Lower Omo during these years (Fukui and Turton 1978), disrupting both subsistence activities and economic exchange. For the Mursi, the most serious conflict was with the Bodi.

Relations between the two groups had been consistently peaceful since the conclusion of an earlier war in the early 1950s. The first signs of trouble came in January 1970, after Mursi cattle had been taken well into Bodi territory to protect them from Hamari raiders. Although this was a strategy that the Mursi had adopted before with the cooperation of the Bodi (most recently in 1966), on this occasion their presence was not welcomed and relations between the two groups began to deteriorate. By May the Mursi were taking cattle up to the highlands to exchange for ammunition in preparation for an all out war with the Bodi that was expected to begin in a month or two's time, when both sides would have taken in their wet season harvests. The first fatality came in June, when a Mursi youth was shot dead north of the River Mara, where he and his father were living and cultivating with Bodi friends.

A 'no-man's land,' 20–30 miles deep, now opened up between the two sides, across which raiding parties of two or three individuals went regularly to and fro, a favorite tactic being to lie in wait for potential victims beside a path or near a watering point. For their part, the Mursi behaved as though the bush and long grass were alive with the Bodi and avoided using well worn paths as much as possible. Those who wore ivory bracelets took the precaution of smearing them with cattle dung so that they would be less visible when traveling, as people preferred to do, at night. The cattle were kept for long periods at the Omo and in the far south of the country, although people continued to cultivate along the Mara and at Kudama, the northernmost Mursi flood cultivation site on the Omo, throughout the war. The biggest single engagement was in late 1971, when a large Bodi force attacked a Mursi settlement at the Omo where several hundred cattle had been concentrated. The attackers, who were better supplied with ammunition than the defenders, succeeded in taking a large number of cattle. They suffered many casualties, however, as they drove them back towards the Mara, under harassment from the Mursi, the narrow path they followed through the bushbelt becoming so littered with corpses that it has since been known as the 'rotten' path.

Not only were the pastoral and (to a lesser extent) agricultural activities of the Mursi disrupted by the war but, equally important at a time of famine, so also was their access to external sources of food. In 1974 the Mursi told me that it had been people who were able to exchange cattle for grain in highland markets who had survived the famine best. Those without cattle took less valuable trade goods, such as buffalo hides and honey, while some were forced to part with rifles, agricultural implements, and personal ornaments. Getting these goods to the nearest market centers, Jinka and Berka, was a dangerous undertaking. The path to Jinka took them across the Mago Valley, where they ran the risk of being attacked and robbed by Hamari, while that to Berka accounted for the largest number of Mursi deaths at the hands of Bodi between 1971 and 1975.

There was no systematic distribution of relief food to the Mursi or, as far as I know, to their immediate neighbors during the 1971–73 famine. Some relief food was obtained by Mursi on an ad hoc basis in Jinka, the *awraja* (district) capital, and some was distributed to Bodi at Hana, the 'Mursi-Bodi' *wareda* (sub-district) capital, which is in Bodi territory, about forty miles north of Mara. At the end of 1973, soon after beginning a second period of fieldwork, I arranged through Oxfam, Christian Aid, and the British Embassy in Addis Ababa for two plane loads of grain to be flown to Hana for the Mursi. The first of these consignments was successfully collected by a party of Mursi, but during the distribution of the second, a month later, a Mursi man was shot dead near the government post, whereupon all the Mursi returned home, leaving the bulk of the grain at Hana.

In the late eighties a new threat loomed for the Mursi, the origins of which lay in national, international, and even superpower politics: the acquisition by their southwestern neighbors, the Nyangatom (often known, in Ethiopia, as Bume and, in Kenya, as Dongiro), of automatic rifles. In February 1987, a large force of Nyangatom, armed with both automatic rifles and with the Mannlicher long rifles and carbines that have been common amongst all the peoples of the Lower Omo since the Second World War, made a surprise attack on the Mursi at the Omo, south of the Dara range. The slaughter was indiscriminate, most of the casualties being women and children. This was, firstly, because a good proportion of the men were with the cattle north of the Dara range, and secondly, because it was easier for men and boys, unencumbered by infants, to scatter and hide in the bush. The majority of the people were killed with spears and knives, having been wounded in the rifle fire. One particularly respected elder, who was well known to the Nyangatom, was deliberately sought out and speared to death. The hands of women and girls were chopped off with bush knives so that their bracelets could be more easily removed. In order to get some idea of the number of people killed, I was told to imagine a packed market square in the nearby administrative town, Jinka. Two families alone lost 64 people between them, and the total number of Mursi deaths mave have reached 500.

Immediately after the attack, the Mursi evacuated the entire southern part of their territory, abandoning in the process their recently harvested sorghum crop. Meanwhile, a whole section of Nyangatom now felt strong enough to move northward and occupy land to the west of the Omo, which had been a contested area between the two groups for many years. When I visited the Mursi in December 1987, I found them fearing for their future as a distinct group. A further onslaught by the Nyangatom, they predicted, would cause them to abandon their territory altogether and seek refuge, as individuals and families, amongst neighboring highland cultivators. Their clan names would survive such a dispersal, but the Mursi would have disappeared. Five years later, however, in 1992, there had been no further Nyangatom attack, and the Mursi had started to acquire automatic weapons of their own (from the Chai). They still felt highly exposed, however, to potential attack from the considerably better armed Nyangatom and had still not permanently re-occupied their southern territory.

WARFARE AND EXPANSION

It is clear that the costs of war are counted, for the Mursi, not only in death and injury for individuals but also in increased economic vulnerability for the community as a whole. And yet, this is a society that is organized for war and in which warlike qualities are inculcated in men from an early age. The military organization of the Mursi is based upon a system of male age sets. Men usually marry in their late twenties or early thirties, while girls are expected to marry in their late teens. This allows older men to practise polygyny and creates a class of physically mature but unmarried men who, since they are without domestic and agricultural responsibilities, are the main source of military manpower. Why, given the obvious negative consequences of warfare for the Mursi, is it such a pervasive feature of their social organization and external relations? This question can be approached from both an ecological and political point of view, corresponding to the two principal, very broad and not mutually exclusive explanations of "indigenous" or "tribal" warfare that have been advanced by anthropologists: that it is a means of adjusting the human population to available resources and that it is a means of maintaining rule-governed relations between autonomous political units in the absence of an overarching authority.

That the Mursi-Bodi war of the early 1970s was related to competition for scare resources seems obvious from the fact that the friction that immediately preceded it arose out of the temporary use by Mursi, under pressure from Hamari raids, of Bodi grazing areas. As I have already explained, however, a permanent northward movement of Mursi had been going on for many years before this as, in their search for new areas of uncleared woodland, they had gradually taken over the buffer zone separating them from the Bodi. The question to be asked, then, is how, regardless of the events that immediately preceded it, was the war related to this long term acquisition of new territory by the Mursi?

It is recounted in Mursi oral history that they entered their present territory from the west, having displaced by force of arms its former occupants, the Bodi, who retreated north of the River Mara (Turton 1987). It is impossible to say when this occupation took place, but it was probably fairly recent — at least 100 but not more than 200 years ago. The Mursi first took over the southern part of the area that had been vacated by the Bodi, and they were still concentrated in the south in 1896, when the Italian explorer Vittorio Bottego was mapping the course of the Lower Omo (Vannutelli and Citerni 1899). The buffer zone between the two groups was eventually eliminated only in the mid-1930s, when the Mursi first began cultivating along the River Mara. This progressive occupation by the Mursi of land that had been occupied many years earlier by the Bodi continued in 1979 when they made a sideways move to the Mago Valley. For this had also been occupied, about 70 years before, by the Bodi.

While it is impossible to reconstruct the circumstances that led to the first permanent crossing by Mursi to the east bank of Omo, it is possible to gain a fairly clear picture of the factors that led to their expansion northward during this century. These can be traced to ecological and political changes that made them increasingly dependent on shifting cultivation: a drastic lowering in the level of Lake Turkana, which fell by 20m. between 1896 and the mid-1950s (Butzer 1971), and the incorporation, also dating from the late 1890s, of the Lower Omo Valley into the Ethiopian state.

The fall in the level of Lake Turkana, which, according to Butzer, was almost entirely due to reduced rainfall over the Omo Basin, led to a progressive diminution of land available for flood retreat cultivation and, because of the consequent reduction in ground water level, to the growth of woody vegetation on land adjacent to the river and along its tributary streams. The lower courses of these tributaries pass today through a dense belt of bushland thicket, 10 to 15 km in width, but older Mursi can remember when this was open grassland used for cattle herding. The Mursi themselves probably also had a hand in bringing about the change, both by cutting down the forest for shifting cultivation and by subjecting the banks of the Omo to heavy dry season grazing. This would have reduced the effectiveness of periodic burning and made it easier for woody plants to establish themselves. The advance of bushland thicket east of the Omo allowed tsetse, already present no doubt in the Omo forest, to penetrate the eastern grassland, a process that is reported by people in their 50s and 60s to have begun in their lifetimes. Thus, not only have flood retreat harvests been deteriorating throughout this century, but herd growth rates have been held back by the steadily increasing tsetse challenge. Demands for tribute and taxes by local administrators of the Emperor Menelik (whose forces occupied the Lower Omo at the turn of the century) and of his successor, Haile Selassie, were also an effective constraint on herd growth (Turton 1987).

In their movement northward during this century, then, the Mursi have been taking over land that had been evacuated many years before by the Bodi. To understand the part played by warfare in this expansion, we have to see it not simply as a means of expelling Bodi from territory later occupied by Mursi, but also as a means of legally and retrospectively ratifying, in the eyes of both groups, an existing occupation. We have to focus, that is, not so much on armed conflict as on its ritual resolution.

Since making peace with the Bodi in 1975, the Mursi have not extended their northern boundary beyond the Mara. On the contrary, those Mursi who had been cultivating before the war with Bodi friends and associates north of the Mara did not resume these links afterwards. What did change as a result of the war was the legal status of the boundary. When the war came to an end, each side 'hosted,' in turn, a peacemaking ritual that was attended by the other side's representatives. The Mursi held theirs on the River Mara and the Bodi held theirs on the Gura, thirty miles further north. These were, in effect, boundary marking rituals, the important point to note being that at the end of the previous Mursi-Bodi war (1952) the Mursi had held their part of the ritual on the River Moizoi, twenty miles south of the Mara, which they had nevertheless been using for cultivation since the 1930s. From the Mursi point of view, the war of the early 1970s was fought to acquire new territory only in a *de jure* sense: to establish their legal right to the Mara, of which they had been in *de facto* occupation for about 40 years.

Another way in which Mursi-Bodi territorial relations were changed by the war was that it gave rise to a new buffer zone, about ten miles deep, north of the Mara, across which the two sides subsequently maintained a respectful distance. From the point of view of the conservation of renewable resources, the creation of this unoccupied zone can therefore be regarded as ecologically adaptive, whichever group occupies it in the future and even though it must have resulted in some loss of resources for both Mursi and Bodi individuals.

The adjustment of population to resources may be achieved, of course, not only by increasing the latter but also by decreasing the former. How might warfare play a part here? An obvious answer is that people are killed in war, but it is a short step from here to the absurd conclusion that the more destructive war is of human life, the greater its adaptive 'efficiency.' The American anthropologist, Marvin Harris, has suggested that it is not "combat *per se*" but the need to produce "combat ready males" that makes warfare among people such as the Mursi an effective means of controlling population growth (1984, pp. 77–8). This is because it exerts a negative influence on the "nuturance of females." Harris is thinking principally of female infanticide, which I have no reason to believe is actually practised by the Mursi. Nor do I have evidence that Mursi mothers are relatively more neglectful of their female children. What is clear, however, is that unmarried adult males, because of their predominantly pastoral lifestyle, are generally the best fed section of the population and the one that is likely to suffer least during times of food shortage. Such men live for most of the year with their local age mates in cattle camps in the eastern grasslands and are the main source of military manpower. If Harris is right that the need to produce and maintain a warrior class does have a negative impact on the survival of females, this could be one of the factors that might help explain the commonly stated finding that mobile herding groups in East Africa have lower population growth rates than sedentary agriculturalists.

WARFARE AND POLITICAL IDENTITY

The contribution of warfare to the survival of a group may also be considered in a political sense. Here, 'survival' means the continuation of the group as a distinct, autonomous, politico-territorial unit, in a system of similar units, and 'warfare' is a reciprocal activity by means of which groups assert their independence of each other and enter into orderly (rule-governed) relations. Viewed this way, then, warfare is not a breaking down in 'normal' political relations, but their very underpinning. This is well illustrated by the part played by warfare and its ritual resolution in defining the changing territorial relationship between the Mursi and the Bodi over the past 100 years. It is clear that, as distinct political units, they are as much products of their periodically hostile relations with each other as they are of their relations with the physical environment. It is even more revealing to consider the repercussions of the Nyangatom attack of February 1987.

This attack upset the normal pattern of Mursi-Nyangatom warfare, not only because of the enormous number of Mursi casualities and because so many of them were women and children, but also because it proclaimed a drastic technological imbalance between the two groups. Although the Nyangatom may have had access to automatic weapons for some time, they had not previously used them against the Mursi. From the point of view of the Nyangatom, the attack was justified by a particularly provocative incident that had occurred a few weeks earlier. Eight Nyangatom, who were guests at a Mursi village on the Omo, had been shot and then hacked to death with bush knives. This in turn was justified by the Mursi by reference to a yet earlier incident in which a defenseless Mursi boy had been shot dead by a Nyangatom after crossing to the west bank of the Omo to collect relief food from a group of missionaries (Alvarsson 1989).

Despite the extremity of their situation, the Mursi I spoke to in December 1987 showed no interest in making peace, even though the

Nyangatom were reportedly ready to do so. My question, "Why do you not make peace?" was met with another: "Who are the Nyangatom to make peace with?" By virtually destroying the southernmost Mursi territorial section, they had destroyed the very group with whom it would have been appropriate for them to hold a peacemaking ritual. A peace that was made now would not provide the Mursi with a guarantee against further attack by the Nyangatom, who would be secretly laughing at them as 'women,' even as they made peace. Such a peace would merely be a temporary convenience for the Nyangatom, enabling them to take in their flood harvest without fear of Mursi snipers. (Less than a month before my visit, two Mursi had crossed the Omo at night and the next morning killed two Nyangatom men who were working on a new dugout canoe.)

There was no doubt that the Mursi wanted an end to hostilities, but it seemed that the only way this could be achieved was by re-establishing the state of balanced opposition that had characterized their relations with the Nyangatom before the February attack. This meant that the Mursi would have to make a comparable attack on the Nyangatom — namely, one involving several hundred men, armed with at least some automatic weapons. One man said that the Mursi would feel able to make such an attack even if they had as few as ten automatics. When I objected that this would surely be suicidal, since the Nyangatom would in due course respond with much greater fire power, he said that a 'return match' (he used the analogy of home and away duelling contests between different Mursi territorial sections) would be seen by both sides as re-establishing the previous balance between them, this being a necessary and sufficient condition of a successful peace. It would not even matter if more Mursi than Nyangatom were killed in the course of the 'return match:' the surviving Mursi would still be able to make a secure peace, thus ensuring their survival also in a political sense. The Nyangatom would understand and respect the 'rules of the game.'

This was not, then, a simple matter of the Mursi needing to 'take revenge' on the Nyangatom, although the individual men I spoke to certainly explained their determination to take part in a counter-attack by referring to relatives of theirs who had been killed in the February massacres. What was at issue, it seemed, was a symbolic, not an actual equivalence, whether of war, casualities, or weapons. As with the peace-making/boundary-marking rituals referred to earlier, we are dealing here with a system of meanings that is shared by both groups. This suggests an analogy with systems of ceremonial gift exchange, which in other parts of the world (notably Melanesia) also provide for rule-governed competition between autonomous political groups. A group that cannot maintain, over the long term, a balance of gift and counter gift with rival groups loses its political autonomy. A group that gains access to items of wealth external to the local subsistence economy — such as cash and motor vehicles — is thereby in a position to 'defeat' any of its rivals who do not have such access. If warfare between the Mursi and their neighbours is seen as a system of inter group 'reciprocity,' we might say that the use by the Nyangatom of automatic weapons had introduced an element of inflation into the system that threatened both literally and symbolically the annihilation of the Mursi.

Another way of putting this would be that warfare itself, and not just the public ritual by which it is concluded, is a common ritual language through which groups make themselves significant to each other and to themselves as independent political entities; it is not *primarily* a means by which an already constituted group seeks to extend or defend its territory, since it is warfare that constitutes the group — or rather the idea of the group — as a separate entity in the first place. The analogy between warfare and dueling, which is clearly relevant for the Mursi themselves, confirms this view of warfare as an essentially ritual activity, the function of which is to create separate political identities.

The dueling weapon is a pole about two meters long and weighing about one kilogram. Bouts take place between individuals and are fast, furious, and short, being brought to an end by the intervention of a referee after about 30 seconds. Such events are sometimes called 'stick fights' in the ethnographic literature, but, at least in the Mursi case, this would give a misleading impression. I use the term 'dueling' or (in past publications) 'ceremonial dueling' to reflect the fact that we are dealing here with a martial art — a highly ritualized and rule-governed activity — rather than with an undisciplined free-for-all.

Contests are held two or three times a year between men of different territorial divisions, or *buranyoga* (sing. *buran*), a term that refers to any order of a territorially defined group, from the whole Mursi population (and including, therefore, neighboring populations such as the Bodi and Nyangatom) down to the members of a single settlement. Contestants, who are always unmarried men, are ritually as well as territorially defined in the sense that they always come from one or the other of two age grades and always duel with members of their own grade. The highest order territorial division of the population, below that of the Mursi as a whole, is into three *buranyoga*, which are named, from south to north, Gongulobibi, Ariholi, and Dola. Although these divisions consist of people who regularly utilize the same cultivation and grazing areas, they are cross-cut by ties of affinity and economic cooperation and exchange that ramify throughout the whole population. Since dueling is the only context in which the lines between one *buran* and another are regularly and visibly drawn, one might say that dueling actually *creates* separate political identities (those of individual *buranyoga*) against a background of close-knit and widely ramifying social ties that work against the drawing of clear-cut and exclusive divisions in everyday life.

If the political subdivisions of the Mursi population are the product of ritualized male violence, it seems reasonable to suggest that Mursi political identity itself will be similarly constructed — that is, through the ritualized male violence that we normally call warfare. Simon Harrison, writing about Avatip in Papua New Guinea, has made an impressive case for viewing warfare in this light:

> War, and the ritual ethic of war, were means used purposefully by men to construct a political identity for their community in the first place, not *just* [emphasis added] as a physical population secure from extermination, but more basically as a conceptual entity free from the normative claims of outsider...They fought and fostered war in their cult, not because they lacked normative ties beyond the village but, quite the opposite, *precisely because they had such ties* and could only define themselves as a polity by acting collectively to overcome and transcend them (1993, p. 000).

These remarks obviously fit well the case of dueling between members of the internal political divisions of the Mursi *buran*. What grounds are there for applying them also to the external relations of the Mursi — that is, to their relations with other *buranyoga*, and particularly with their principal enemies of recent years, the Bodi and Nyangatom?

Firstly, these relations certainly do not exclude 'normative ties,' as the incident that sparked the Nyangatom attack of February 1987 illustrates. The Nyangatom guests who were hacked to death in a Mursi settlement had come to obtain grain, a frequent item of exchange between the Mursi and Nyangatom in times of hunger. Earthenware cooking and water pots, made by Mursi women, are also in demand among the Nyangatom, from whom the Mursi traditionally obtain goats. Relations between Mursi and Bodi are, if anything, closer. During my first period of fieldwork, just before the last Mursi-Bodi war of the early 1970s, several Mursi were cultivating on a regular basis with Bodi friends north of the River Mara.

Secondly, like duelling, warfare is a specifically male activity that men engage in as part of a ritually defined category of the population — an age set. If age set ritual is the equivalent, in this context, of the men's cult at Avatip — the institutional focus of Mursi political identity — this would help to explain the timing and the significance of the most recent Mursi age set formation ceremony, or *nitha*, held at Kurum in southern Mursiland in January 1991 (Woodhead 1991a and 1991b). Kurum is the historical center, or 'stomach' of Mursiland, it being the place that was first occupied by the ancestors of the present Mursi when they crossed the Omo from the west bank about 200 years ago. It had been evacuated following the 1987 massacre and, in 1991, was still only being utilized during the dry season for flood retreat cultivation.

The 1991 *nitha* was considered long overdue, the last one having been held in 1961. When on previous visits I had asked about this delay, I had been told that social and environmental conditions had simply not been good enough to allow the organization of such an important event. And yet these conditions could hardly have been less propitious in January 1991. Not only were the Mursi, who were still without automatic weapons of their own, in constant fear of further Nyangatom attacks, but food was in short supply because of poor rain and flood harvests in both 1990 and 1991, and only five months earlier, about 200 people had died in a meningitis epidemic that particularly affected the southern Mursi. There are grounds for arguing, however, that the *nitha* was held when and where it was *because*, rather than despite these difficult and threatening circumstances.

In the first place, it can be seen as a symbolic assertion by the Mursi of their historical right to the territory they had been forced to evacuate four years earlier. The main events of the *nitha* take place around a specially constructed enclosure of branches with a tree at its center and two openings opposite each other. The enclosure at Kurum was built around a young and highly unimpressive looking tree about six feet tall. The choice, however, was deliberate: the tree had a long life ahead of it and would therefore 'grow-up' with the members of the new age set who were thus identified, not only with the tree but also with the place where it was rooted. In the future, the fact that the *nitha* had been held at Kurum, a fact concretely symbolized by the tree, could be used to validate Mursi claims to this territory, which was still considered too insecure for permanent occupation.

In the second place, the 1991 *nitha* can be seen as an essential step in preparing the way for a Mursi response to the 1987 massacre and therefore to re-establishing peaceful and yet politically equal relations between the Mursi and the Nyangatom. The point here is that the men whose responsibility it would be to make this response — those between the ages of approximately 20 and 45 — had not yet become jural adults (*zuo*) and members of an age set because of the period that had elapsed since the last *nitha*. They were, of course, perfectly capable, in a physical and organizational sense, of responding to the Nyangatom attack. What the *nitha* did was transform them ritually into a category of men whose 'official' role it was to engage in warfare. It also ensured that those who would die in the process — of whom there would obviously be very many, given the new technology of automatic weapons — would 'die as adults.' Indeed it is quite likely that one of the pressures that was brought to bear on the older men, to persuade them to hold the *nitha*, was the unwillingness of the younger men to risk dying as 'boys' in a 'return match' with the Nyangatom. To say that warfare is an activity of a ritually defined category of the population is to say more, therefore, than that a ritual 'stamp' must be given to what is already the case. It is the ritual definition which *makes* the case: until formed into an age set, these men were not *able* to make the required military response, not in the sense that they would not otherwise have had the necessary stamina or training, but in the sense that their action would not otherwise have carried the necessary message, whether to themselves or to the Nyangatom.

CONCLUSION

It is clear that the direction and rate of Mursi expansion against the Bodi have been determined by ecological change and that warfare has played a key role in making that expansion possible. On the other hand, it is also clear that the role of warfare has been as much ritual as military: the Mursi do not fight the Bodi to acquire new territory except in a *de jure* sense. Fighting appears to be a necessary preliminary to the real, ritual business of periodically defining and communicating to themselves and their neighbors their common territorial boundary. Thus the materialist 'explanation' that warfare is a means of adjusting population to scarce resources is not complete without the political 'explanation' that warfare is a means of establishing and maintaining the separate political identities of neighboring groups. *Wars* may be fought, in the Lower Omo Valley as elsewhere, for material ends, but *warfare* exists to create the entities that pursue those ends: it is a cause rather than a consequence of political identity.[1]

NOTES

1. An earlier version of this chapter, with the title "Warfare, Vulnerability and Survival: A Case from Southwestern Ethiopia" appeared in *Cambridge Anthropology* 13:2, 1988–9, pp. 67–85 and in *Disasters* 15:3, 1991, pp. 254–64.

REFERENCES

Alvarsson, J. (1989). *Starvation and Peace or Food and War? Aspects of Armed Conflict in the Lower Omo Valley.* Uppsala: Uppsala Research Reports in Cultural Anthropology.

Butzer, K. (1971). *Recent History of an Ethiopian Delta: The Omo River and the Level of Lake Turkana.* Chicago: University of Chicago Press.

Fukui, K. and D. Turton (1978). *Warfare among East African Herders.* Senri Ethnological Studies, 3, Osaka: National Museum of Ethnology.

Harris, M. (1984). "A Cultural Materialist Theory of Band and Village Warfare: The Yanomamo Test." In B. Ferguson (ed) *Warfare, Culture and Environment.* New York: Academic Press.

Harrison, S. (1993). *The Mask of War: Violence, Ritual and the Self in Melanesia.* Manchester: Manchester University Press.

Lydall, J. (1977). "Hamer." In M. L. Bender (ed) *The Non-Semitic Languages of Ethiopia.* East Lansing: Michigan State University.

Turton, D. (1977). "Response to Drought: The Mursi of South West Ethiopia." In J. P. Garlick and R. W. J. Kay (eds) *Human Ecology in the Tropics.* London: Taylor and Francis.

———— (1978). "War, Peace and Mursi Identity." In K. Fukui and D. Turton (eds) *Warfare Among East African Herders.* Senri Ethnological Studies, 3, Osaka: National Museum of Ethnology, pp. 179–210.

———— (1987). "Looking for a Cool Place: The Mursi, 1890s to 1980s." In D. Johnson and D. Anderson (eds) *The Ecology of Survival: Case Studies from Northeast African History.* London/Boulder: Lester Crook Academic Publishing/Westview Press.

———— (1993). "We Must Teach them to be Peaceful: Mursi Views on Being Human and Being Mursi." *Nomadic Peoples,* 31, pp. 19–33.

Turton, D. and P. Turton (1984) "Spontaneous Resettlement after Drought: an Ethiopian Example." *Disasters,* 8, pp. 178–89.

Vannutelli, L. and C. Citerni (1899). *L'Omo: Viaggi d'Esplorazione nell' Africa Orientale.* Milan: Hoepli.

Woodhead, L. (1991a) *The Land is Bad, Disappearing World* Series, Granada T.V., (52 mins. Colour). Anthropologist: David Turton.

———— (1991b). *Nitha, Disappearing World* Series, Granada T.V., (52 mins. Colour). Anthropologist: David Turton.

Chapter SIX

Requiem for the Rational War

Carolyn Nordstrom
*Department of Anthropology and
Knoc Institute of International
Peace Studies
University of Notre Dame*

Nordstrom's article, like that of Turton, asks that readers contemplate the politics of capaitalist states against those who resisted them. It concerns civil conflict in post-Independence Mozambique where a movement called Renamo fought a very 'dirty war' against the Marxist-Leninist government of Mozambique in the 1980s. Renamo, however, was controlled to a considerable extent by the armed forces of Apartheid South Africa, and the fighting in Mozambique was but one theater in a larger war that South Africa waged at the time throughout southern Africa, to destabilize anti-capitalist regimes. There had been heavy U.S. investment in South Africa, so the U.S. government supported its South African ally in this war. In other words, the U.S. used South Africa as its proxy to wage a war in which South Africa, in turn, used Renamo as its proxy, and Renamo fought a 'dirty war'. What parties in this sad circuit of normal monstrosities were guilty of crimes against humanity?

The Social indicators describing Mozambique paint a grim portrayal of the war that undermined the country for over fifteen years. In 1991, during my fieldwork there:

One fourth of the Mozambicans lived as refugees or internally displaced people.

One third of all schools and health care units had been shut down or destroyed by the war.

40 percent of the population was malnourished, and over half of the country's inhabitants were in need of direct food aid.

Approximately one million war-related casualties occurred in the last decade, and over 200,000 children have been orphaned by violence against civilians.

With 90 percent of the population living in proverty and 60 percent in absolute poverty, Mozambique is one of the poorest countries in the world, ensuring that few resources exist to ameliorate the crippling effects of the war on the nation. (UNICEF 1990; UNICEF 1989; UNICEF/Ministry of cooperation 1990; Ministerio Da Saude/UNICEF 1988; World Health Organization 1990).

While statistics chronicle the destruction of lives and social infrastructure, they can not capture one important aspect of the war. War's destruction of cultural integrity — the undermining of knowledge and action frameworks necessary to life — remains an often unrecognized casualty of civilian-targeting warfare. Statistics can tell us that Mozambique had the highest infant mortality rate in the world, primarily as a result of the war (UNICEF 1990), but they do not tell us how a culture of violence develops nor how a culture of terror is lived as experience.

The true impact of the war can be seen in the narratives that emerged from the frontlines of the conflict, frontlines populated primarily by civilians. Horror stories circulated daily: children were forced to watch, or even participate, in the mutilation and murder of family and friends, women were gang raped and kidnapped to rebel bases while their husbands and children stood helplessly by, and men and children were taken by the paramilitary to provide forced porterage, labor, and even paramilitary 'recruits.' The people who escape detection by the paramilitary forces had their own stories of dread: lost family members, destroyed communities, seemingly endless refugee treks, starvation, and the hypervigilance that becomes part of a life of 'waiting for the next attack.'

In order to study these questions, I introduce here the ethnography of a warzone. This will take us from the frontline experience of warfare to the formation of military mentalities and cultures of violence that make such warfare possible, and finally, to an analysis of power (and the powerful ironies) driving war. In this ethnography of a warzone, it is a process, and not a place per se, that is of focal interest. Because war is a cultural system and violence a learned behavior (Foster 1986; Foster and Rubinstein 1986; Mead 1940), the processes of war, and not a specific locale, provide the 'site' of the ethnography. As 90 % of all war casualties in the world today are civilians (the figure is even higher in Mozambique), the ethnography of a warzone essentially entails an ethnography of normal people in decidedly abnormal circumstances, and worse, what happens when the abnormal — warfare and the culture of terror it perpetuates — comes to define the norm.

My research covered eight of Mozambique's ten Provinces in collecting a spectrum of in-depth interviews that included average civilians, people caught in acute war-related crises, refugees and displaced people, government officials, soldiers, and captives. The largest portion of my year and a half fieldstay (during the years 1988–1991) was spent in Zambezia, the Province most severely affected by the war. In each Province, I followed the ebb and flow of the war from urban centers to rural outposts, visiting locations on the peripheries of the war, locales that had recently been attacked, and villages and towns that had changed hands from the government to the rebel forces a number of times. While I worked in areas where the rebels were in close proximity, I never actually worked in rebel occupied areas.

THE QUESTIONABLE VALIDITY OF THE TERM 'INTERNAL WAR': THE DEVELOPMENT OF THE WAR IN MOZAMBIQUE

Mozambique was conceded independence by Portugal in 1975 after a decade of struggle against colonial rule. The revolutionary movement, Frelimo, formed a black-majority government at this time. As Mozambicans point out, they were colonized by a country that was itself essentially underdeveloped by Western standards, leaving Mozambique critically impoverished at independence.

In the year immediately after independence, Frelimo formalized a Marxist-Leninist political system and a dedication to assisting the anti-apartheid liberation movements in Rhodesia and South Africa. These two actions set the stage for the development of the rebel group, Renamo. The government of Ian Smith in Rhodesia made a strategic decision to form Renamo in order to destabilize Mozambique and thus undermine any assistance the country could extend to the guerrilla forces fighting for independence. The fact that Rhodesian forces raided Mozambican prisons for a core of Renamo soldiers suggests that popular support for Renamo inside Mozambique was minimal at best, and Minter's (1989) estimate that roughly 90 percent of Renamo's troops were kidnapped in raids and instrumentalized into fighting indicates that Renamo's popularity did not increase.

When Rhodesia became independent Zimbabwe in 1980, control of Renamo was taken over by South Africa's military intelligence, and like their predecessors, their goal was destabilization. Retaining military and ideological control over Renamo, the South Africans developed an essentially ragtag force of several thousand into a much more lethal force estimated at between 20,000 and 30,000 troops. The extent and destructiveness of the war escalated dramatically at this time. (Excellent comprehensive books on Mozambique include: Finnegan 1992; Geffray 1990; Hanlon 1984, 1991; Issacman and Issacman 1983; Johnson and Martin 1986; Legum 1989; Munslow 1983; Urdang 1989, Vail and White 1980; Vines 1991.)

Renamo claimed to champion traditional culture and authority (chiefs and traditional healers) and democratic process, but for the most part it controlled people largely through force and intimidation, with little attempt to provide political ideology or infrastructure. Forced labor and the extraction of resources and taxes from occupied areas seemed to be Renamo's primary goal. While some traditional leaders at first elected to assist Renamo, many became increasingly disillusioned by the rebel force's oppression and brutality, and sought to distance themselves from the group.

Conflicts that develop in such a manner beg the question of whether the term "internal" war is at all appropriate. If the impetus for conflict develops externally, if the strategists, supplies, and grounding ideologies come from outside the country, and if all of these are structured principally to benefit foreign goals, what is the relevance of the concept 'internal war?' This external control has a direct bearing on the way the war is played out: What loyalties do foreign strategists and mercenaries have to a country not their own to ensure that some semblance of a 'just war' ideology exists (if, it can be argued, such a concept as 'just war' is anything more than an oxymoron)?

THE EXPERIENCE OF WAR — THE CIVILIANS

War Realities: Social Process

We sometimes speak of 'war' as if it were a singular, monolithic, homogeneous experience. But war covers an endlessly complex and fluid set of behaviors. The people who are mutilated in individual acts of terror, the villages that are totally destroyed, the communities that bribe paramilitary soldiers not to harm them, the children kidnapped and forcefully trained to become soldiers, the refugees who continually flee war and never see it — but lose family members to starvation and deprivation caused by the war, the people who make fortunes selling information about captives and war booty, the war orphans who have seen their parents killed — each experiences a different war, and all these experiences are as central to war as the experiences of soldiers. It is the sum total of all these stories, told and untold, that defines the dynamics of war. In contrast, the classical approaches to war that focus on formal politico-military institutions of war, the formal ideologies governing these, and the battlefield strategies and outcomes between contending troops represent a very limited picture of war.

The following excerpts from my fieldnotes and the literature demonstrate the vast range of expressions of the war in Mozambique, and the multitude of ways it is endured by its victims.

Mozambique 1:

An area is under the control of Renamo (the oppositional forces). The troops demand food, labor, women, and ideological loyalty from the civilians. Sometimes they demand limbs and lives – in the name of vendetta, publishment, or perversion. Frelimo (government) troops take the area and gather the population around them, after killing those deemed to have been Renamo collaborators. This serves to keep civilians out of Renamo's hands and help, and to create a buffer zone between the troops and their opponents. Unable to maintain normal crop and trade productivity, the population often begins to starve, with death and disease rising dramatically. A government official, a reporter, a non-governmental organization gets wind of this, and with great hue and cry sets up an emergency airlift of food and other essentials. The ones with guns and connections "receive" preferential access, while the population gathers and waits. Renamo, also suffering a lack of supplies because of their reliance on destabilization tactics, follows the relief planes to the drop sites. Should Renamo attack, it is the buffer zone of unarmed and starving citizens that most frequently serves as the battleground. If Renamo recaptures the area, they gather the population around them, after killing those deemed to be Frelimo collaborators. Sometimes they just loot the locale of people and goods and conduct a forced march to a secure base. If the airlift dries up and the troops themselves cannot procure sufficient supplies, Frelimo and Renamo both melt away to other more productive areas, abandoning the area to the hungry and homeless until the site becomes strategic once again. Unattended by government troops and open to Renamo reprisal, journalists and relief personnel no longer have safe access to the area. Reports dry up like the food, and people continue to starve and fight and die, only they no longer do so in the public eye.

— Fieldnotes, Mozambique, 1991: culled from an informal conversation among Mozambican and foreign journalists, relief workers and civilians on 'this bitch of a war.'

Mozambique 2:

Gersony (1988), in his now classic study of Mozambican refugee conflict experiences, details three other common scenarios based on Renoma operations: tax areas, control areas, and destruction areas.

Tax areas were generally located in rural locales with dispersed population and settlement patterns. Renamo demanded 'contributions' of food, clothes, women for sex, and adults to porter supplies, but instances of brutality, murder, and kidnapping were not the norm.

In control areas, the population generally surrounded a Renamo base, and both the demands placed upon the population and the measures for controlling and punishing them were more extensive and brutal than in tax areas. The civilians were forced to devote six days of work a week providing for Renamo, and were allowed one day a week to produce all their own requirements for survival, including crops, housing, and other essentials. Failure to produce for Renamo resulted in severe penalties, such as beatings, mutilation, and death. The civilians received no remuneration from Renamo for their toils and, as Gersony notes: "the only reciprocity the captives appear to receive or expect is the opportunity to remain alive." A failed attempt to escape from a control area resulted in death; in the event of a successful escape, members of the escapee's family were often put to death.

Even the opportunity to remain alive was denied those in Gersony's third category, destruction areas. These areas frequently had some form of Frelimo governmental representation (political and possibly military), or served as a government-sponsored refugee location. The government presence might have been no more than one or several administrative officials, possibly a government-sponsored health clinic and/or school, and in some instances a small contingent of Frelimo troops. When Renamo targeted such an area, it attacked civilians and officials alike, structure and infrastructure simultaneously. Goods were looted and people kidnapped to porter them. Other civilians were wantonly tortured and killed: Gersony explains: "a large number of civilians in these attacks and other contexts were reported to be victims of purposeful shooting deaths and executions, of axing, knifing, bayoneting, burning to death, forced drowning and asphyxiation, and other forms of murder where no meaningful resistance or defense in present" (1988: 32).

Mozambique 3:

> And I saw my children crushed, disembowelled, rent with bayonets or their heads blown open by a burst from a machine-gun. And I heard it being said that there was civil war in Mozambique. Civil war?! What is civil war? Wars, whether civil or not, are waged between armed contingents. That's not what's happening in Mozambique. There's no civil war in Mozambique. In Mozambique there is genocide perpetrated by armed men against defenseless populations (Magaia 1988: 17).

Lina Magaia's book on peasant tales of tragedy in Mozambique (from which the preceding quote is taken), brings another perspective to the war in Mozambique. Working in the Ministry of Agriculture as a Frelimo official, Magaia traveled about the country listening to endless stories of Renamo's unprovoked brutality against peasants. Unlike Gersony, Magaia did not work with refugees, nor did she identify military areas. Her story is the story of Mozambique's peasants, neither controlled by Renamo nor free of them, and periodically subjected to the most horrifying random brutality. Renamo emerges through the vignettes told by average villagers not as a coherent military force, but as small roving bands who appear specter-like to demand food, goods, services, retribution for an unnamed affront, and blood sport, and then move on. Violence and not ideology, cruelty and not logic, the personal and not the military, define these accounts.

Mozambique 4:

> I love this country and I hate it. It is my country, its blood flows in my veins. I want to leave, but I cannot, I must stay and try to help cure

it. No one who has not lived like this can understand. The war has gotten into us all, it lives in us, affecting our every move and thought. If I walk outside, I wonder if today is the day I will die. If my brother is late coming to visit me, I wonder if he has been kidnapped or killed, and the terror lives in me. I have not heard from my mother — she lives in an uncertain area behind Renamo control, and I live daily not knowing if she is dead or alive, whether her spirits are calling for me to do a proper ceremony for her, or if her body is calling for food and family. You do not have to see the war, and the war lives in all of us.
—Fieldnotes, Niassa District, Mozambique,1991.

Mozambique 5:

The armed bandits (Renamo) kidnapped my mother-in-law, and it took my husband and me two years and all our money to find her. We had to pay a jackal – you know, the men who fought on no side but profit from all sides in a war.
—Fieldnotes, Zambezia Province, Mozambique, 1990.

These five vignettes only begin to introduce the complexity of the war in Mozambique — a war where the oppositional forces relied far more on terror tactics directed against civilians than on any plan to "win the hearts and minds of the population." In this war, the social fabric of the entire nation has been seriously, and possibly in some ways irreparably, damaged. And if one gathered together a sampling of this war's victims — the peasants who are occasionlly set upon by Renamo troops demanding a part of their produce, the women who have been senselessly mutilated, the villagers who fled when their village was burned to the ground, and the children who have been kidnapped by Renamo — and left them to talk amongst themselves, they might find it surprising that they were all enmeshed in one and the same conflict process.

War Realities: Cultural/Experiential Process.

In order to understand the true effects of this war, it is necessary to ground the foregoing discussion in the context of the *lived experience* of war — to grasp the impact of the tactics and terrors of war on the lives and life-worlds of the predominantly noncombatant casualties.

While maimed and murdered civilians and ruined social infrastructure may be the most visible and dramatic 'casualties' of Renamo's dirty war, they are not the only ones. Socio-cultural process — that by which we define who we are and (how to be in) the world at large — is rooted in the social institutions of every day life. And this process generates 'reality' in its most fundamental sense (Schutz and Luckman 1973; Bourdieu 1977; de Certeau 1980). It is what creates a world simultaneously 'made up' and 'made real' (Taussig 1993). When ordinary social process is severely disrupted (as it is in dirty wars), cultural integrity is undermined for the affected population at large.

Life-world viability is disrupted not only by public acts intended to horrify (public maimings, gang rapes, excessive beatings, and desecration of bodies), and by action intended to destabilize social institutions basic to society (the destruction of education, health, economic, and family systems crucial to survival), but also by the way of life forced upon a population living in a warzone. One Mozambican summarized the dehumanizing effects for me:

> They have made us inhuman. We sleep in the jungle like animals every night to avoid attack. We run from every sound like the animals we hunt, we scavenge for food in the countryside like animals because we cannot maintain our crops like men. Our family is scattered on the wind – we don't know where children and parents are, or even if they are alive. We can't even help and protect them – we are even worse than animals in that sense. Do you know what this does to a person, living like this? Do you know what this does, facing inhumanity, being forced to live inhumanity?
> —Fieldnotes, Mozambique, 1991

Such comments were legion among the war-affected population of Mozambique — a constant indication of the social toll of violence, of the 'wounding' of identity and the dismantling of the world of significances. Another Mozambican confided:

> They attacked my village, stole my things, destroyed what they couldn't carry, burned my house, and killed my animals. They managed to kidnap and kill some of my family and friends. Those of us who escaped ran in all different directions, and I don't know where the rest of my family is. They have taken everything from me. They have taken me from me: who am I without the sons I have fathered, my lands and the house I have built and my ancestors who protected all of this, the clothes that I know and the bed of my marriage. Who am I? I am nothing.
> —Fieldnotes, Mozambique, 1990

And another:

> They have not just killed my family and taken my home, they have killed my soul. They have spit on it and killed it.
> —Fieldnotes, Nozambique, 1991

THE (RE)PRODUCTION OF WAR — THE SOLDIERS

I want to turn now from a discussion of the experience of war to the question of *how* such a dirty war as this can come to take place. The question takes on added significance when we consider that in Mozambique some 20,000 to 30,000 Renamo troops and an equal number of Frelimo troops have generated some 1,000,000 war-related deaths, over 4,000,000 refugees and displaced people, and directly affected a further 2,500,000 people.

The following analysis develops the notion of the simultaneity of two related, yet contradictory, dynamics: the top-down (re)creation of cultures of violence and terror as strategy, and the bottom-up subversion of these as personal biography and agency are inserted where "power becomes force." Within this analysis, power — as a concept, as a phenomenon, and as an experienced reality — emerges as fundamentally, and ironically, contested.

The Dirty War: Construct(ion)s of Brutality and Terror

Contemporary anthropological theory points to the conclusion that violence is not innate but is culturally constructed (Foster 1986; Mead 1940; May 1964). If we accept this conclusion, we are confronted with the question of how certain individuals are induced to mutilate and murder their brethren. [For those who argue that violence is innate to human behavior, I would like to point out that in all wars, very few people perpetrate conflict, while a great many simply suffer it. Specifically, in the case of Mozambique, recruits are not flocking to Renamo: Minter's (1989) widely accepted figures place the number of Renamo troops who have been kidnapped and then instrumentalized into fighting at 90 percent.]

In the case of recruits who have been kidnapped and forced into fighting, it is not difficult to understand how they come to perpetuate brutality. Most are youths, and the process by which they are indoctrinated into Renamo soldierhood is itself so brutal and dehumanizing that it cannot be said these people are demonstrating free will or natural tendencies. The question then becomes, How is it that the leaders of a (para)military organization come to justify dirty war tactics as an acceptable military strategy?

It might be assumed that dirty war tactics are expedient (terrorize the population into submission and therefore control 'political process') and generic (mutilation and massacre are mutilation and massacre wherever they occur). I would like to argue that neither of these suppositions is true. I have suggested elsewhere that while dirty war tactics do undermine culture and identity, they simultaneously provoke resistance among those affected — which ultimately undermines the ability of terror to control (Nordstrom 1992a, 1992b). Therefore dirty war tactics may be more 'habit' than 'logic.'

It has long been recognized that the us/them constructs (Memmi 1967) people apply in conflict models allow a far greater degree of violence to be done to 'them' than to 'us.' Dehumanization precedes violence (Keen 1986; Bernard et al. 1971; Duster 1971). Once 'they' are dehumanized, 'inhuman' acts become allowable and even strangely obligatory — a construct that produces a compelling spiral of violence.

When an 'internal war' is externally orchestrated, the us/them construct is 'always already' in the conflict dynamic. If foreign, and clearly antagonistic, military advisors have control over the training and leadership of troops fighting in another country, ideologies and practices that dehumanize the 'enemy' can easily become justified as strategy.

The data from Mozambique support these conclusions. While people acknowledge that Frelimo troops have engaged in unconscionable brutality at times, and many chafed at the degree of control the politico-military system imposed — most agree that it was primarily Renamo that was associated with the sheer volume of grotesque terror-warfare. Gersony (1988) reports that while Mozambicans cited instances of brutal behavior on the parts of both Frelimo and Renamo, over 90 percent of the *atrocities* committed were attributed to Renamo.

The violence imposed by the us/them construct has a visible impact on women in war (Hartsock, 1990). Jeichande (1990), in conjunction with the Organization of Mozambican Women, interviewed women in difficult situations — refugees, displaced people, and women who had been kidnapped by Renamo and later escaped. Most of the stories are chronicles of pain and suffering. I noted in reading the texts of the interviews that a number of women stated that when 'white men' (presumably foreigner commanders) were present, the level of brutality was much worse. For example, a woman may be raped, even gang raped, by local Renamo forces, but if a foreign soldier was present, she was likely to be raped, beaten, and possibly killed.

Clearly, then, the reliance upon dirty war techniques and the construction of a culture of violence and terror was introduced into the war in Mozambique from the inception of Renamo. Because culture, war included, tends to reproduce itself across time and space, even if the strategic focus on dirty war principles abates, the actual dirty war practices may not, for they have come to define the 'reality' of the war. Only a concerted effort to redefine the way in which the war is to be conducted may be able to redirect war behaviors.

The history of the war in Mozambique illustrates the difficulty of cleaning up a dirty war. Frelimo's proof, based on documents captured from Renamo's headquarter's at Casa Banana in Gorongosa and subsequently made available worldwide, that South Africa had not only violated the Nkomati Accord, but had done so relying on incontestably dirty strategies, swung world opinion towards Mozambique. Subsequently, world opinion was increasingly swayed by the growing recognition of Renamo's massacres of civilians. Even the United States Congress made a formal statement against Renamo, calling them the Khmer Rouge of Africa and Mozambique the Killing Fields (Frelick 1989).

Renamo realized that financial and political support was drying up in response to the expanding documentation of their atrocities, and Renamo leaders tried (at least in their public pronouncements) to temper their troop's reliance on dirty tactics. While some changes in the way Renamo conducted its war were noticeable, for the most part the wishes of the leaders did not translate down to the practices of the soldiers in the field. They continued to employ violence as they learned it — reproducing war as it was first (re)produced to them.

The difficulty leaders face in controlling the course of war once it is set in motion is especially pronounced in locations like Mozambique. The country is nearly twice the size of California, and its extensive rural areas are isolated, unconnected by reliable communication or transportation infrastructure. While leaders may be able to communicate fairly easily with certain groups of crack troops directly under their command, they may not even be able to reach other factions 'under their control' at all. The strategies of the top, once the war is in progress, may have little influence on battlefield behaviors.

International Conflict Process, the Cultural Construction of Violence, and the (Para)Military Mentality

The character of the Mozambican war was directly molded by larger international socio-political conflict processes. Internal conflicts, far from being particular expressions of unique conditions and specific tensions, are in fact strongly influenced by military cultures of violent conflict operating throughout the world.

Highly developed international relationships link various 'internal' conflicts across the globe. A significant amount of information, strategy, supplies, weapons, and personnel are transferred among like-minded military organizations. State-sponsored support is complemented by private formal organizations, both legal and illegal, and the activities of individual sponsors and mercenaries. A great deal of ideological presupposition and cultural assumptions are simultaneously transferred with these goods, services, and alliances.

These international networks of alliances, antipathies, and mercenaries enable core strategies and specific (tactical) practices to be transferred from group to group across international boundaries and political alliances. Transferred with these are the cultural belief systems in which strategic knowledge and action are embedded; beliefs about what constitute acceptable, and necessary, processes of war, violence, and control in the quest for power. Like specific strategies, these core cultural assumptions defining the fundamental relationships of power and violence have long since been forged, continuously transmitted, shared, reformulated, and reproduced across time and space as goods and personnel move around the globe. Understandably, only politico-military leaders, and not the common soldier, have the privilege to travel, train, and interact with leaders of other country's (para)military organizations. And it is they who set strategic policy in their home country.

The Wild Card: Translating Ideology into Action.

This raises the question of how military paradigms of thought and action are translated from privileged politico-military leaders to the ground forces, from the institution to the enactment of war. The question of military strategy and practice proves to be more complex, and far less rational, than traditional political science analysis would have it.

Consider a conversation I had with two recently captured Renamo soldiers, both, like many of their confederates, young teenage men. One youth, slightly older than the other, did the majority of the talking, and in the following exchange it is he who is answering:

> CN: Why were you fighting?
> Renamo: Cuz they told us to.
> CN: What were you fighting for?
> Renamo: I forgot

CN: You forgot?
Renamo: Ah, yeah.
CN: But your leaders must have told you something?
Renamo: Ah...that the government is bad and we need to run the country.
CN: But why?
Renamo: (*Sigh*)...Cuz they're bad.

This dialogue is not repeated here to belittle the soldier's mentality. Rather, it demonstrations the low level of commitment many soldiers have. Both of these youths were kidnapped at a young age by Renamo and trained to fight under extremely harsh conditions. They were both barefoot and dressed in very tattered shorts and the remnants of shirts far from any military issue — ground soldiers in the bush. They admitted that they were not sad to be captured because they were sick of living and sleeping in the bush, always on the move, and always eating poorly. It was not a good life by any means, they confessed, and they hoped to be able to return to their homelands and families and forget the war.

Adult Renamo soldiers may be more eloquent, but the import of their words may not differ much from that of the teenagers. Another recent captive told me:

> Why did I fight? [Laughs] I'll tell you why I fought. I was kidnapped from my home when my village was attacked by Renamo and forced to walk endless days into another Province. I was kept on a guarded base and beaten and told if I tried to escape they would continue to beat me until I was dead. I was told to pick up a gun and at gunpoint told to go with the soldiers on raids. The choice wasn't great – do what they say or get shot. I did what they said.

Not all 'recruits' to Renamo are kidnapped. But those who chose to fight with Renamo may not have done so for the ideological reasons their commanders and political leaders would have us believe. Consider another Renamo soldier, who told me he fought because:

> My land was poor what with the drought and all, and the work was backbreaking, the same shit day after day, month after month, and what do you get? Well, I wanted to get something more.

And the village youth who told me he ran off to join Renamo soldiers who came through his area because:

> I wanted a pair of shoes.

Taussig (1987) has called acts of terror-warfare 'rituals.' But we can take the analysis further: terror-warfare, indeed warfare in general, is transmitted through ritually-structured action (Kertzer 1988). Bootcamp, whether voluntary or by forced conscription, is clearly a rite of passage (Van Gennep 1960) in a ritual process (Turner 1969) to forge new identities and behaviors. Soldiers are 'trained'; they are not 'educated.' Mimetic (re)actions (Girard 1977) and scripted behaviors are encouraged through repetition passed top-down. Punishment, not explanation, enforces rules.

History and research demonstrate that the average person is not predisposed to maim and massacre fellow humans (Rapoport 1989), and thus training based on violent desensitization and inhumanization (often of both the 'enemy' and the recruit) have consistently been used to create soldiers capable of torture and murder (Gibson and Haritos-Fatouros 1986). Cultures of violence are not only produced externally, they are reproduced internally. The rituals of training become the scripts for action on the battleground. Through this training process, cultures of violence gleaned from international conflict processes are assimilated into local aggressions.

It is important to point out, however, that top-down (para)military orientations do **not** control the character of the war as it is played out on the ground. The wild card of personal biography is inserted at every level of command, training, and action.

Individual action in the field becomes defined by, precisely, individual action: the ideologies and strategic orientations of the generals and the financiers of war have little significance on the ground. Personal motivation, immediate context, and individual attitudes toward violence come to determine actual agency on the ground level. Commanders insert their own personalities into their training and strategic objectives; soldiers renegotiate these to fit their own capabilities, needs, and circumstances.

While those far removed from the frontlines of war may not be alert to the importance of ground-level agency in the process of warfare, the noncombatants living in the midst of the war are acutely alert to it: their survival depends on it. They know each (para)military group in the area, its habits, and its tendencies toward violence. They know whom they can bribe, whom they can avoid, and from whom they must run. And they know the 'statements' issued by the power elites — whether about cease fires, strategic targets, or 'just war' promises — have virtually no effect on the processes of war as they are living them: it is a long way from the offices of the power brokers to the realities of the frontlines.

(IR)RATIONALITY IN THE POWER EQUATION

If the distance between the institutions and the manifestation of power are as great as my argument suggests, Lukes' (1974) assertion that power is essentially contested takes on a fundamental irony.

In grappling with the issue of power, it is important to recognize that power is not a totalizing phenomenon. Like all human endeavor, it is born in and through complex social relationships and cultural potentialities: negotiated, subverted, and renegotiated over space and time.

Most importantly, power is not a monolithic construct. Following Foucault (1972, 1979, 1980, 1982) and Gramsci (1968, 1971), most scholars accept the wisdom that power is decentered in and through both society and discourse, knowledge and action. Anthropologists like Bourdieu (1977, 1989), Comaroff (1985, 1991), and Feldman (1991) have pointed out ways in which power is symbolically as well as socially (re)produced and resisted in the complex unfolding of daily social dramas through time. Scott (1985, 1990) underscores the nuances of resistance by chronicling overt and covert strategies that the dominated themselves employ in the face of domination and the abuses of power. Finally, Nietzche (1956, 1968) has thrown the whole issue of agency into question by focusing on the performance, and not the sponsorship, of power. It is not the institution but the actor that is relevant to him, and no simple lines of authority align the two. In his words: "the doing is everything" (1956:179).

Acknowledging the contributions of these scholars as fundamental to my analysis of power, I would like to underscore the considerable distance — the competing horizons of thought and action — that exists between the power figureheads, whether political, military, or charismatic, and the minions who carry out their 'will and demands.' The classical textbook assertion that a direct link exists between the power source and its site of implementation would have us belive that political leaders forge ideology to determine action, military commanders forge strategy to carry out the former's vision, and the troops act to accomplish these ends. This scenario, however theoretically uncluttered, is quixotic. The politico-military 'institution' of war is an abstract, idea(l) construct — wholly divorced from the vagaries and the dynamics of minute-to-minute human action, social interaction, individual will, personal foibles, competitive vested interests, and the constantly negotiated tension between (intentional) agency and the (unintentional) unconscious.

When we put human actors into the power equation, we find that power is constantly reformulated as it moves from command to action. The soldier clearly gains the legitimation (power) to act by his association with a centralized politico-military institution. (Without this legitimation, his actions would be sanctioned as individual banditry.) Yet if ground soldiers bring their own personalities, traditions, ignorances, ideals, and vested interests to the fore of their actions — as they must — and if these are negotiated in the actual context of the war among others with their own personalities, traditions, vested interests, etc, — they are not only responsible for the actual wielding of force, *they are essentially constructing the reality of the way in which power is expressed.*

Clearly there is no such thing as an uninterrupted top-down flow of power. More importantly, if soldiers *can* respond to the question "why are you fighting?" with "I dunno" or "I wanted a pair of shoes," how much rationality can be said to exist in fundamental power equations?

The ironies of politico-military agency carry a step further: power brokers have the option of either accepting sponsorship of ground-level actions or risking the appearance that they do not fully control the power process. As the latter is generally unpalatable, power brokers often prefer to invoke a (mythologized) time sequence whereby they take authorship of actions after the fact *as if* the action actually derived from their institutional authority.

CONCLUSION

During the final work on this article, a fragile peace accord was signed and a cease-fire took place in October, 1992. As I write this in the first week of 1993, no one knows if the accord will hold, or if Mozambique will follow the route of Angola and descend back into violence.

But, many fear that solving the conflict itself is not the only critical issue facing Mozambique. Numerous Mozambicans refer to the present generation of children in their country as the 'lost generation.' Having been exposed to the horrors of war — the broken and fleeing families trying to get out of the war's path, the physical stunting of starvation and the emotional and intellectual stunting that has come of ruined infrastructures and burned villages — this generation will never be able to grow and live a normal life. And Mozambicans worry what impact this will have on the future of their society and culture as these children grow up.

If first Rhodesia and then South Africa wanted to set into motion a movement that would undermine the very fabric of society, it might be argued, they could hardly have come up with a better scheme than Renamo.

Even if the goals were purely political and concerned with control through destabilization, it could further be argued that because terror-warfare undermines not only social cohesion but cultural integrity, it is a logically constructed strategy intended to cripple a society's will to resist and thereby to create political acquiescence among the population at large. That the strategy of 'winning hearts and minds' has been replaced with the tactics of controlling them may be the result of simple expediency: it is easier to torture a person and torch a village than it is to develop strong systems of political and social support.

However pervasive dirty war strategies are in the world today, they cannot be called rational responses to conflicts interest and contests of power. Any study of the wars that have used violence and terror against civilian populations to effect political acquiescence shows that sooner or later the people rebel and the systems of force and authority upon which control was erected break down. Ethnographies of these wars show that the seeds of resistance are implanted by the very acts of terror-warfare.

Dirty war, then, is (re)produced more as a habit than as a carefully considered option. As I have pointed out, Renamo's strategies were not forged in a social and cultural vacuum. The production of the (dirty) war in Mozambique has been reproduced within larger international political and military cultures that have strongly shaped the expression of the war in this country. The culture of war reproduced internationally tends to accept uncritically the reality of power/violence equations, and, increasingly, dirty war is condoned in the exercise of power and control. If this seems a strong statement, consider the fact that in the present century the ratio of combatant to noncombatant casualties has changed from 80 percent soldier and 20 percent civilian at the beginning of the 1900s to the present inversion, in which 80 to 90 percent of all war-related casualties are noncombatants (Sivard 1990).

The destruction of socio-cultural process (including such fundamental human prerequisites as epistemological coherency (Schutz and Luckman 1973) and ontological security (Giddens 1991) as well as that of life and limb discussed in the first part of this paper) may in part be a conscious goal of dirty war strategies. But it is also an unacknowledged result of the many competing, conflicting, only partially controlled violences inflicted at the ground level, where power becomes force in such a way that personal history and personality, ideas of vengeance and gain, ignorance or sadism, and the chaos of circumstances combine to create the true manifestation of war.

This analysis suggests that in order to understand better the processes of war and their impact on a society and upon culture, we should pay as much attention to the experiential reality of war as to the definitions of its formal institutions. Certainly, this approach will result in more accurate portrayals of the nature of power and its relationship to the processes of force and the enactment of violence. But as well, as the people living on the frontlines of the war in Mozambique variously demonstrate, giving voice to the experiential, or 'lived' reality of socio-political violence can help forge more realistic, and humane, approaches to conflict resolution and the amelioration of war wounds, both physical and socio-cultural.

The people who refer to the 'lost generation' of war-ravaged Mozambicans could also benefit from an analysis of experiential reality at the ground level — at the frontlines of the war. It is true that the victims of the war are legion and that some will be impaired for life. But my research shows that the very people who suffer the worst of the war develop innovative ways of dealing with it. During the war, traditional healers provided sophisticated treatments for the war-traumatized. They provided 'treatments' that were in essence conflict resolution measures, such as finding ways to remove Renamo soldiers from their units, "taking the war out of them," as the healers say, and finding ways to reintegrate them into a healthy community life. Peasant traders braved war zones to carry goods, messages, and hope to link war-torn communities, and informal networks were set up to find and return kidnapped people to their villages and their families. Community wide ceremonies were instituted to reintroduce traditional values capable of combatting the cultures of terror and violence brought by the war. And all of this took place not only in a continuing scenario of warfare, but as well in the parasitic conditions of blackmarketeering, crime, usury, Janus-faced collaboration, and banditry that feeds on war's chaos. Possibly considering the irrationality in the power equation, an old Mozambican villager, recently burned out of his home and village, summed up to me: "If the governments and all those other outsiders who think they know what is going on would just get out of this, we could cure this country in no time."

REFERENCES

Bedjaoui, Mohammed, ed. (1986). Modern Wars. London: Zed Books Ltd.
Berger, Peter and Thomas Luckman (1966). The Social Construction of Reality. Garden City: Doubleday and Company.
Bernard, Viola, Perry Ottenberg, and Fritz Redl (1971). Dehumanization. In Sanctions for Evil. N. Sanford and C. Comstock, eds. pp. 102–24. San Francisco: Jossey-Bass.
Bourdieu, Pierre (1977). Outline of a Theory of Practice. Cambridge: Cambridge University Press.
——— (1989). Social Space and Symbolic Power. Sociological Theory 7(1): 14–25.
Comaroff, Jean (1985). Body of Power, Spirit of Resistance. Chicago: The University of Chicago Press.
Comaroff, Jean and John Comaroff (1991). Of Revelation and Revolution: Christianity, Colonialism, and Consciousness in South Africa. Vol. 1. Chicago: University of Chicago Press.
de Certeau (1980). On the Oppositional Practices of Everyday Life. Social Text, Fall 1980: 3–43.
——— (1984). The Practice of Everyday Life. Translated by S. S. Rendall. Berkeley: University of California Press.
Duster, Troy (1971). Conditions for a Guilt-Free Massacre. In Sanctions for Evil. N. Sanford and C. Comstock, eds. pp. 25–36. San Francisco: Jossey-Bass.
Feldman, Allen (1991). Formations of Violence. Chicago: University of Chicago Press.
Finnegan, William (1992). A Complicated War: The Harrowing of Mozambique. Berkeley: University of California Press.
Foster, Mary LeCron (1986). Is War Necessary? In Peace and War. M. Foster and R. Rubinstein, eds. pp. 71–8. New Brunswick: Transaction Books.
——— and Robert A. Rubinstein, eds. (1986). Peace and War: Cross-Cultural Perpectives. New Brunswick: Transaction Books.
Foucault, Michel (1972). Power/Knowledge. New York: Pantheon Books.
——— (1979). Discipline and Punish: The Birth of the Prison. Translated by A. Sheridan. New York: Vintage Books.
——— (1980). The History of Sexuality, Volume 1: An Introduction. Translated by R. Hurley. New York: Vintage Books.
——— (1982). The Subject and Power. In Michel Foucault: Beyond Structuralism and Hermeneutics. H. Dreyfus and P. Rabinow, eds. pp. 208–26. Chicago: The University of Chicago Press.
Frelick, Bill (1989). Renamo: The Khmer Rouge of Africa; Mozambique, Its Killing Field. Testimony before the House Subcommittee on Foreign Operations. Washington, D.C., February 8, 1989.
Geffray, Christian (1990). La Cause des Armes au Mozambique: Antropologie d'une Guerre Civile. Paris: Editions Karthala.
Geffray, Christian and Morgens Pederson (1986). Sobre a guerra na provincia de Nampula. Elementos de analise e hipoteses sobre as determinacoes e

consequencias socio-economicas locais. Revista Internacional de Estudos Africanos 4/5, 303–18, Janeiro-Dezembro, 1986.
Gersony, Robert (1988). Rebels Create Havoc in Mozambique. Cultural Survival Quarterly 12(2): 31–40.
―――――― (1988). Summary of Mozambican Refugee Accounts of Principally Conflict-Related Experience in Mozambique. Report submitted to Ambassador Jonathon Moore: Director, Bureau for Refugees Program and Dr. Chester Crocker: Assistant Secretary of African Affairs. April, 1988.
Gibson, Janice T. and Mika Haritos-Fatouros (1986). The Education of a Torturer. Psychology Today 20 (11): 50–8.
Giddens, Anthony (1991). Modernity and Self-Identity. Stanford: Stanford University Press.
Girard, R (1977). Violence and the Sacred. Baltimore: Johns Hopkins Press.
Gramsci, Antonio (1968). The Modern Prince and Other Writings. 3rd Printing. New York: International Publishers.
―――――― (1971). Selections from the Prison Notebooks. London: Lawrence and Wishart.
Hanlon, Joseph (1984). Mozambique: The Revolution Under Fire. London: Zed Books.
―――――― (1991). Mozambique: Who Calls the Shots? Bloomington: Indiana University Press.
Hartsock, Nancy (1990). Foucault on Power: A Theory for Women? In Feminism/Postmodernism. L. Nicholson, ed. pp. 157–75. New York: Routledge.
Issacman, Allen and Barbara Issacman. (1983) Mozambique: From Colonialism to Revolution 1900–1982. Hampshire, England: Gower.
Jeichande Ivette Illas (1990). Mulheres Deslocadas em Maputo, Zambezia e Inhambane (Mulher em Situacao Dificil). OMM — UNICEF, Maputo, Marco 1990.
Johnson, Phyllis and David Martin (1986). Destructive Engagement. Harare: Zimbabwe Publishing House.
Keen, Sam (1986). Faces of the Enemy. San Francisco: Harper and Row.
Kertzer, David I. (1988). Ritual, Politics and Power. New Haven: Yale University Press.
Legum, Colim, ed. (1988). Mozambique: Facing up to Desperate Hardships in Post-Machel Era. Africa Contemporary Record, Volume 19: 1986–1987, pp. B681–B701. New York: African Publishing Co.
Lukes, Steven (1974). Power: A Radical View. London: MacMillan.
Magaia, Lina (1988). Dumba Nengue: Run For Your Life. Peasant Tales of Tragedy in Mozambique. Trenton: Africa World Press.
May, Mark A. (1964). War, Peace, and Social learning. In War. L. Bramson and G. Goethals, eds. pp. 151–58. New York: Basic Books.
Mead, Margaret (1940). Warfare is Only an Invention — Not a Biological Necessity. Asia XL: 402–05.
Memmi, Albert (1967). The Colonizer and the Colonized. Boston: Beacon Press.

Ministerio Da Saude/UNICEF (1988). Analise da Situacao da Saude. Maputo, Septembro 1988.

Minter, William (1989). The Mozambican National Resistance (Renamo) as Described by Ex-participants. Research Report Submitted to Ford Foundation and Swedish International Development Agency. March 1989.

Munslow, Barry (1983). Mozambique: the Revolution and its Origins. London: Longman.

Nietzche, Friedrich (1956). The Genealogy of Morals. In The Birth of Tragedy & The Genealogy of Morals. Trans. by Francis Golffing. New York: Doubleday.

————— (1968). The Will to Power. Garden City, NY: Doubleday.

Nordstrom, Carolyn (1992a). The Backyard Front. In The Paths to Domination, Resistance, and Terror. C. Nordstrom and J. Martin, eds. pp. 260–74. Berkeley: University of California Press.

————— (1992b). The Dirty War: Culture of Violence in Mozambique and Sri Lanka. In Internal Conflicts and Governance. K. Rupesinghe, ed. pp. 27–43. New York: St. Martin's Press.

Rapoport, Anatol (1989). The Origins of Violence: Approaches to the Study of Conflict. New York: Paragon House.

Schutz, Alfred and Thomas Luckman (1973). The Structures of the Life-World. Evanston: Northwestern University Press.

Scott, James C. (1985). Weapons of the Weak: Everyday Forms of Peasant Resistance. New Haven: Yale University Press.

————— (1990). Domination and the Arts of Resistance. New Haven: Yale University Press.

Sivard, Ruth Leger (1990). World Military and Social Expenditures. Leesburg, VA: World Priorities.

Suárez-Orozco, Marcelo (1987). The Treatment of Childern in the "Dirty War": Ideology, State Terrorism, and the Abuse of Childern in Argentina. In Child Survival. N. Scheper-Hughes, ed. pp. 227–46. Boston: D. Reidel Publishing.

Taussig, Michael (1987). Shamanism, Colonialism, and the Wild Man. Chicago: University of Chicago Press.

————— (1993). Mimesis and Alterity. New York: Routledge Press.

Turner, Victor (1969). The Ritual Process. Ithaca: Cornell University Press.

UNICEF (1989). Childern on the Frontline, 1989 Update. Geneva: UNICEF.

————— (1990). Annual Report; Mozambique 1990. Maputo.

————— Ministry of Cooperation (1990). The Situation of Women and Childern in Mozambique. Maputo.

Urdang, Stephanie (1989). And Still They Dance. London: Earthscan.

Vail, Leroy and Landeg White (1980). Capitalism and Colonialism in Mozambique. London: Heinemann.

Van Gennep, Arnold (1960). The Rites of Passage. Chicago: The University of Chicago Press.

Vines, Alex (1991). Renamo: Terrorism in Mozambique. Bloomington: Indiana University Press.

World Health Organization (1990). WHO/Mozambique Cooperation. Organizacao Mundial Da Saude Representacao em Mocambique, Maputo, March 1990.

Chapter
SEVEN

The Politics of Ethnic Conflict in a Transboundary Context, the Senegal River Valley[1]

John Magistro

Magistro's article and that of Bonte, which follows, deal with the region in Africa known as the Sahel. This an immense, arid, poor area immediately south of the Sahara that extends from the Atlantic Ocean to Chad. The Sahel has since Independence known its share of ethnic violence. Magistro deals with fighting between Maures and peoples of sub-Saharan ethnic groups that broke out in the west along the Senegal River, which divides Senegal from Mauritania. His analysis concentrates upon the way in which this river valley is being integrated into advanced capitalist economies through the construction of irrigation development schemes. In this instance development is, indeed, deadly because it provokes ethnic conflict.

INTRODUCTION

As the waters of the Senegal River retreat to a shallow ebb at the height of the dry season, the border separating northern Senegal from southern Mauritania narrows to a thin, incandescent band of blue, reflecting the intense sunlight of the arid Sahel. In the middle Senegal Valley border town of Matam, situated on the river's left bank (Figure 7.1), the morning of April 20th, 1989 dawned as another serene and uneventful day, the heat of the tropical sun keeping town residents at bay, sequestered in their mud-thatch dwellings and rectangular tin-roof houses. The calm of the mid-morning air soon gave way, however, to the faint sound of a peculiar drone, much like that of a distant rumbling train.

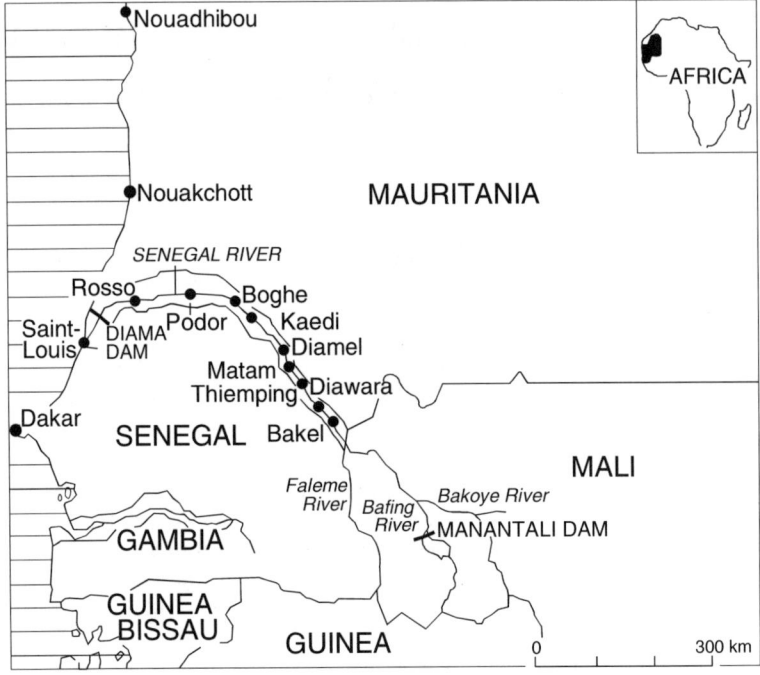

Figure 7.1. The Senegal River Valley.

Gazing from the top of the high clay banks of the river, a large gathering of people could be seen some distance below, amassed as a human fortress wall in the middle of the river. Facing off a short distance away on the right bank, a throng of assailants moved about at a frenzied pace, running up and down the sandy incline of the river, hurling large rocks and bits of wood upon the horde of angry bodies in the river below. The clash was marked by an occasional duel as attackers wielding large chunks of wood as clubs swung frantically at one another.

From high above on the banks of Matam, women and children in the fishing quarters of the village scurried about between mud huts, calling out to one another as they gathered rocks and bits of wood. The fresh stocks of ammunition were passed rapidly in a gauntlet down the slope of the river to the men below. Meanwhile, youth raced along the narrow pathways between the mud dwellings carrying small ruminants belonging to their attackers from across the river. In the early morning hours, these animals had been confiscated after entering river garden plots belonging to the fishing community and grazing on the fertile beds of grass and the dry stover of maize, beans, and garden vegetables.

This violent clash of neighboring riverine communities — a bloody confrontation of black Haalpulaar fishers and cultivators, and black *haratin* Maures[2] — continued unabated well into the day. By nightfall, two men, one from each community, had died. Both had been brutally tortured and beaten. This incident of ethnic violence on the northern boundary of Senegal occurred in the wake of a similar border dispute eleven days earlier between Mauritanian herders and Senegalese farmers on the river island of Doundou Khore at Diawara (near Bakel in the upper valley) where two Senegalese died.[3] In the aftermath of these skirmishes on the remote sahelian frontier, the grisly truncheoning, mutilation, and indiscriminate execution of hundreds of innocent victims several days later in the towns and cities of Senegal and Mauritania caught the most astute social critics of political relations between the two countries by surprise. The black-on-black conflict that initially erupted at Diawara and then Matam set off a deadly chain of events from the upper valley to the Atlantic coastal port of Saint Louis. Residents in town after town along the Senegal border took to the streets venting their rage and hostility at Mauritanians in their country.

Initially, the assault targeted personal property and items belonging to "white" Maure shopkeepers or *bidan*,[4] who are found in many of the towns and villages of Senegal, where they dominate petty trade and markets in the retail sector. By the time the unrest spread to the capitals of Nouakchott and Dakar, however, people as well as property fell victim to the violent outburst.

In the brief span of a few days in late April, mayhem ruled the streets of the major towns and cities in each country. It is estimated that between 15,000 to 40,000 Mauritanian shops in Senegal (Fall 1989a: 33; Park et al. 1990: 2) were pillaged and destroyed.[5] Eyewitness accounts chronicle macabre scenes in Mauritania such as the mutilation of children's genitalia and women's breasts by bands of *haratin* assailants. During "Black Tuesday" in Nouakchott, at least 200 black Africans died at the hands of black *haratin* death squads trucked in from the countryside to carry out systematic executions under the supervision of white *bidan* patrons (Doyle 1989: 15, 16; Coupe 1990: 369–71). A representative rendering of the gruesome acts of violence is found in the following account by the West African news magazine *Jeune Afrique*:

> In Dakar, in Nouakchott as in the principal cities of the two countries, the scenes of pillage and of vandalism had been, everywhere, accompanied by acts of incredible savagery: mutilated bodies, heads cut off, women disemboweled, children's throats slit, etc. (Diallo 1989: 26).

The bloodbath unfolded as a series of reprisals and counter reprisals between Nouakchott and Dakar as rumors of mutilation and widespread execution filtered back to the capitals, inciting hysteria and violence among mobs of youth in Senegal and *haratin* in Mauritania.[6] By the end of April, when the bloodletting finally subsided, over 50 Maures had died in Senegal (Doyle 1989: 16). The number of Senegalese killed in Nouakchott and the countryside is somewhere between 200 and 1,000 (Dahmani 1989:24; Africa Confidential 1989: 2). Soon after the eruption of violence, the heads of state in each country declared states of emergency, imposing curfews under military supervision. A massive international airlift of approximately 100,000 repatriates from both countries was launched soon after the pogroms ended (Parker 1991: 160). The quelling of unrest in the towns and cities gave way to a new round of tragedy, however, as black subsaharan Africans — primarily of Haalpulaar ethnicity — were systematically rounded up and deported from Mauritania. By May, 1989, a huge wave of refugees — many of Mauritanian nationality living on the right bank of the Senegal River — began crossing the border into Senegal.[7] At the same time, large numbers of Mauritanian nationals were expelled from Senegal. By late October, 1991, an estimated 70,000 people had sought refuge in Senegal, another 13,000 having fled to Mali (GAVD 1991: 2; UNHCR 1991: 80 in de Sherbinin 1992: 16). In June, 1989 the refugee count of Mauritanians returning to their homeland was approximately 170,000 (Belotteau 1989: 41, 42). In recent years, the left bank of the Senegal River has become the holding area for thousands of refugees separated from family members and former lives in Mauritania. These dispossessed dream of being reunited with kin and resuming normal lives as cultivators, fishermen, livestock producers, and day laborers in their villages and towns of origin.

CONCEPTUALIZING CONFLICT

The Senegal-Mauritania conflict is symptomatic of a trend within modern states of heightened competition among various groups for human and natural resources (i.e., group entitlements in employment, health, education, land, loan guarantees, etc.). Journalists and social scientists alike have attempted to identify the causes underlying the ethnic fratricide in Senegal and Mauritania. Numerous commentaries have been advanced, the majority of which use a structural materialist approach to explain the ethnic violence. The focus has largely been on the issue of resource access, particularly access to land, which is today a highly prized commodity in the Senegal Valley. Since completion of the Manantali Dam in Mali in 1987, and the anti-saline intrusion barrage at Diama near the river's mouth in 1986, regional development efforts have concentrated on commodified rice production in irrigated perimeters. In the haste to bolster agricultural production, the conversion of some of the most fertile recession farmlands to irrigation has provoked volatile land disputes among peasant smallholders and urban elites and sparked serious debate among scholars and experts about the future path of development to be taken in the region.[8] Authors offer different interpretations of the weight to be assigned to the environment and physical ecology (Santoir 1990a), political ecology and economy (Horowitz 1989, 1991), domestic and inter-state political relations (Parker 1991), and Arab-African national identity (Baduel 1989, Stewart 1989, Santoir 1990b) in spawning widespread violence and unrest across national boundaries.

This essay seeks to demonstrate how structural and material conditions in tandem with the motivating forces of the individual or group actor give rise to conflict. The macroanalytical focus on structure and the micro-level emphasis on individual and group actors merge in the synthesis of two recent exposés on ethnic conflict. The different theoretical views on ethnic discord of Horowitz (1985) and Tambiah (1989) are complementary paradigms when understood in a broader context. What follows is a brief summary of the authors' perspectives.

In his comprehensive work, *Ethnic Groups in Conflict*, Horowitz (1985: 140) argues that paradigms that cast ethnic rivalries in either a materialist mold, as the product of modernization, or in a cultural idiom, as the result of invidious plural ethnic tendencies, do not go far enough in explaining "the important role of ethnic-group anxiety and apprehension....None treats the intensity and violent character of ethnic conflict as specially worthy of explanation."

> Attention needs to be paid to developing theory that links elite and mass concerns and answers the insistent question of why the followers follow. The role of apprehension and group psychology needs specification, as does the importance of symbolic controversies in ethnic conflict. The sheer passion expended in pursuing ethnic conflict calls out for an explanation that does justice to the realm of the feelings. It is necessary to account, not merely for ambition, but for antipathy. A bloody phenomenon cannot be explained by a bloodless theory (*ibid.*).

Horowitz's critique of a materialist approach to ethnic conflict is reflected in a 1989 essay by Tambiah, who elaborates on the increasing "ethnic politicization" taking place within the framework of a capitalist world economy. Contradictory processes of global cultural homogenization and local socioeconomic diversification and differentiation (Roseberry 1982: 202; Tambiah 1989: 341) exist concurrently. According to Tambiah, what separates contemporary anthropological discourse from its recent Barthian past in the quest for a more profound understanding of "ethnicity" is the endeavor to explain the present ground swell of ethnic militancy in the world today. In the 1960s, anthropologists studying ethnic identity were preoccupied with the investigation of permeability and process (Barth 1969). Today, Tambiah (1989: 339, 341) turns our attention to the new challenge that confronts anthropology — to make sense of the heightened "politicization of ethnicity" in contemporary states:

> ...Barth's edited volume...seems now, scarcely two decades later, too benign and tranquil for the study of the ethnic conflicts accompanied by collective violence that rage today....The central problems posed by our present phase of ethnic conflicts are startingly [sic] different, arising out of an intensified "politicization of ethnicity" and issuing in conflicts between member groups of a state and polity, which itself is thought to be in crisis ("the crisis of the state")....the main problem to be explained is "why ethnicity becomes more easily politicizable in

modern society and in those societies on the threshold of modernization, as compared with earlier phases of history" (Tägil 1984: 36). The present context of politicized ethnicity is distinctly a marked phase in the political and economic history of newly independent countries.

In sum, whereas Tambiah attributes ethnic conflict to the strain of differential resource allocation in a competitive world capitalist order, Horowitz attributes the collective violence of individual elites and their constituent ethnic groups to factors such as "ethnic-group anxiety and apprehension" and the role of "relative group worth" (1985: 140, 143, 213). The global or external conceptualization of conflict (materialist structural paradigm of Tambiah) and the local or internal configuration (group psychological actor-oriented model of Horowitz) need not be mutually exclusive. In reinterpreting the conflict between Senegal and Mauritania, this essay suggests that the distinct group psychology of ethnic collectivities as constituted by processes of self-identity (which Horowitz [1985: 143, 185] equates with concepts such as "relative group worth," "group legitimacy," "group entitlement," and "group cleavage and comparison"), has as its structural underpinning a political economic dynamic of capitalist expansion and economic differentiation.

Enmities among ethnic groups are the product of years of intergroup contestation over territory and resources. The bloodletting on the streets of Dakar and Nouakchott in 1989, as well as sporadic incidents of violence on the northern border in the wake of the urban melee, must be placed within their proper historical, cultural, and socio-political context. What is presented here is the unique sequencing of events, that over time created sentiments of mutual distrust and hostility. The border incidents at Diawara and Matam awakened these latent antagonisms, and in so doing set off the deadly spark that cost the lives and loss of property for many, brought serious physical injury to hundreds of people, and triggered the forcible expulsion of thousands of foreign and national residents from each country.

The bases of group identity and self-legitimation and the forces of modernization intersect when the issue of group entitlement is situated in diachronic perspective. By briefly tracing three phases of regional history — 1) the permeability of pre-colonial boundaries by agrarian communities on the northern Senegal frontier, 2) French colonial policies of cultural, political, and economic hegemony over black sub-saharan Africans and Arabo-Berber Maures, and 3) post-colonial state initiatives of agrarian land reform and agricultural modernization in the Senegal Valley — it will be shown that state policies of resource disbursement have been instrumental in distancing black and Arabo-Berber populations. In effect, the historical process of evolving use rights over land and political participation in multi-ethnic nation building (with important implications for group entitlements to land, legitimation of cultural identities through language preservation, and economic opportunity through political networks of state access) are the basis for understanding how "group cleavages" and "group comparisons" are formed (ibid.: 143). The transboundary division of ethnic communities in the Senegal Valley by means of inter-state policies of inclusion or exclusion to land, linguistic parity, and political autonomy has bred periodic bouts of anxiety, apprehension, and finally — conflict — spilling over both banks of the river on a massive scale in recent times.

Tambiah (1989: 346) identifies three critical scenarios in which the subjugation of an ethnic minority to the discriminatory policies of an ethnic majority leads to a deterioration of inter-community relations and ultimately to an outbreak of hostilities among competing groups. These are: 1) a "severe erosion of niche-equilibrium" among foreign specialized minorities (commonly referred to in the literature as "middlemen minorities" [Bonacich 1973]); 2) the slow and progressive physical displacement of "satellite ethnic/tribal minorities" from their peripheral frontier homelands by "majorities entrenched at the center;" and 3) "differential incorporation" whereby the claims by a particular ethnic collectivity to political ascendance based on demographic superiority and/or historical precedence of occupation lead to a process of "structural asymmetrical pluralism" that is resented and contested by the ethnic minority. Collectively, these scenarios are central in understanding the interplay of group psychology and global capital in ethnic conflict. In each case, a close parallel may be drawn to the context of violence as it occurred in Senegal and Mauritania. Attention now turns to the regional history and geographical context in which the three scenarios mentioned above have been played out at the crossroads of the Sahel, where North and South, Arabian Maghreb and sub-saharan Africa, adjoin.

ENMITIES OLD AND NEW: HISTORICAL ANTECEDENTS OF CONFLICT

In the early 20th century, the Senegal River was designated by the French colonial government as the boundary separating Senegal from Mauritania. The fertile soils at the river's edge and in the adjacent lateral floodplain supported a mosaic of ethnic communities engaged in riverine fishing, floodplain and dryland farming, and transhumant and nomadic livestock production. For centuries, the river basin functioned as an oasis in a semi-desert region, enabling humans and animals alike to prevail over intermittent drought and climatic variability in this harsh sahelian landscape.

Directly north of the Senegal River in the western Sahara, the vast barren desert region of *Shinquit* (present day Mauritania) became home to a nomadic population of Muslim scholars (*zawiya*), descendants of the Sanhadja Berbers (Almoravids) who migrated into the region between the 8th and 11th centuries (Chassey 1977: 32). Arab warriors (*hassani*) of the Banu Ma'qil tribe (from which Hassaniya, the official Mauritanian language is taken) occupied the same region several centuries later, arriving during the late 14th century (Stewart 1973: 13). Descending from these two principal groups are Mauritanians of Arabo-Berber stock, known as *bidan* ("white" in Arabic). Today, they are at the apex of a three-tiered Maure social hierarchy of nobles, middle laborers (former slaves or *haratin*) and tributaries, and slaves (*'abid*), musicians, and artisans (Chassey 1977: 84–90, 1984: 27, 28; Coupe 1990: 60).[9]

Until the recent period of protracted sahelian drought beginning in the late 1960s, many *bidan* eked out a modest existence in the desert as nomadic herders.[10] The *haratin*, who farmed the fertile floodplains on the right bank of the Senegal River, provided tribute in grains to their *bidan* superiors. The *'abid* slaves lived in the remote desert interior cultivating oasis lands and tending the herds of their *bidan* masters under conditions of harsh exploitation and poverty.

Prior to the French policy of regional pacification in the late 19th century, the Senegal River valley served as a corridor for the movement of trade goods and people between the Maghreb and sub-saharan Sudan. Settled principally on the left bank of the Senegal River before the mid-18th century were three ethnic polities: the Wolof in the Kingdom of Waalo in the lower valley, the Haalpulaar of Fuuta Tooro in the middle valley, and the Soninke of Gajaaga in the upper valley (see Figure 7.2). On the right bank were the Maure emirates of Trarza, Brakna, and Tagant.[11] Frontier relations were often hostile as warring bands of Mauritanian warriors (*hassani*) would descend from the northern desert, slip unchecked across the river, and raid isolated encampments and small farming enclaves in the floodplain and adjacent upland plateau, capturing young women, men, and children as slaves, and simultaneously pillaging goods, food and animals. Santoir (1990a: 556) notes that this customary form of raiding, or *razzia*, was not carried out exclusively in the middle valley by *hassani* warriors, but rather was a common practice of FulBe and Haalpulaar warriors as well, constituting an institutionalized "mode of transfer" of resources within an integrated regional economy.

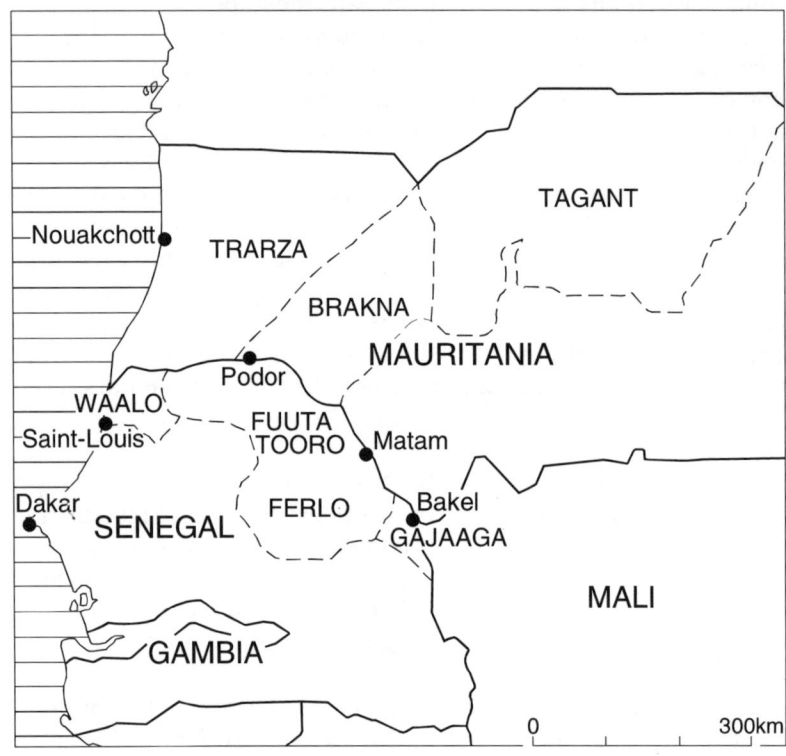

Figure 7.2. Pre-Eighteenth Century Ethnic Polities in the Senegal River Valley.

In addition to being the central location of raiding parties across the river, the northern frontier also attracted FulBe herders in search of nutrient-rich pasture. During the rains, Senegalese herders would move north across the river, grazing their animals on the seasonal grasslands of southern Mauritania. With the onset of the dry season, FulBe herders in the Mauritanian interior would move south across the river, pasturing their animals on the crop residues of the floodplain after harvest. During this post-harvest period of open grazing, known as the *ñaangal*, the manuring of farmers' fields and the exchange of dairy products for grain and fish would assure the reproductive survival of herding, farming, and fishing communities. Thus, the river frontier during pre-colonial history was characterized by a high degree of temporal and spatial permeability and flux of populations. Relations among the neighboring Maure and black African populations became characterized by mutual but contradictory associations of complementarity and conflict (ibid.: 559).

The Taming of the Northern Frontier: French Merchant Capital and Colonial Pacification

With the arrival in the 18th century of French merchant capital eager to extend its sphere of commercial control into the heart of Africa, relations among inhabitants on both sides of the river were ineluctably altered. The relevance of French colonial dominion over sub-saharan and Arabo-Berber peoples of the Senegal basin in fostering ethnic dissonance has not been adequately explored.

Colonial conquest and the consolidation of disparate and, for the most part, inimical ethnic bodies within a corporate French polity, bound by coercive measures of commercial regulation, codification of law, and mandatory tax policy (Tambiah 1989: 341), left an indelible mark on the collective conscience of the *bidan* Maure community. French interest in the region initially took the form of mercantile trade. Trade evolved along the Senegal River at trading entrepots or "escales" such as Podor, Matam, and Bakel. Salt from the Sahara was exchanged for grain and livestock from Senegal and gum harvested by *haratin* Maures was traded for imported guinée cloth via the French colonial capital at Saint Louis (Schmitz 1989: 70). Ongoing warfare and raiding for slaves between the Maure emirates and Senegalese powers south of the river eventually led to French pacification of the region in the late 19th century. By the turn of the century, Wolof and Haalpulaar communities had managed to recover and cultivate lands lost earlier to the Trarza and Brakna emirates on the north bank during slave raids that forced blacks to flee south into Senegal (Park et al. 1990: 9).

The early 20th century witnessed the progressive resettlement and recuperation of right bank land by left bank inhabitants and the increased presence of FulBe herders in southern Mauritania. Santoir (1990a: 560) attributes resettlement of the right bank by the Haalpulaar to three main factors: 1) lower livestock population densities allowing for a larger pastoral reserve during drought years as well as during periods of abundant rainfall after 1950; 2) livestock requisitioning by France during the two world wars as well as livestock epidemics forcing herders to flee north; and 3) evasion of taxation on animals by colonial administrative authorities. The movement of black Africans north across the river coincided with a reverse migration of *bidan* south into Senegal's groundnut basin, where they opened small retail shops in small towns and cities to capitalize on the burgeoning groundnut trade in the region. Strong religious affinities between Mauritania and Senegal were also established at this time through Muslim brotherhoods (Qadiriyya and Tijaniyya). The marked shift in commerce to the groundnut basin also contributed to the regional decline of the Senegal Valley and extensive outmigration by the latter half of the 20th century (Becker and Lericollais 1989: 151).

In 1903, Mauritania was declared a protectorate of France and colonial officials based in Saint Louis administered control of the Mauritanian hinterlands through a policy of indirect rule akin to that of the British, placing regional authority in the hands of *hassani* emirs (Stewart 1972: 385, 386). Soon after, however, French authorities began delegating more political tasks to francophone black Africans educated and trained in Senegal, assigning them to important administrative posts in the Mauritanian outback (Stewart 1989: 162). The northern desert lands were administered as a subsidiary of French commercial interests in Senegal. Imported goods destined for Mauritania were shipped north by land to Saint Louis, before proceeding further north. Overall, French policy aims and infrastructural development in the region were largely directed toward Senegal, with Mauritania serving more as a satellite to be incorporated within the administrative colonial core at Saint Louis (ibid.: 162, 163).

Ethnic Cleavage and the Quest for National Identity in Mauritania

The French policy of geopolitical consolidation of Maure society under a francophone black African regional polity precipitated political debate among Mauritanians in the 1950s over the direction the emerging nation's identity should take at independence. Mauritania found itself at the crossroads of a crisis of national cultural identity, forced to forge one of two paths: that of political inclusion (implying a pluralistic culture of Arab/black African identity), or political exclusion (based on a monolithic Arab identity).

The political debate over national identity found its overt expression prior to independence in the establishment of several regional political parties. The UPM Party (*Union Progressiste Mauritanienne*) espoused a pro-French policy of regional integration, favoring the merger of Mauritania with Senegal and Mali in a pluralist society of

Arab-black African unity. The EM Party (*Entente Mauritanienne*) sought an exclusive Arab nationalist polity. Finally, the FNLM (*Front National de Libération Mauritanien*) advocated the pan-Arab union of Mauritania with Greater Morocco (Baduel 1989: 16, 17). The early voices of dissent among black Mauritanians in the Senegal River Valley opposed to any political platform of national Arab identity united in forming two party blocks, the BDG (*Bloc Démocratique du Gorgol*) in 1956, and the UOVF (*Union des Originaires de la Vallée du Fleuve*) in 1957 (Stewart 1972: 388, 389; Baduel 1989: 18). These two groups were the precursors to a more militant, politicized movement for black African parity known as FLAM (*Forces de Libération Africaine de Mauritanie*) that was to emerge out of growing political unrest and dissent among black Mauritanians in the 1980s.

The partisan views of the pro-Arab and black African parties on the political orientation to be adopted by the Mauritanian state were vociferously expressed during the National Congress at Aleg in 1958 (Baduel 1989: 25, 26). Stewart (1972: 392) notes that during this period, the incipient rise of a black non-Maure political conscience served as the primary catalyst in the emergence of a new Maure identity in which past animosities between *hassani* warriors and *zawiya* marabouts were laid to rest.

In sum, the ethno-politicization of black Mauritanians at independence and a colonial legacy of French political and economic domination gave rise to a concerted policy of arabization by *bidan* Mauritanians in the post-independence period.

Group Entitlement and Arabization at Independence

Several scholars writing on ethnicity have underscored the significance of language in conferring political advantage in a multicultural context. Horowitz (1985: 219, 220) refers to language as "a symbol of domination....the quintessential entitlement issue." Tambiah (1989: 345) reaffirms this position, suggesting that "'language' is not a mere communicative device, but has implications for educational advantage, occupation and historical legitimation of social precedence." In Mauritania, shortly after independence, arabization played a key role in conferring political advantage and "entitlement" to *bidan* Maures who had staunchly resisted attempts at cultural assimilation and participation in the colonial system of French education, and who moved quickly to assume control of the government bureaucracy at the expense of a black non-Arab speaking population in the Senegal Valley. Thus blacks, who had previously gained favor with the French as a result of their active participation in the colonial school system, now suddenly found themselves disadvantaged vis-à-vis Maures.

Soon after Mauritanian independence, President Ould Daddah proclaimed Arabic as the national language in 1961 (French maintaining the status of "official language") (Park et al. 1990: 12). Movement on the part of the *bidan* government to extricate itself from any postcolonial French allegiance gathered momentum in 1965 via departure from the OAM (*Organisation Africaine et Malgache*) and the promulgation of laws 65–025 and 65–026 mandating Arabic in all primary and secondary schools (Baduel 1989: 24). The educational decrees had the incendiary effect of fomenting unrest and formal protest among black lycée students and teachers in Nouakchott on 4 January, 1966. The protests were immediately and forcefully put down by bands of armed *haratin* mobilized under the supervision of *bidan* nobles.[12] During the incident, 6 people died and an estimated 70 more were injured (ibid.: 26).

In protest of the violence and systematic under-representation of blacks in positions of government political authority, a Manifesto of 19 was issued in February, 1966. Language again resurfaced as the source of controversy in 1979 when another government decree was issued augmenting the role of Arabic in education (Omaar and Fleischman 1991: 36). Protests and violence again erupted leaving 2 dead (Park et al. 1990: 5). In addition to educational policies promoting arabization of Maure society, other commentaries have noted a concerted strategy on the part of the government to project an exclusively Arab image void of any black African presence through the media, in bank notes, stamps, airline advertising, and other forms of public relations (Omaar and Fleischman 1991: 38; FLAM 1991: 18).

Additional measures taken by the government in favor of a pro-Arab/anti-French stance included creation of a national currency and abandonment of the zone franc in 1973, membership in the Arab League in 1973, and nationalization of the mining industry in 1974 (Baduel 1989: 22–24). Between 1972 and 1974, Mauritania steered a new course in international relations, shifting its political allegiances away from the West in favor of the arab Middle East (ibid.).

CAPITAL TRANSFER FROM THE CORE TO THE PERIPHERY

Following independence in Senegal and Mauritania in 1960, ethnic tensions between *bidan* Maures and black communities in the Senegal Valley worsened. The deterioration in relations may be attributed to two factors that strongly effected structural change in the domestic economies of both countries during the 1970s and 1980s: 1) massive donor lending and foreign capital investment in the damming of the Senegal River, a strategy intended to modernize the agricultural sector and boost food production after two decades of sahelian drought, and 2) a foreign debt crisis prompting drastic reductions in domestic spending and the dismantling of public sector finance under the rigorous guidelines of structural adjustment laid down by the World Bank.

As capital flows and development resources under the purview of the *aprés-barrages* or post-dam initiative began to be funneled to the northern valley in the mid-1970s for investment in modern pump irrigation agriculture, the issue of group entitlement, most notably concerning land, emerged once again as the Achilles heel of ethnic discourse.

Redefining the Landscape: Drought and Development on the Borderlands

The onset of drought conditions in the Sahel in the late 1960s exacerbated longstanding differences among farmers and herders on both sides of the river, and became the pivotal force in reshaping the region's physical and socio-political landscape. The devastating losses of livestock to herders in Mauritania profoundly transformed a predominantly pastoral society into a nation of urban squatters huddled at the margins of desert towns like Nouakchott and Nouadhibou in poor shanty-like quarters or *bidonvilles*. Estimates cite a drop in the nomadic population of Mauritania from 80–85 percent of the national total between 1965–70 to 17–23 percent between 1980–85 (Andriamirado 1989a: 34; Baduel 1989: 38). The urban population rose precipitously from 2 percent in 1950 to 40 percent in 1990 (Baduel 1989: 38), and national herd losses were estimated at 45 percent (cattle 54 percent, camels 10 percent, sheep and goats 17 percent) during the drought years of 1968–73, 1976, and 1982–84 (Ould Cheikh 1983, in Coupe 1990: 141).

Santoir (1990a: 571) observes that in the drought years after 1972, the near extinction of semi-nomadism as a way of life among the *bidan* Maures was accompanied by the rural exodus of a servile labor reserve of *haratin* and *'abid* sharecroppers cultivating the recession floodplains and desert oases of their *bidan* patrons. *Haratin* and *'abid* alike sought out the sanctuary of towns and cities staffed with government services and international famine relief for victims of the drought. The abrupt diminution of a *bidan* presence in the pastoral sector and their increasing presence in the petty retail trade (notably in Senegal) left abandoned grazing lands open to colonization by FulBe herders by the mid-1970s (ibid.). At the same time, *haratin* dromedary nomads were forced by the drought to move south into Haalpulaar farmlands in search of better pasture (ibid.: 573). This reconfiguration of social and spatial boundaries, along with a new campaign on the part of the *bidan* government to administer post-drought taxes on livestock and appropriate land and animals by informal modes of coercion heightened tensions between *bidan* and *haratin* Maures on the one hand, and black farmers and herders (largely Haalpulaar and nomadic FulBe) on the other.

By the end of the 1970s and a decade of near constant drought, both the Senegalese and Mauritanian economies were in need of vigorous revival through massive infusions of investment capital. The construction of the Manantali and Diama dams on the Senegal River, financed by Arab and European funds,[13] was hailed as the perfect elixir for the economic woes of both countries. The dams are intended to provide a cheap source of hydroelectric power and shore up food production deficits and mounting trade imbalances in grain imports that have been rising steadily over the past three decades. The optimistic prospect of introducing a double season rice crop is touted by ardent supporters of the project (GERSAR/CACG et al. 1989, 1990) as the silver bullet solution to the agroeconomic ills of the region.

The introduction of irrigated agriculture began in earnest in the mid-1970s, and after nearly two decades, 56,000 hectares (40,000 in Senegal, 16,000 in Mauritania) have come under development. The long range goal for the region is to develop approximately 375,000 hectares (240,000 in Senegal, 125,000 in Mauritania, and 9,000 in Mali), of which 100,000 are to be irrigated by the year 2015, at a net annual increase of just over 2,500 hectares (Horowitz 1991: 173). Even with the projected expansion, grain production will fall far short of meeting planners expectations of the highly touted "ricebowl" region to feed the populations of both nations.[14]

In Mauritania, the devastating effects of drought on the economic wellbeing of the country were compounded by a second disaster of human rather than natural agency — involvement in the Polisario conflict. Between 1975 and 1982, the war effort in the Spanish Sahara accounted for 30–40 percent of the national budget. With the marked drop in world market prices for copper and iron (Baduel 1989: 31), the country's total foreign debt mushroomed from $600 million in 1978 to $1.8 billion by 1987, or approximately 250 percent of its GDP, making Mauritania one of the world's most indebted countries per capita (Jeune Afrique 1990, in Baduel 1989: 41). This ruinous foreign policy, dovetailing with the infirmities of drought, brought the nation financially to its knees. Feeling its back to the wall, the *bidan* administration turned its full attention to the Senegal River Valley, where it hoped to rise from the abyss of fiscal disaster. In casting all its eggs in the basket of agrarian land reform and privatized tenure, the Maure government had prepared its nest for the birth of a new modern creature — irrigation agriculture.

Agrarian Land Reform and Rising Tensions in the Senegal Valley

Eager to transform a long neglected regional economy into an agrarian heartland, the Senegalese and Mauritanian governments embarked on a program of national land reform aimed at reapportioning resources both to state and private sector interests, foreign as well as national, capable of investing heavily in rice irrigation. Under the criterion of *mise en valeur* (ie., capital valorization), national land reforms in Mauritania (1960) and Senegal (1964), followed by additional decrees in the 1970s and 1980s, set in motion the institutional jural mechanisms facilitating the progressive erosion and transfer of common property rights from the smallholding peasantry to an elite cadre of government functionaries, private commercial entrepreneurs, and maraboutic clerisy of Islamic sectarian leaders.[15]

While both countries attempted to shift customary ownership and use rights from communal to individualized collectivities for the purposes of rice irrigation, the government policy in Mauritania took on a more capitalized form, allowing for the disposition of land rights through purchase and entitlement.[16] The initial Mauritanian decree (No. 60.139) in 1960 granting the state eminent domain over vacant lands (*terre morte*) after ten years (Park et al. 1990: 12; Ba 1991: 260), set the stage for a new era of land speculation in the 1980s. Land ordinances in Mauritania in 1983 and 1984 (Nos. 83.127/CSMN and 84.009) effectively individualized tenure, thereby opening the door for state access to large tracts of land for irrigation development (Park et al. 1990: 15; Ba 1991: 264).

This was followed soon after by a series of ministerial directives or "*circulaires*" in April of 1984 (No. 0005) and July–August, 1985 (Nos. 007 and 00020) enabling *bidan* government officials to circumvent certain restrictions on the size of land holdings for appropriation and to "set up agricultural development schemes without passing through the verification of ownership and compensation procedures of the 1983–84 legislation" (Park et al. 1990: 15). With this legislation the state took away local control over conflict resolution in land disputes. As Park et al., (ibid.: 17) note, the consequences of this state action were often grim:

> Traditionally, cultivators could always reach an agreement because each community knew the limits of its territory and its holdings. Even if there was conflict on the border of their territories, customary law, seconded by *shari'a*, provided a means of resolution. With the abolition of traditional tenure and the application of the 1983–84 legislation, only the government can settle tenure issues....this has led to many casualties and even to whole villages being eliminated by the government.

By 1985–1986, additional government circulars (Nos. 020/MINT and 00013/MINT/SG/DAT) from the Interior Minister to regional administrators accelerated the pace of expropriation of peasant land holdings to private sector interests from Nouakchott and other urban areas (Coupe 1990: 348, 349; Crousse 1991: 284). Innumerable instances have been documented of acts of land grabbing by *bidan* entrepreneurs and government elites from Nouakchott and elsewhere. Among the most noteworthy accounts of land expropriation, are the loss of 21,356 hectares of classified forests, traditional grazing routes, and national highway land between Boghe and Rosso in the Trarza region to *bidan* entrepreneurs from Nouakchott; the loss of *haratin* lands at R'Gheywat; and the seizure of Wolof lands at Bren (Ba 1991: 266, 267). In Rosso and neighboring departments of the Trarza, Ba (ibid.: 267) also exposes the abuses of defective land entitlement procedure, where 8,245 hectares were registered under the names of 56 people (an equivalent of 147 ha/person), many of them fictitious. In addition, land purchases of 20 hectares for 200,000 UM (Mauritanian *ouguiya*) by regional administrators and businessmen became commonplace on the Mauritanian right bank (ibid.).

A 1987 report of the Mauritanian parastatal SONADER (National Society of Rural Development), promoting irrigation agriculture in the region, provides a candid commentary on the frontier ethic (Bloom 1990) of land expropriation by well-positioned elites:

> Now a peasant can get up one morning to begin the work of clearing new land belonging to him, and find an urban entrepreneur already working there without his having been informed (Ministère du Développement Rural, SONADER 1987: 1, in Coupe 1990: 354).

Accompanying the changes in land valorization for purposes of rice irrigation in Mauritania was the formation of a new social class of rural proletarian field labor composed of black *haratin*, sedentarized FulBe agropastoralists, and Senegalese and Malian farmers who were paid 3–4,000 UM/month for long, onerous hours on the rice schemes (Ba 1991: 268, 269). Senegalese technicians were routinely hired as skilled equipment operators on the perimeters as well (Coupe 1990: 349).

The proliferation of land seizures predates the circulars of 1985–86 noted above. The Minister of the Interior himself ironically acknowledges the abuses of illegal land concessions by regional authorities and chides his subordinates in 1984 for their excesses and liberal interpretations of the land code:

> Finally, I turn your attention to the innumerable abuses of power committed by administrative authorities with regards to state land concessions. Several authorities have accorded rural concessions while they have no authorization before the present decree [No. 0005/MINT of 14 April, 1984]. This attitude denotes not only an ignorance of the law...even negligence of the rights of the State that the territorial authority must faithfully represent. In any event, the breaches of the present circular, and the acts of concession issued in defiance of the reglementation will be severely sanctioned (Crousse 1991: 294).

Despite culpability acknowledged on the part of *bidan* government officials themselves, land privatization continued unabated after the decrees of 1985–86.[17] It finally reached its apogee when a local directive (No. 119/DB) initiated in 1988 by the prefect of Boghe in the middle valley reapportioned nine plots varying in size from 20–689 hectares to *bidan* speculators from the north (Andriamirado 1989a: 34; Park et al. 1990: 17). This event, along with numerous other land seizures, prompted black leaders of the Tijaniyya Islamic caliphate in the Senegal Valley to call for the organization of self-defense militias to resist land seizures by the state and to warn the Mauritanian government in June, 1988 that "if it [the border situation] is not firmly resolved in reasonable time this problem may bring grave consequences to the peace of the northern frontier and the surrounding sub-region" (Andriamirado 1989a: 34, 36). The pernicious seizure of valuable floodplain lands belonging to black Senegalese and Mauritanian farmers, mostly Haalpulaar, and a general state trend toward "bidanization" of government resources and services (arabization of education, preferential hiring of *bidan* in government posts, etc.) prompted black Haalpulaar leaders and intellectuals in 1986 to form a militant organization, FLAM (African Liberation Force in Mauritania), in defense of black Mauritanian interests. FLAM members distributed the "Manifesto of Oppressed Black Mauritanians" at the 1986 OAU (Organization of

African Unity) summit in Harare calling for violent resistance to continued land sales and seizures by Maure merchants (Coupe 1990: 351).

FLAM leaders also protested the preferential disbursement of loans and credit through national banks to *bidan* entrepreneurs for agricultural investment in large-scale irrigation schemes. A Mauritanian government crackdown on FLAM dissidents and intellectuals including the author of the manifesto, Tene Youssef Gueye, resulted in arrests, imprisonment, and torture. This fueled protests in Nouakchott, Nouadhibou, Boghe, and Kaedi (Coupe 1990: 352–354). Further violence and rioting in Mauritanian cities in 1988 was triggered by the execution of three high-ranking officers and the pronouncement of eighteen life sentences in Oualata prison following an aborted coup attempt in October, 1987 by Haalpulaar military officers. By late 1988, Gueye and two officers of the coup had died while in prison (ibid.: 355–360).

Violent confrontation over land had been escalating prior to 1988, as black Senegalese farmers were forcibly expelled from their farm lands on the right bank by *haratin* communities defending the capital interests of their *bidan* superiors.[18] The clashes on the border prompted an August, 1988 meeting of Senegalese and Mauritanian officials and the formation of an inter-state commission to identify affected areas of land dispute and to institute measures assuring the maintenance of transborder mobility of populations and the equitable access to farmlands by parties on both banks of the river. Disagreements between the two parties following visits to village sites of land contestation led to the failure of border diplomacy and a resumption of inter-ethnic hostilities over farmlands on the right bank.

Upping the Ante: Frontier Retribution and the Prelude to Chaos

With tensions mounting along the border prior to the ethnic clashes in 1989, a chain of events spurred by the governments of each country fanned discord among inhabitants on both sides of the river. Annoyed by what was perceived to be an outright assault on the transboundary farmlands of their northern border residents, Senegalese officials retaliated in November, 1988, by enforcing an earlier government decree (No. 322 on 11 March, 1986) restricting dromedary grazing below a line extending across the Ferlo region from Potou to Dara, Linguere, and Matam. The total number of camels was not to exceed 6,000 head and only 2 males and 1 female were permitted per family (Santoir 1990a: 570). Mauritanian herders lost 20,000 camels (in addition to 30,000 cattle and 100,000 sheep) during the seizures (Dahmani 1989: 24) and responded soon after by setting up a temporary embargo along the border to prevent entry of Senegalese trucks carrying vegetable oil, animal feed, and fresh vegetables. The Senegalese immediately responded in kind, instituting a blockade at the border town of Rosso on all fresh fish, mineral water, and food imports from Mauritania.

This low-level trade dispute finally ceased in February, 1989. At this time, only two months prior to the eruption of hostilities at Diawara, the Mauritanian government took the long awaited step of joining the Maghreb Union, and in so doing, intensified the inflamed racial sensibilities of black communities settled in the region.

The Epilogue to Conflict: Frontier Raiders, Forlorn Victims, Forsaken Lands

In the aftermath of the violence of April, 1989, diplomatic relations were severed between the two states. The Mauritanian government pressed its claim of indemnization for large losses of property belonging to Maure shopkeepers, the confiscation of livestock, and assets frozen in Senegal's banks. Senegal advanced irredentist claims to land on the right bank and called for the redrawing of the northern boundary based on a 1933 French colonial charter. Both nations stood teetering at the brink of warfare by December, 1989, as minor military clashes along the river went either unnoticed or underreported by the international press. Heavy exchanges of artillery fire on the border occurred on numerous occasions as did Mauritanian training missions near the river where loud explosions were frequent by late 1989 and early 1990. One of the most sustained military engagements occurred on 20 December, 1989 at Diamel, a small fishing village on the left bank 2 kilometers downstream from Matam. This confrontation, and several others, as well as sporadic gunfire by armed *haratin* civil militia at Senegalese fishermen on the river and at left bank farmers, resulted in scores of casualties, including on occasion, innocent women and children. Several sources documented the Iraqi shipment of arms, mortars, SAM-7 missiles, rocket launchers, and Iraqi military advisors in anticipation of ensuing warfare (Africa Confidential 1990: 3, 1991: 6; King 1990: 18; Andriamirado 1989b: 32; Soudan 1990: 42).

During the height of the conflict in 1989, thousands of black Senegalese and Mauritanian nationals were forcibly expelled from

Mauritania while many others voluntarily fled their villages to avoid threats of physical attack and loss of property. Many crossed the river on foot or by boat, arriving in Senegal tired, hungry, and with few if any belongings.[19] A large number claiming Mauritanian nationality appear to have been expelled either as a result of putative Senegalese descent, or because Mauritanian identity cards were obtained after 1966, in some instances fraudulently (New York Times 1989: 1, 4; Park et al. 1990: 20). Contesting the claims of Mauritanian authorities, one survey of FulBe refugees in the middle valley (Matam department) reveals that an overwhelming majority (>90 percent) were born in Mauritania (Santoir 1990b: 595). Many villages on the right bank are alleged to have been torched and razed or systematically emptied of black Haalpulaar residents. Park et al., (1990: 2) report the clearing of 140 Mauritanian villages of their entire population, and cite an estimate by Soulier (1989) that 50 percent of the Haalpulaar community downstream from Podor was expelled from the right bank by mid-1989. Many of these villages were then repopulated by *haratin* Maures relocated in the valley to farm new irrigation schemes. In addition to serving as a convenient labor reserve, this population of relocatees functions as the armed guard of the *bidan* government, positioned on the front line of defense against FulBe herders, and Haalpulaar fishermen and farmers attempting to cross the river (El Hassan 1992 in Sherbinin 1992: 7; Omaar and Fleischman 1991: 38).

By 30 June, 1989, the Matam department had received more than 26,000 refugees of which an estimated 80 percent were FulBe herders.[20] Three-quarters of them cultivated floodplain lands in Mauritania (Santoir 1990b: 581). A geographical survey undertaken by Lericollais and Diallo (1980) in 1973 provides the only exhaustive assessment of the magnitude of transboundary farming. Seck's (1991: 305) recent analysis of the 1973 data reveals that 11.7 percent (37,498) of all floodplain farmers in the Senegal Valley cultivated fields on the opposite side of the river. The Senegalese, moreover, represented 79 percent (29,771) of all transborder farmers, while their Mauritanian counterparts accounted for only 21 percent (7,727) (ibid.). Although these figures are now dated, they provide, nonetheless, a rough measure of the proportional losses of highly valued floodplain lands to both Senegalese and Mauritanian farmers since closure of the northern boundary.

As farmers and herders fled each country, significant numbers of ruminant livestock were confiscated or abandoned. The animals reported by Matam officials as missing, stolen, or confiscated as of

30 June, 1989 include: 1) Mauritanian livestock: 9,399 bovines, 16,543 ovines and caprines; 2) Senegalese livestock: 3,190 bovines, 4,012 ovines and caprines.

To recuperate personal herds, as well as those of individual clients, FulBe "commandos" or *ruggiyankooBe* deported from Mauritania began launching night time raiding parties, slipping back across the border.[21] By the end of 1989, late night FulBe raiding excursions into Mauritania had become a lucrative enterprise for many. Santoir (1990b: 590) notes the payment of 500,000 FCFA (approximately $1,800) by one client for recovery of his lost herds. It is interesting that the recent episodes of ethnic conflict in Senegal and Mauritania have witnessed a reactivation of customary raiding patterns in both urban and rural settings — the alliance of *bidan-haratin* ties (patron-clientelism) during the *razzia* in Mauritanian towns and cities, and the revival of the *ruggo* among FulBe herders on the border. All too frequently, casualties of Mauritanian civilians and military, and FulBe herders alike resulted from these furtive missions. The unchecked success of these raids in terms of substantial herd losses in Mauritania was central in pushing border tensions to the brink of full-scale warfare by early 1990.

The sudden, massive influx of deportees, many with extended family ties to members in the receiving villages, overwhelmed the resource capacity of local communities to feed and clothe large numbers of destitute people. In the middle valley, the Matam department experienced a 50 percent population increase almost overnight as refugees spilled across the border in the initial months after April, 1989 (Santoir 1990b: 590). Data presented below from a survey of refugees in one border village provide an example of the degree of wealth in farmland and livestock lost by some farmers and herders.

Located 17 kilometers upstream from Matam on the Senegal River, the village of Thiemping became sanctuary to 392 Haalpulaar farmers, fishers, and FulBe herders from area villages and hamlets across the river. Between May and July, 1989, the village population rose by almost 32 percent. Two-thirds of the incoming refugees were transhumant FulBe pastoralists, the remaining one-third Haalpulaar agropastoralists and fishers. Among the deported, 47.2 percent claimed status as Senegalese nationals (6.6 percent as repatriates, 40.6 percent as displacees or "uprooted"), while the remaining 52.8 percent (refugees) identified themselves as Mauritanian citizens. Of the Haalpulaar repatriated, almost all were close kin to Thiemping villagers. FulBe families claimed no affiliation to village members. The gender composition of the deported community was balanced.

Fifty percent of refugees were under the age of 15, and the average period of residence in Mauritania for adults above age 30 was 23 years. The high proportion of individuals surveyed claiming Mauritanian citizenship and the lengthy period of residence of adults in the country (most claiming birth there) seriously calls into question the official position of the Mauritanian government that no citizens of their country were deported.

Haalpulaar farmers and FulBe herders alike suffered heavy losses of livestock. Of 4,732 animals owned (12 head per capita), only 891 (2.3 head per capita) or 18.8 percent were recovered. Per capita livestock holdings were much greater among FulBe herders (15.8) than among Haalpulaar farmers (4.9). Recovery rates as well were much higher among the former group (3.1 vs. 0.6). Losses were proportionately higher for large ruminants and browsers (cattle, horses/donkeys, camels) than for small ones, but at 22.4 percent, recovery rates were higher for small ruminants (sheep/goats). Overall, the FulBe recovered 19.9 percent of their animals, while the Haalpulaar recuperated only 12.3 percent. Data on animal losses sustained and rates of recovery are presented in Table 7.1.

Table 7.1. Herd Loss and Recovery Rates among Thiemping Refugees, 1989.

	Cattle			Horses/ Donkeys			Sheep/Goats			Camels			Total		
	*O	L	R	O	L	R	O	L	R	O	L	R	O	L	R
	n	n	%	n	n	%	n	n	%	n	n	%	n	n	%
Herders	1009	916	9.2	80	73	8.8	2992	2281	23.8	2	2	0	4083	3272	19.9
Farmers	174	157	9.8	21	18	14.3	454	394	13.2	0	0	0	649	569	12.3
Total	1183	1073	9.3	101	91	9.9	3446	2675	22.4	2	2	0	4732	3841	18.8

*O=Ownership, L=Loss, R=Recovery

A survey of the land cultivated in 1988–89 by the refugee population reveals the importance of transboundary farming in the region and the extent of land lost by riverine farmers and herders (Table 7.2). Nearly four-fifths (79.3 percent) of the land farmed was located in Mauritania, the remaining one-fifth in Senegal. In Mauritania, rainfed uplands (*jeeri*) made up almost one-half (49.6 percent) of all plots farmed, another one-third (34 percent) were in recession agriculture (*waalo* bottomlands 15.5 percent, *falo* river gardens 12.2 percent, *foonde* high plains 6.3 percent), followed by 16.4 percent in irrigation (PIV or *Périmètre Irrigué Villageois*). The refugee population owned most of this land (92.4 percent), the remainder being farmed on a usufruct basis through tenancy, lease, and loan arrangements.

While the refugees owned and farmed most of their fields in Mauritania, the proportion of fields owned in Senegal remains significantly high (32 of 62 plots, or 51.6 percent). Floodplain lands (*waalo, falo, foonde*) represent the quasi-totality (96.8 percent) of all plots farmed, with *waalo* bottomlands accounting for 64.5 percent. In examining the portfolio of agricultural lands cultivated by the refugee sample, several important facts emerge: 1) four-fifths of all land farmed and lost was located in Mauritania; 2) the bulk of land (84 percent) was owned and farmed by the herder-farmer population itself; and 3) recession lands (*waalo, falo, foonde*) comprised almost one-half (46.9 percent) of all the holdings lost.

These data corroborate the findings of the 1973 transborder land survey cited above (Lericollais and Diallo 1980, and discussion by Seck 1991). They illustrate the saliency of seasonal mobility for agropastoral communities and show clearly how agrarian livelihoods and landholdings in African river basin ecosystems often transcend international boundaries.

Table 7.2. Transborder Landholding Status Among Thiemping Refugees, 1989.

	Mauritania Landholding Status											
H	Waalo		Falo		Foonde		Jeeri		PIV		Subtotal	Total
GH	*LH	UR	LH	UR	LH	UR	LH	UR	LH	UR	LH UR	
	n	n	n	n	n	n	n	n	n	n	n n	n
Herders	23	4	13	2	5	1	64	6	25	2	130 15	145
Farmers	10	0	12	2	8	1	48	0	12	0	90 3	93
Total	33	4	25	4	13	2	112	6	37	2	220 18	238
%	15.5		12.2		6.3		49.6		16.4		−	100.0

	Senegal Landholding Status											
	Waalo		Falo		Foonde		Jeeri		PIV		Subtotal	Total
	*LH	UR	LH	UR	LH	UR	LH	UR	LH	UR	LH UR	
	n	n	n	n	n	n	n	n	n	n	n n	n
Herders	2	22	0	3	0	0	0	0	1	0	3 25	28
Farmers	11	5	9	0	8	0	1	0	0	0	29 5	34
Total	13	27	9	3	8	0	1	0	1	0	32 30	62
%	64.5		19.4		12.9		1.6		1.6		−	100.0

Table 7.2. (contd.)

Total Transborder Landholdings

	Waalo		Falo		Foonde		Jeeri		PIV		Subtotal		Total
	*LH	UR	LH	UR	LH	UR	LH	UR	LH	UR	LH	UR	
	%	%	%	%	%	%	%	%	%	%	%	%	%
**RIM	11.0	1.3	8.3	1.3	4.3	0.7	37.3	2.0	12.3	0.7	73.3	6.0	79.3
Senegai	4.3	9.0	3.0	1.0	2.7	0.0	0.3	0.0	0.3	0.0	10.7	10.0	20.7
Total	25.6		13.6		7.7		39.6		13.3		–		100.0

* LH=Landholdings, Ur=Use Rights (tenancy, lease, loan)
** RIM=Republic of Mauritania

CONCLUSION

This essay, in focusing on a distant, obscure locale at the margin of the African Sahel, has attempted to shed light on a violent ethnic confrontation that has received scant attention and little critical analysis in both social science circles and the American popular press. The fatal turn of events of 1989 is complex and multidimensional in nature — the fusion of history, ethnic identity, ecology, and political economy.

Tambiah (1989: 346) describes three scenarios leading to ethnic conflict that are effectively illustrated in the Senegal-Mauritania case: the "severe erosion of niche-equilibrium," the marginalization of "satellite ethnic/tribal minorities," and the "differential incorporation" of ethnic collectivities giving rise to a phenomenon of "structural asymmetrical pluralism." The erosion and reconfiguration of "niche-equilibriums," induced by natural and anthropogenic forces, has radically altered the physical and cultural landscape of both countries. Persistent drought in the 1970s provoked a mass exodus of *bidan* herders from the countryside to the towns and cities of Senegal and Mauritania, where they created a new occupational niche for themselves in the petty retail sector. This spatial and socio-occupational void was soon filled by black FulBe herders who reoccupied the semi-desert niche. Many bond servants (*'abid*) and freed slaves (*haratin*), also fleeing the vagaries of drought, abandoned their previous agropastoral activities for the safety of urban centers. Finally, drought coupled with economic stagnation precipitated the migration north of black Africans into urban areas of Mauritania where manual and semi-skilled jobs were created in the post-drought years.

Since the drought, the occupational and physical landscape has been redefined and restructured by human agency. *Bidan* access to black farmlands on the right bank of the Senegal River for private sector irrigation, aided by the redeployment of servile labor from the oases and river floodplains to the perimeters, has forced Haalpulaar farmers and herders to flee their homes and take up residence as refugees in Senegal. Finally, the abrupt departure of *bidan* shopkeepers from the urban setting in Senegal, and their forced relocation in Mauritania, leaves the issue of future niche-equilibrium in that country as yet undefined.

The "bidanization" of Haalpulaar lands in Mauritania illustrates Tambiah's second point as well: the retreat of "satellite ethnic/tribal minorities" at the hands of an encroaching ethnic majority well ensconced in the political and economic nucleus of the state. The arabization of formal schooling and the privatization of prime farmlands in the river basin under a series of land reform decrees in the 1980s consolidated the *bidan* hold on the urban core and paved the way for the transfer and investment of capital to the rural periphery.

A third scenario instigating ethnic conflict is that of "differential incorporation," whereby the political economic ascendance of *bidan* elites is buttressed by claims of a demographic majority and historical precedence of occupation.[22] The end result has been a disproportionate overrepresentation of *bidan* authority and influence in both public and private sectors of the economy and a marked underrepresentation of blacks — symptomatic of Tambiah's reference to "structural asymmetrical pluralism."[23]

Finally, this essay asserts that the Senegal-Mauritania conflict is the result not only of the territorial competition over commodified resources, but the product of internecine strife and ethnic antagonism conditioned by historical perceptions of the "other" as adversary. The recurrence of phenomena such as slave raiding and the *razzia* by the Maures, *"ruggo"* raiding parties by the FulBe, and the contestation over farmlands and pastoral reserves by black Haalpulaar farmers and Maure nomads adds an important and deep-seated social-psychological dimension of group apprehension and anxiety to ethnic conflict. Ethnic animosities borne out of historical struggle, and reinforced by more recent exclusionary practices such as the apportioning of group entitlements in language, land, economic opportunity, and political office to *bidan* rather than black Mauritanians, have produced a self-perpetuating cycle of distrust and vilification between the rival groups. Distorted perceptions of the "enemy," amplified by rumor and innuendo, have never become more evident between black Africans and light-skinned (as well as black) Maures than during the violent clashes of April, 1989, when each group brutally lashed out, hacking and pummeling one another in a grotesque fashion.

Recent initiatives to expand the agricultural productivity of the region by means of hydro-technological development of the river basin have had the unforeseen effect of heightening longstanding enmities among ethnic communities on both sides of the river. After a brief rendezvous with mob mayhem and a spontaneous maelstrom of terror and bloodletting on the streets of Dakar and Nouakchott in late April, 1989, it is hoped that government authorities, development planners, and social scientists alike will move beyond a position of passivity in "[coping] with the phenomenon of destructive violence" (Tambiah 1989: 348). Concerted action is required to adopt effective policy measures that will mitigate against the likelihood of another tragic outbreak of ethnic violence in the foreseeable future.

NOTES

1. This essay draws from data gathered by the author in the middle Senegal River Valley while conducting doctoral field research under the auspices of the Institute for Development Anthropology for the SRBMA I (Senegal River Basin Monitoring Activity) Project between 1988 and 1990. Dissertation write-up support under an Africa Program Dissertation Fellowship Research Grant has been provided by the Social Science Research Council of the United States. The author gratefully acknowledges the financial support of these two institutions.

    I am also deeply indebted to numerous mentors and colleagues for their generous support, editorial assistance, and constructive commentary in the writing of this paper. They include Michael Horowitz, Peter Little, Michael Painter, Monica Sella, Matthew Richard, Mary Ellen Zuppan, and Jean-Michel Jolly. Any interpretive or factual errors, however, remain those of the author.

2. The Haalpulaar population (meaning literally "speakers of Pulaar") in the northern Senegal Valley is a cultural mélange of black sub-saharan agropastoralists who farm, fish, and raise ruminant livestock along the river's edge and on the adjacent lateral floodplains, and who reside primarily in the intermediate catchment zone of the river's broadly extending basin known as the middle valley. In addition, a semi-nomadic population of FulBe herders dwelling directly south of the floodplain belt

in a sandy upland plateau region (known as the Ferlo) are subsumed within the ethnic category of the Haalpulaar described here. When necessary to make an unambiguous distinction among these communities, however, FulBe herders will be referred to separately from Haalpulaar farmers and fishers.

The *haratin* are freed slaves or serfs of black sub-saharan descent who speak Hassaniya, a Mauritanian Arab dialect. *Haratin* (sing, *hartani*) refers historically to a population cultivating the palm grove oases of the Sahara who "constitute ... a kind of caste, formed of men theoretically free but of an inferior status, ranking between the *ahrar* 'free men' and the *'abid* 'slaves, captives': peasants" (Colin 1971: 230).

3. For an eyewitness account of the 9 April, 1989 Diawara incident by a Senegalese national taken hostage in Mauritania during the crisis see *Jeune Afrique* (1989: 88, 89).

4. The term *bidan* as described by Stewart (1973: 8) refers to "the white race" and derives from the Arabic term *bayd*, the plural feminine construction of *abyad* meaning "white." While primarily of Arabo-Berber origin, *bidan* historically intermarried with *aerobe* or black sub-saharan Africans, leading Stewart to claim that the term is "essentially a social rather than colour classification," and that *bidan* status "requires a genealogy claiming Arab descent which is socially acceptable, i.e., which is credible to other [*bidan*]" (ibid.).

5. Doyle (1989: 14), a foreign correspondent assigned to Dakar during the bedlam, estimates between 300,000–500,000 Maure shopkeepers in Senegal. In all, they account for about 85% of the country's small retail trade (Fall 1989a: 33).

6. The precipitating conflict in the northern valley at Diawara and the chain of violence involving the wholesale destruction of Maure shops and the seesaw pattern of urban pogroms is extensively documented by national and foreign correspondents reporting on the events as they transpired. For detailed accounts of the inter-state conflict, the sources are numerous, including: the 1989–90 issues of popular African news magazines (*Jeune Afrique, Africa Report, West Africa*), African and European newspapers (*Le Soleil, Sopi, Sudhebdo, Le Monde, La Croix — l'Evénement, Libération*), and bulletin news summaries and political reports covering African affairs (*Africa Confidential, Africa Research Bulletin, Economist Intelligence Unit*). Reporting in the American press (*New York Times, Washington Post, Christian Science Monitor, Newsweek, Time*), on the other hand, has been much more sparse.

This essay does not attempt to recount the lengthy chronicle of events as they have been reported in the sources above. Rather, attention is drawn to the structural linkages of society, history, politics, and the environment as they mediate process and change between the urban core and the rural periphery.

7. Discussion of the plight of the refugee population follows in the latter half of this essay.

8. For detailed accounts of the conflict placing the phenomenon of "land grabbing" at the heart of the debate, see Horowitz 1989, 1991; Coupe 1990; Park et al. 1990; Bâ 1991; Crousse 1991; and Seck 1991.
9. "Subordinate to the hassanis were zawiya tribes and several strata of tributaries: the *zenegha* or *lahma* who were bidanis, *haratine* or freed slaves, *abid* or slaves, *mallemin* or smiths, and *iggawen* or musicians and bards" (Stewart 1972: 379).
10. "For the Bidan, acts of physical labor implied the control of one individual over another's labor: to engage in any form of physical labor was to admit some degree of dependence and some degree of ignobility" (Webb 1984: 36).
11. While ethnic polities are statically portrayed here as having fixed geopolitical boundaries dissected by the physiognomy of the Senegal River, in fact, a considerable flux of populations occurred, both seasonal and long-term, moving back and forth across the river.
12. A freed slave once interviewed about the nature of relations existing between the *bidan* and servile *haratin* provided the following metaphor: "the Moors rule by an alliance of the rider and his horse" (Mercer 1984, in Coupe 1990: 334).

   This alliance of white patron and black client has been interpreted by one observer of urban violence in Nouakchott as a modified form of the traditional *razzia* undertaken by the *hassani* warrior and his faithful *haratin* tributaries (Coupe 1990: 334).

   It is essential to note that despite differences of color, the white *bidan* and black *haratin* are inexorably bound by language and culture. During incidents of ethnic unrest (both past and present) between *bidan* Maures and black Africans, the *haratin* have steadfastly defended the interests of their *bidan* superiors — pitting themselves against other sub-saharan blacks.
13. As of 1990, dam costs (all infrastructure including dam supervision, access roads, population resettlement, and forest clearing) had reached $ 620 million ($506 million for Manantali, $114 million for Diama [$1=316 FCFA]) (Zolty 1990: 33). Cost sharing to be borne by the tri-member states is as follows: Senegal 42.1 percent, Mali 35.5 percent, Mauritania 22.6 percent. The reimbursement of energy-related costs (hydroturbines, transmission lines, etc.) will be shared primarily by Mali at 52 percent, followed by Senegal at 33 percent and Mauritania at 15 percent (Fall 1989b: 40).
14. By 1991, grain output in Mauritania reached 82,414 metric tons, or only 23 percent of the nation's food needs (FEWS 1992, in Sherbinin 1992: 12) while irrigation agriculture in Senegal is expected to produce 583,000 tons or only 31 percent of the nation's requirements in grain by the year 2000 (Fall 1989b: 40).
15. For more exhaustive treatments of land tenure policy and reform in Mauritania see Park et al. (1990), Crousse (1984, 1986, 1991), and Ba (1986, 1991). For Senegal, see Niang (1982), Seck (1985), Engelhard and Ben Abdallah (1986), and OMVS/CEPC (1986).

16. The critical distinction to be made between Senegalese and Mauritanian land reform policy is one of structural mediation or its lack thereof, between the state and the peasantry. Seck (1991: 309) comments on the key role of the Rural Community (*Communauté Rurale*), a locally elected body of rural village elders responsible for all jural procedures of land disposition and registration, as the mediatory mechanism of the state instituted under the 1972 Senegalese agrarian administrative reform (NPA or Nouvelle Politique Agricole). In Mauritania, the stark absence of any modality for arbitration enables the state to intervene directly via local government officials (district governors and departmental prefects) in the usurpation of peasant lands. It is this blatant disregard by the state of peasant rights to land that has fostered resentment and periodic outbreaks of violence against the *bidan* establishment by black farmers.
17. A recent World Bank report (in Sherbinin 1992: 8) indicates that between 1984–85 and 1987–88, the total surface area of private rice perimeters in Mauritania increased 17-fold, from 500 to 8,500 hectares.
18. Numerous instances have been documented of ongoing contestation between neighboring villages on opposite sides of the river over right bank floodplain bottomlands (*waalo*) and river bank gardens (*falo*) converted for irrigation use. One of the most vehemently disputed, volatile confrontations over such lands, took place between the *haratin* Maure community of Dolol Siwre (on the right bank) and the Haalpulaar village of Odobere (on the left) in the middle valley, dating back prior to 1986. For accounts of specific village incidents, see Sy and Tall 1989, in FLAM 1989, Fleischman 1991: 15, and journalistic coverage by *Sud Hebdo* in 1989.
19. Coverage of the plight and pillage of border refugees is chronicled in the sources cited in note 6 above. These accounts describe the systematic confiscation of personal items including jewelry, watches, clothing, and money, and the destruction of national identification cards by Mauritanian authorities.

    The maltreatment of those deported from Mauritania, as well as an extensive history of human rights violations such as the imprisonment, torture, and extra-judicial execution of political prisoners has been documented by human rights organization such as Amnesty International (1990), and Africa Watch (1990, 1992). In addition, FLAM (1989, 1991) has reported at length on the deliberate actions of the state to institute a discriminatory policy against blacks in Mauritania reminiscent of the policies of apartheid in South Africa.
20. In order to qualify for national and international human relief services such as food aid, the Senegal government has identified three subcategories of "refugees:" 1). *réfugiés* — black Africans of Mauritanian nationality, 2). *rapatriés* — Senegalese citizens who resided or worked in Mauritania, and 3). *déguerpis* — displaced or uprooted Senegalese citizens who farmed the right bank of the Senegal River (Horowitz 1989: 6). Among the deported in the Matam department, 17,774 were

refugees, 7,122 were repatriates, and 1,360 were uprooted as of 30 June, 1989 (figures obtained from the Matam Prefecture in June, 1989).
21. Santoir (1990b: 589) denotes the root of the term *ruggiyankooBe* from the FulBe noun *ruggo*, which is a ritual practice of institutionalized livestock raiding among neighboring camps of FulBe youth as a demonstration of virility and courage.
22. The *bidan* government claim of demographic superiority has been contested by numerous sources, the most vociferous opposition coming from FLAM (1989, 1991). National census figures from 1977 and 1988 have never been officially released, leading many to question the government claim of a *bidan* demographic majority. Data from the 1960 census reveal 75 percent of the population as speaking Hassaniya, 17 percent Pulaar, 5 percent Soninke, and 10 percent mixed (Parker 1991: 167).

A 1964–65 study from the Mauritanian Center of Demographic and Social Studies extrapolating from a representative sample of the population provides very different figures, indicating a clear black majority: white Maures 43 percent, black Africans 16 percent, other servile groups (largely black) 41 percent (Ould Cheikh 1986, in Coupe 1990: 59).

Any claims of historical precedence of occupation may be mute as well, since the earliest known settlement of the western Sahara is purported to have been a black population of "Bafour" hunters and gatherers during the Neolithic who were slowly pushed southward by the dessication of the Sahara and the invasion of the Almoravids from the north (Chassey 1977: 23; Gerteiny 1981: 32).
23. For documentation on the disproportional underrepresentation of blacks in favor of the *bidan* in high posts of the government, commerce, and military, see FLAM (1989: 16–29).

REFERENCES

Africa Confidential (1989). Mauritania: War on Black Citizens. Africa Confidential 30(14): 2–3.
——— (1990). Mauritania: The Politics of a Pogrom. Africa Confidential 31(13): 3–4.
——— (1991). Mauritania: Friends of Saddam. Africa Confidential 32(3): 6–7.
Africa Watch (1990). Mauritania-Slavery: Alive and Well, Ten Years After it was Abolished, Washington.
Amnesty International (1990). Mauritania: Human Rights Violations in the Senegal River Valley, London.
Andriamirado, Sennen (1989a). Sénégal-Mauritanie. Le dossier du conflit. Première Partie. Comment Nouakchott et Dakar ont géré la crise. Jeune Afrique 1491 (August 2): 34–39.

——————— (1989b). Sénégal-Mauritanie. Le fleuve baisse, la tension monte. Jeune Afrique 1508 (November 27): 32–34.

Ba, Boubakar M. (1986). Les systèmes agraires de la vallée du Sénégal en Mauritanie. Rapport de consultation. Dakar: OMVS/CEPC.

——————— (1991). La question foncière dans le bassin du fleuve Sénégal. *In* La vallée du fleuve Sénégal. Evaluations et perspectives d'une décennie d'aménagements (1980–1990). Bernard Crousse, Paul Mathieu, and Sidy M. Seck, eds. pp. 255–275. Paris: Editions Karthala.

Baduel, Pierre Robert (1989). Mauritanie 1945–1990 ou L'Etat Face à la Nation. Revue du Monde Musulman et de la Méditerranée 54(4): 11–51.

Barth, Frederick (1969). Ethnic Groups and Boundaries. Boston: Little, Brown.

Becker, Charles and André Lericollais (1989). Le problème frontalier dans le conflit sénégalo-mauritanien. Politique Africaine 35: 149–155.

Belotteau, Jacques (1989). Sénégal-Mauritanie: les graves événements du printemps 1989. Afrique contemporaine 152(4): 41–42.

Bloom, Evan (1990). Frontier Ethics and the Senegal River Valley. Africa Notes December: 1–2.

Bonacich, Edna (1973). A Theory of Middleman Minorities. American Sociological Review 38(5): 583–594.

Chassey, Francis de (1977). L'étrier, la houe et le livre. Paris: Editions Anthropos.

——————— (1984). Mauritanie, 1900–1975. Paris: Editions l'Harmattan.

Colin, G. S. (1971). Ḥarṭānī. *In* The Encyclopaedia of Islam. New Edition. B. Lewis, V. L. Ménage, Ch. Pellat and T. J. Schacht, eds. Leiden: E. J. Brill.

Coupe, Jeffrey A. (1990). Political Instability in Urban Africa: The Case of Nouakchott, Mauritania. Master of Arts Thesis, University of Florida.

Crousse, Bernard (1984). Logique traditionnelle et logique d'Etat. Conflicts de pratiques et de stratégies foncières dans le projet d'aménagement de M'Bagne en Mauritanie. *In* Espaces disputés en Afrique noire, Pratiques foncières locales. B. Crousse, E. Le Bris, E. Le Roy, eds. pp. 199–215. Paris: Karthala.

——————— (1986). Etatisation ou individualisation: La réforme foncière mauritanienne de 1983. Politique Africaine 21: 63–76.

——————— (1991). L'influence des réglementations foncières modernes dans l'aménagement de la vallée. *In* La vallée du fleuve Sénégal. Evaluations et perspectives d'une décennie d'aménagements (1980–1990). Bernard Crousse, Paul Mathieu, and Sidy M. Seck, eds. pp. 277–295. Paris: Editions Karthala.

Dahmani, Abdelaziz (1989). Mauritanie éteindre vite l'incendie. Jeune Afrique 1481 (May 24): 24–25.

Diallo, Siradiou (1989). Mauritanie-Sénégal: après le cauchemar. Jeune Afrique 1480 (May 17): 26–29.

Doyle, Mark (1989). Blood Brothers. West Africa (July–August): 13–16.

Engelhard, Philippe and Taoufik Ben Abdallah, eds. (1986). Enjeux de l'après-barrage. Vallée du Sénégal. Dakar: ENDA and Ministère de la Coopération.

Fall, Elimane (1989a). Dakar: un étrange sentiment de malaise. Jeune Afrique 1480 (May 17): 30–33.
────────── (1989b). Sénégal-Mauritanie. Le dossier du conflit. Première Partie. Les enjeux de l'après-barrages. Jeune Afrique 1491 (August 2): 39–44.
FLAM (Forces de Libération Africaines de Mauritanie) (1989). Mauritanie: (1960–1989) 30 ans d'un APARTHEID méconnu. October.
────────── (1991). Livre blanc sur la situation des noirs en Mauritania. January.
Fleischman, Janet (1991). The Dispossessed. Africa Events (May): 14–15.
GAVD (Groupe Africain des Volontaires pour le Développement) (1991). La Situation des Réfugiés Mauritaniens dans la Vallée du Fleuve Sénégal (Rive Gauche). Etude de Cas des Camps de Ogo, Sinthou Garba, et Faboli dans le Département de Matam. Unpublished manuscript.
GERSAR/CACG., Euroconsult, Sir Alexander Gibb & Partners, SONED-Afrique (1989). Plan Directeur de Développement Intégré pour la Rive Gauche de la Vallée du Fleuve Sénégal. Rapport d'Etape, Decembre.
────────── (1990). Plan Directeur de Développement Intégré pour la Rive Gauche de la Vallée du Fleuve Sénégal. Document Provisoire, Juin.
Gerteiny, Alfred G. (1981). Historical Dictionary of Mauritania. Metuchen, N.J.: The Scarecrow Press, Inc.
Horowitz, Donald L. (1985). Ethnic Groups in Conflict. Berkeley: University of California Press.
Horowitz, Michael M. (1989). Victims of Development. Development Anthropology Network 7(2): 1–8.
────────── (1991). Victims Upstream and Down. Journal of Refugee Studies 4(2): 164–181.
Jeune Afrique (1989). Honteux massacres fratricides. No. 1483 (June 7): 82–95.
King, John (1990). Iraq's Growing Involvement in Mauritania. Middle East International (August 3): 18–19.
Lericollais, André and Y. Diallo (1980). Peuplement et cultures de saison sèche dans la vallée du Sénégal. 7 cartes et notices. Dakar: ORSTOM.
Levtzion, Nehemia (1985). The Early States of the Western Sudan to 1500. *In* History of West Africa, vol. 1. J. F. A. Ajayi and M. Crowder, eds. pp. 87–128. New York: Longman Inc.
Mason, David (1986). Introduction. Controversies and Continuities in Race and Ethnic Relations Theory. *In* Theories of Race and Ethnic Relations. John Rex and David Mason, eds. pp. 1–19. Cambridge: Cambridge University Press.
New York Times (1989). An African Exodus With Racial Overtones. (July 22).
Niang, Mamadou (1982). Réflexions sur la réforme foncière sénégalaise de 1964. *In* Enjeux Fonciers en Afrique Noire. E. Le Bris et al., eds. pp. 219–227. Paris: Karthala.
Omaar, Rakiya and Janet Fleischman (1991). Arab vs. African. Africa Report July–August: 34–38.
OMVS/CEPC (1986). Aspects fonciers et organisationnels dans le développement de la culture irriguée. Dakar: OMVS/CEPC.

Park, Thomas K., Mamadou Baro and Tidiane Ngaido (1990). Conflicts Over Land and the Crisis of Nationalism in Mauritania. Madison: University of Wisconsin Land Tenure Center.
Parker, Ron (1991). The Senegal-Mauritania Conflict of 1989: A Fragile Equilibrium. The Journal of Modern African Studies 29(1): 155–171.
Roseberry, William (1982). Coffee and Capitalism in the Venezuelan Andes. Austin: University of Texas Press.
Santoir, Christian (1990a). Le Conflit Mauritano-Sénégalais: La Genèse. Cahiers des Sciences Humaines 26(4): 553–576.
—————(1990b). Les Peul 'Refusés:' Les Peul Mauritaniens Réfugiés au Sénégal. Cahiers des Sciences Humaines 26(4): 577–603.
Schmitz, Jean (1989). Le fleuve Sénégal: ligne de front ou voie de passage. Afrique Contemporaine 154: 70–74.
Seck, Sidy M. (1985). Aspects fonciers et organisationnels dans le développement de la culture irriguée (dans le bassin du Sénégal), Saint Louis: OMVS/CEPC.
————— (1991). Les cultivateurs "transfrontaliers" de décrue face à la question foncière. In La vallée du fleuve Sénégal. Evaluations et perspectives d'une décennie d'aménagements (1980–1990). Bernard Crousse, Paul Mathieu, and Sidy M. Seck, eds. pp. 297–320. Paris: Editions Karthala.
Sherbinin, Alexander M. de (1992). Mauritanian Refugees: Casualties of Rural Development? Paper presented at the 1992 annual meetings of the Association of American Geographers, San Diego, California.
Soudan, François (1990). L'offensive africaine de Saddam Hussein. Jeune Afrique 1516 (January 22): 40–42.
Stewart, Charles C. (1972). Political Authority and Social Stratification in Mauritania. In Arabs and Berbers: From Tribe to Nation in North Africa. Ernest Gellner and Charles Micaud, eds. pp. 375–393. Lexington, Mass: Lexington Books.
————— (1973). Islam and Social Order in Mauritania. A Case Study from the Nineteenth Century. Oxford: Clarendon Press.
————— (1989). Une Interprétation du Conflit Sénégalo-Mauritanien. Revue du Monde Musulman et de la Méditerranée 54(4): 161–170.
Tambiah, Stanley (1989). Ethnic Conflict in the World Today. American Ethnologist 16(2): 335–349.
Webb, James L. A. (1984). Shifting Sands: An Economic History of the Mauritanian Sahara, 1500–1850. Unpublished Ph.D. dissertation in history, The Johns Hopkins University.
Zolty, Alain (1990). Hydro-agriculture au Sud du Sahara. Afrique Agriculture 177: 1–72.

Chapter EIGHT

Ethnicity and Land Tenure in the Sahel

P. Bonte,
Director of Research
CNRS Laboratory of Social Anthropology, Paris

Bonte extends the analysis of Sahelian ethnic disharmony to include the situations in Niger, Mali, and Mauritania. Sahelian societies, as is the case throughout much of the African continent, are still predominantly agricultural. Access to land is survival. Land in Africa had been largely equitably distributed in the past. Bonte reports that Sahelian land tenure systems are currently changing in less equitable directions, with members of certain ethnic groups acquiring disproportionate amounts of land, largely for capitalist farming. This, then, is a transformation of historic significance, one that is raising ethnic conflicts.

It is not usual to construct the objects of anthropological research on a scale as vast as that of a region like the Sahel,[1] which is rather of interest as such to geographers, economists, or geopoliticians. I hope that the choice will prove to be justified by the nature of the question treated. Before introducing it, I will rapidly summarize some of the general characteristics of this region whose exposition will be useful for the discussion.

The Sahel, corresponding to its meaning of "shore" in Arabic, is a zone of low precipitation (200 to 600 mm) between the desert, the Sahara, and the Sudanian savannah. It is also a zone of contact between two types of civilizations and modes of life: nomadic herders, "Whites," belonging to the mediterranean peoples of the north, and village farmers, "Blacks," belonging to the Sudanese peoples of the south.

It is no doubt in large part due to this situation of contacts and exchanges, cultural, human, and commercial, that the Sahel is a privileged and ancient zone of great African states. From Ghana (around the VIIth century) via Mali and Songhai, as well as Bornu and Kanem, to the states born of the *jihads*[2] of the 19th century, the existence of these states has left an enduring impression on the organization of the populations of this zone.

These sahelian populations are generally divided into large groups that are significant for the number of people that they contain and the size of the territories they cover. These groups are relatively homogeneous, in spite of the existence of widespread and massive diffusion linked to the geopolitical context, the construction of states, or to the mode of life, as in the case of the Fulani herders distributed throughout the region. Authors often hesitate to speak of these vast ensembles as ethnic groups, although they do share certain features of ethnicity, language, and culture; the term "nation" could sometimes be quite as appropriate, even in earlier periods. Diversity is marked in these ensembles: at the territorial level one can also speak of "countries." Functional variations, underlining these levels of specialization and integration on a larger scale, are often observable, both among these population groups (Fulani herders, Bozo fishers, Wangara traders in the past, Dioula at present, etc.) and within them, where often are found a large number of specialized "castes" (smiths, potters, weavers, fishers, etc.), which are generally said to be of foreign origin.

In the course of this history prior to the shock of colonization, the notion of "ethnic minority" seems not to have been very pertinent, so important were the factors of economic, political, and religious integration that prevented closure and could even lead in a short period of time to the formation of new populations, as in the case of the Toucouleurs in the Senegal valley.[3] This capacity for integration and receptivity is in large part characteristic of the states, often organized by and around a dominant group,[4] but in a mode more federalizing than centralizing. The diffusion on a large regional scale of certain patronymics from Senegal to Niger, for example, testifies to these intermixtures.[5]

Even though they are rare, there are exceptions. One may speak historically of "minority" in the case of the Dogons, agriculturalists refuged in their inaccessible cliffs. They have, relatively speaking, preserved their individuality from political and religious (Islamic) enterprises, without forgetting, however, that they represent numerically one of the most important linguistic groups in present day Mali.

In this sahelian society, true minorities are more likely to be social rather than ethnic in nature, and they correspond to the generalization of slavery and the servile status that continues to exist even when the slaves have been "freed." They constitute distinct groups, such as the Moorish *harâtîn*, the Twareg *ighawelen*, and the Fulani *rimaybe*, that can constitute demographically the majority of the society. Servile status is often associated with modes of categorization that transcend "ethnic" categories: "Whites" and "Blacks,"[6] Muslims and non-Muslims.

The broad outlines of the context of these remarks having been presented, we can now turn to the argument that I propose to develop. Since their colonization more than a century ago, *the issue of land seems to be a generalized process at the heart of these sahelian societies producing new forms of ethnicity and, simultaneously, ethnic minorities*. This process has only become more accentuated since colonization and the constitution of independent states.

Let me try to summarize rapidly the hypotheses that I will develop in this contribution. The armed coflicts that have become widespread since independence in sahelian societies simultaneously reveal a displacement of the land issue that is tied to evolutionary changes in technology and economics as well as to demographic pressure and the importance it assumes in the political context of the sahelian states. Beyond the appearances of the ideologies and political practices developed by the elites who monopolize political power, a general reclassification is actually taking place of the position of the local groups that they represent and to which they are linked by multiple relations of interests — kinship, matrimonial, clientship, economic, or political — as the weight of democratic numbers enters into the equation. It has become increasingly clear in recent years that it is when this reclassification implicates a major displacement of the local relations of power that the ethnic dimension of conflicts develop and the latter take on an exacerbated form, becoming a source of uncontrolled massacres or implacable resistance.

COLONIAL AND POST-COLONIAL EVOLUTION OF THE LAND TENURE SITUATION.

It is difficult to draw a quick sketch of the land tenure situation prior to colonization,[7] if only because of the diversity of the types found. As above, therefore, I will only introduce a few points of a general order useful for the development of my argument.

The pre-colonial land tenure regime is characterized first of all by the importance of *common property*. This regime is primarily confined to the pastoral domain among herders, but it is also quite widespread in agricultural societies where access to the land is mediated by collective membership: membership in a lineage or other politico-religious group.

This level of *collective control, political and/or ritual,* of access to land is the keystone of these systems.[8] In the Moorish and Twareg pastoral societies, it is membership in the tribe, a cognatic group, even if it sees its structure as unilinear, that mediates access to land.[9] This structurally cognatic character of the tribe opens it up widely to alliances and the integration of foreign elements (Bonte 1991). Among farmers, "masters of the land" or "masters of the ground"[10] carry out the rituals necessary for the crops and intervene decisively in the distribution of the land; they can also ensure the integration of foreign elements into the lineage group, or the population concerned,[11] to the degree that the ritual authority, along with its social and economic effects, of the first settlers is recognized.

There is, therefore, no real closure of the land tenure system, and this situation has favored the mixing and diffusion of "ethnic" groups that I have referred to above. Indeed, there is only one absolute restriction on access to land in these land tenure systems. It concerns the servile categories, slaves but also former slaves, who obtain this right through their masters or former masters. In pastoral societies these groups, *hâratîn, ighawelen,* or *rimaybe,* constituted villages of farmers having access to the land in the cadre of the collective tribal property. One could also find villages of slave origin in farming village societies where slaves and former slaves remained integrated in the village structure in which their access to land remained precarious.[12] It is known that slavery, although ancient, was particularly developed in the 19th century within the new state structures then being elaborated.

These characteristics of the land tenure regime result in most cases in a *superposing of land rights*, distinguishing, for example, rights of political control, ritual rights, rights of usage, etc., favorable to the coexistence in the same space of differentiated groups. Thus one arrives at very complex systems, such as the Dina, which under the control of the Fulani state of Macina regulated access to the resources of the interior delta of the Niger (Mali).[13] Among Twareg and Moorish herders it is not unusual for tribes to succeed each other in the same territory that they exploit seasonally according to the species raised.[14] Fulani herders, thanks to exchanges of milk and manure for cereals, negotiate the use of agricultural lands after the harvest.

This superposing of rights and the coexistence of groups naturally did not prevent *conflicts over land*, which were settled by negotiation, either ritual (sacrifies among the Dogon, for example) or economic (exchanges between Fulani and farmers), and, of course, by relations of politico-military force. Before colonization, the balance of forces among distinct groups was expressed by the creation of vast uninhabited hinterlands, forest zones corresponding often to the poorest soils, such as H. Barth described at the time of his voyage in Africa in the middle of the 19th century between the Hausa "countries" surrounding their city-states.

It is in this context that colonial land policy was carried out, a policy initiated very early in the years 1899–1901 and expressed within the AOF (French West Africa) in the land decree of 1932 and the domanial decree of 1935.

One should perhaps recall first of all that this land legislation was not associated with a colonial settlement policy, non-existent in the Sahelian zone, but rather with control of the indigenous populations, with development in the sense of the monetarization and commercialization of production, and more recently with the "development" of these populations.

The uniform principle[15] of colonial land policy was *to make the public domain serve the diffusion of private property*. The point of departure was the constitution of the eminent domain of the state over land — in the context of the "colony" at first, and then in that of the states created by independence — consisting of the totality of lands not registered. The registration procedure consists in registering a piece of real estate at the end of a complex administrative process that transforms it into individual or collective property. In fact, this procedure has been little utilized in the rural (pastoral or agricultural) domains. To this extent the quasi totality of this rural domain, whether it is a question of cultivated lands, zones of pasturage, or of any other form of exploitation of forests or water, etc., has become the eminent domain of the state.

The difficulties of registration are due not only to the complexity of the procedure and to the relative lack of interest on the part of the colonial administration to apply it. They correspond also to the contradiction between the principle of absolute property in land and the land tenure regime that we will henceforth refer to as "customary" that regulates access to it in the populations concerned. It is impossible to preserve the forms of common property and the diversified rights that can be exercised on the same land. Sahelian herders and farmers were all the less motivated to modify the land tenure regime in place, closely articulated to the social structure, since the *land and domanial laws* confirmed *the exercise of these customary rights* "in so far as the state does not need the lands on which they are exercised." The feeble degree of development of these Sahelian zones and the absence of any colonial settlement policy have contributed to leaving vast extents of these precolonial regimes in place.

The fact that these "customary" rights of usage were at least tolerated, if not recognized, so long as they did not contradict the needs of the state does not mean that they were not profoundly modified. The impact of the land and domanial laws in this regard manifests itself in two ways.

On lands claimed by the state these customary rights are legally voided. This is the case with the programs for large-scale irrigation works, the most celebrated example of which during the colonial period and also the most sinister because of its human cost, is that of the *Office du Niger* in the region of Ségou in Mali. In this case, as in most of the other projects of this type, the policy followed has remained the same after independence. The expropriation of "customary users" in no way implies that they accede to new forms of private property on those developed perimeters, which continue to be managed under state control and administration. The state maintains its property rights, sometimes reinforcing them by proceeding to register the land in its own name.[16]

The "purging" of customary usage rights is not limited to these development projects; it also concerns on a much larger scale the establishment of forests and other "classified" sites brought under a special jurisdiction, that of the Forestry Code, and managed by a specific administration that applies a regulation excluding all traditional rights of usage — cutting, hunting, etc. — and all possibilities of clearing or pasture.

The law thus regulates the right to clear new lands subject to authorization and a particular tax. This measure is not applied systematically, thanks essentially to a lack of means of control and enforcement. It reflects, however, the legal authority that the land and domanial laws give to colonial and neocolonial administrations. The precariousness of customary rights of usage is utilized as a means of administration, allowing the punishment of some people and the favoring of others, the initiation of agricultural policies in pastoral zones, policies for commercial crops in agricultural zones, etc. Thus customary land tenure rules are progressively weakened from the inside even as they seem to be perpetuated.

In the last analysis one notes the coexistence of a legal land tenure system and a "real" one governed by customary rules but whose application is perturbed by newly installed administrative and state mechanisms that are applied in an increasingly competitive context.

The development of this *competition in land* is manifested as much by the evolution of conflicts over land as by the multiplication of the forms of devolution of land (sale, rent, cession), which often borrow procedures deriving from customary law but which pervert them by monetarizing the contractual relationship and which develop them on a large scale in certain groups.

This competition in land falls within the framework of the duality mentioned above and it favors it to the degree that the "real" system is disconnected from the "legal" system and from the colonial politico-administrative framework in which the latter develops. Ultimately, the relations of politico-military force among the groups concerned, which derived from the connection between the land system *stricto sensu* and the politico-ritual system in which it operated, and were the ultimate protections in pre-colonial society, no longer function. Certain agricultural groups thus start processes of colonization and clearing of new lands, the pressure being particularly strong and competitive at the limits of the pastoral and agricultural zones. Similarly, Fulani herders, more mobile, penetrate on a broad scale into the pastoral zone formerly occupied exclusively by Moorish and Twareg herders.

Other factors, which I will only rapidly enumerate, serve to aggravate the competition in land.

The most obvious is the growing demographic pressure, to which is added economic pressure in those regions where commercial crops are being developed (peanuts and cotton), which limits the areas devoted to food crops.

I have already referred to the constraints that resulted in colonial times from the policy of development (large-scale works) and territorial improvements (forestry code), in so far as they restricted usage rights, as well as from the intervention in the land-tenure domain to facilitate the economic policies dictated by the administration. These disruptions also affected the general equilibrium of relations among "ethnic" groups. A good example is the process of regional specialization that is becoming established in the western part of the Sahel as a consequence of the early development of the peanut zone in Senegal.[17] This zone corresponds almost exactly to Wolof territory. Its favorable soils close to the sea lend a particular weight to this group, which is starting a movement to clear neighboring agricultural lands.[18] The Toucouleurs of the Senegal River Valley, who had represented a hegemonic pole in the 19th century,[19] remain specialized in the production of food cereals, while the Moors supply slaughter animals to the Senegalese market.[20]

The evolution of the relations among ethnic groups has also seen the monetarization of exchange relations. I have shown on two occasions, both among the Twaregs and Moors, that the tendency during the entire colonial period had been toward an evolution in the respective prices of cattle and cereal products to the benefit of the latter, hence of the farmers (Bonte 1969; Bonte and Abd el-Wedoud ould Cheikh 1983). We will see later the consequences in a particular case — the evolution of the relations between the Fulanis and Dogons in Mali.

Finally, although this list is by no means exhaustive, there is another factor that contributes to the aggravation of competition over land. It concerns the growing demand of the servile categories to have the right of direct access to land. This demand is a source of local competition[21] and may favor movements of agricultural colonization, as in the case of Twareg *ighawelen* (Bonte 1975).

These last developments will serve as a transition to approach the evolution of the land question since the sahelian states have achieved independence,[22] for the factors of this evolution previously defined have been just as operative since independence as they were before. Demographic and economic pressures on the land contribute to the ecological degradation that the latest periods of drought have revealed, and they raise competition in land to the level of a matter of life or death for certain sahelian populations.

The "development" policies that already characterized the last decade of colonization have had their full effect after independence, resulting in the multiplication of development works, essentially hydro-agricultural. The most striking example on the regional level is that along the course of the Senegal River, to which we will return. Rice is increasingly replacing millet and sorghum in production and consumption among the sahelian populations. Subject to the rise and fall of world market prices, commercial crops have also increased considerably.

These transformations have taken place with respect to land in the framework of land and domanial laws, rewritten, of course, by the independent states, but without modifying the dispositions of colonial laws and sometimes even making them more severe.[23]

On one point, however, independence has brought a profound modification, one that bears on the nature of the relation between that which I have called the "real" land tenure system and the legal one. Whereas the colonial state, the political apparatus that controlled the "legal" system, was outside the groups concerned with the rules of the "real" system, the post-independence state is accessible to them and has become a stake in the competition for land.[24] This has led to an ethnic colorization of the state. One has only to think of the role of the Wolofs in Senegal, the Bambara in Mali, the Zarma-Songhai in Niger, or even the arabophone policy in Mauritania, on which I will not expand. Other authors have, in fact, already explored this theme and its multiple manifestations, whether it is a question of linguistic policy, the distribution of charges and payments in the administration or army, or of the control of economic networks.

Although less evident at first glance, the manner in which the *land issue* arises in this context is perhaps more fundamental, *for the production, both on a material and symbolic level, of new identities, of a new dimension of ethnicity along with its conflicting political consequences, and the constitution of ethnic minorities are at play in this domain.*

This is true first of all on a material level, for it is evident that the demographic weight of these ethnic groups and the territory that they occupy are going to play a determining role in the relations that are formed among them with respect to the state. The dominant ethnic groups that we have cited are all of important size, but they are not always the most numerous in their countries, for other factors play a role. One notices, for example, that the capitals of these countries are all situated in a region where these groups are in the majority. The economic power that they have been able to acquire is also a decisive factor, as is their access to modern educational systems and to the new technical elites that result from them, etc.

On the symbolic level, even though the decision-making powers at the heart of the state are apparently to a large degree removed from the rural sector and do not derive from the territorial basis of the ethnic group, the latter and its representatives in the state apparatus often attach a primordial importance to its roots and to the land dimension of ethnic membership. The investments in such and such a region, the "projects" shared in by the sahelian populations and financial organisms, are often stakes that elude economic rationality.

Certainly, even in the absence of democracy in the western sense of "one man one vote," local supports, ethnic or tribal clientelism, play an important role in the contemporary political life of these states. However, I will cite an example that underscores the purely symbolic dimension of certain of the conflicts that develop on this occasion.

In Mauritania dams have been built with state aid on certain wadis to improve traditional recession cultivation of sorghum. With few exceptions, these constructions have proved to be not very productive, out of proportion to the investment made, and sometimes, for various reasons (technical design, location, climatic conditions) production has been practically non-existent. However, serious conflicts over land have developed around these dams, opposing tribal groups, or more frequently *harâtîn* farmers of servile origin and their former *bidan* masters, who under present conditions (drought and degradation of pastures) sometimes practise farming. These conflicts develop around the assertion of collective tribal property, either against other competing groups or against former dependents who claim access to land no longer mediated by the *bidans*. There is no economic interest. It is simply a matter of affirming the local existence of the tribe. One can even ask if the original decision to construct the dam did not have this single goal.

The ensemble of these determinations — material, political, and symbolic — organizing themselves to a significant degree around the issue of land, define what I call the new dimension of ethnicity. In the second section of this study we will analyze its manifestations and consequences by studying various concrete cases.

ETHNICITY AND THE COMPETITION FOR LAND IN THE SAHEL

The cases, presented very succinctly, are on different scales, local (Séno in Mali), regional (interior delta of the Niger in Mali), national (valley of the Senegal in Mauritania), and even international in the case of the Twaregs. Thus they underline the continuity in action of the same mechanisms at these different levels. It is the interplay of these mechanisms that contributes to the construction of what I have called the *new face of ethnicity* in its triple dimension: land (territorial), identity (ethnic), and politics (state).

Before arriving at the exposition of these four cases I will construct a kind of reading grid by distinguishing the broad lines of the mechanisms at work.

Competition and conflicts over land. The exacerbation of the competition over land and the conflicts that result from it are underlined by the weakening of the modalities of regulation, particularly among ethnic groups. Intervention by the state, which, as a function of the relations of political power at the center above these groups, is exercised in favor of one or the other party, can lead to the displacement of the conflict into the arena of state politics.

Expansion and dispossession. Aggravated by demographic and ecological pressures, expansionist movements, most often agricultural, yet sometimes pastoral as in the case of the Fulani, increase the competition and lead to an evolution in relations among ethnic groups that are reflected, furthermore, in monetary and trade relations. In extreme cases, less and less rare, the process ends with the territorial dispossession of one group.

Marginalization. When these tendencies are combined with the marginalization of the ethnic group within the state, for a variety of reasons, ethnic minorities are produced in a context illustrated by numerous political and military conflicts in the Sahel.

Fulanis and Dogons at Séno Mango (Mali)

The Séno is a massif of fossilized dunes where precipitation (about 300mm) and the absence of easily accessible subterranean water have intensified pastoralism. At the moment of colonial intervention, the region was dominated by two powerful chiefdoms of Fulani herders and warriors[25] who practised agriculture marginally through the intermediary of *rimaybe* slave villages. The Dogon farmers were for the most part installed on their famous cliffs, with the exception of the ancient implanation of some lineages in the plain between the Séno and the cliffs. Strongly specialized in either herding or farming, those groups practised daily exchanges of milk and cereals.

Colonial pacification allowed the Dogons to undertake a vast movement of colonization on the plain, one facilitated by the expansionist character of their social and land tenure system[26], stopping, however, for lack of water sources at the limits of the Séno. A certain equilibrium was established between the Fulanis and the Dogons. The first provided manure and milk and were able to continue their pastoral vocation despite the restriction of pasturage by having access to Dogon cereals and to zones left open by long periods of fallow.

Since independence the degradation of the terms of exchange between milk and cereals, linked to the rise in prices of food products, demographic and economic pressures (augumentation of areas cultivated following the increased value of cereals on the market), and the growing access of the Dogons to cattle, in which cereal revenues are invested, have brought a new expansion by the Dogons. The installation of a pastoral project, the ODEM,[27] has become an opportunity for them to occupy the pastoral lands of the Séno.

A series of wells has been dug to facilitate the pastoral exploitation of the zone. Thanks to the support of the local and national administrations, the Dogons are transforming these wells into centers for the introduction of agriculture, which allows them to clear the periphery permanently. Simultaneously they are increasing their pastoral investments.

The Fulanis continue to herd in a reduced area. The degradation of the terms of exchange between milk and cereals and their non-monetarization,[28] leads the Fulanis to sell the agricultural lands they had, entailing a progressive reduction of their herds. At this point they can only choose between migration toward supposedly better lands[29] or reduction to the status of guardians of Dogon herds.

The interior delta of the Niger (Mali).

The interior delta presents a quite distinct ecological particularity in the sahelian zone. It corresponds to the fossil delta of the Niger River (upstream) before it joins the Niger (downstream) that empties into the Gulf of Guinea. The former delta, situated in a very dry zone (100 to 500 mm.) represents a vast flood zone during the annual floods. The receding waters give place to crops (rice and sorghum) and pastures, in particular the famous *bourgoutières* capable of supporting a very heavy pastoral charge.[30]

The economic importance of the delta — which also has very important resources in fish — explains its historical destiny. Two of the principal former sahelian cities, Timbuktu and Djénné, are situated on its periphery and river commerce has always played a determining role. The delta has been included in all the great sudanese states and was often a stake in extremely bitter political struggles. At the start of the 19th century the theocratic Fulani state of Macina established itself there and gave it a new organization, the Dina.

The Dina is a political and territorial system (divided into *leydi*) centered on herding, the principal activity of the Fulani founders of this state. It favors a partial settlement of the Fulani herders by organizing during the flood the annual transhumance outside the delta of a part of the herd, leaving the milch cows in reserved areas. Access to the flood pastures (*bourgoutières*), the trails, and the stop-over points for the cattle are regulated spatially and temporally by the authority of the *dyoro*. The development of farming is limited by these rules. It is practised by the *rimaybe* of the Fulanis, who control their access to the soil, and by free farmers whose rights are recognized, as are those of the *Bozo* fishermen. The fundamental principle of this land use system is religious, as it is founded on Islam and the rights of the ritual masters of the land and water.

Colonization broke the power of the Fulanis and facilitated the autonomy of the farmers, Fulani slaves and others, leading to an extension of cultivation. Other herders as well, in growing numbers, could enter the delta, respecting, however, the authority over land and ritual of the Fulani *dyoro*, for these outside herds only had access to the *bourgoutières* after the native Fulani herds. The growing charge on the pastures was partially compensated for by the commercialization of cattle (and fishing).[31]

Since independence the situation has deteriorated sharply. The large-scale hydro-agricultural programs had been developed on the peripheries of the delta (Office du Niger in the region of Ségou); since then they have been installed in the heart of the delta: the 40,000 hectares put into rice cultivation by the ORM[32] have been only moderately productive and have made inroads on the flood pastures. In the pastoral domain, to try to relieve pastoral pressure on the delta, ODEM has adopted a policy of creating pastoral wells in the peripheral zone outside the floods that serves as refuge to the delta herds during the flood. This policy facilitates the development of agriculture, as I have shown in the case of the Séno, or the installation of new herders, without, however, having any effect on the situation in the delta and while creating problems of overstocking in the unflooded zone.

The climatic crisis has become an ecological catastrophe in the delta with the decrease in the extent of the flood, which greatly diminishes the area of the *bourgoutières*[33] and favors the transformation of part of them into rice fields. Production figures, both for herding and fishing, have fallen by half and the development of agriculture seems more like a transfer of activities than as a true advance. The pressure from outside herders, in particular Fulanis and especially Twaregs chased from their pastures by the drought and the development of farming, becomes increasingly strong, leading to a social and political crisis.

However, the *dyoro* have preserved a part of their control over land, even if they use it now to sell land to farmers. The monetarization of the conditions of access to the *bourgoutières* and the commercial role of certain Fulani groups have contributed to the perpetuation of a certain land tenure structure and to the preservation of an equilibrium among the ethnic groups who join forces to keep new pretenders, particularly the Twaregs, outside the delta.

This equilibrium has been realized to the benefit of a stratum of notables, enriched by commerce, who maintain privileged relations with state powers.

The Senegal River valley

The central zone of the Senegal valley, the Futa Toro, was formerly occupied by a peasantry of heterogeneous origin that exploited highly productive flood recession lands (*walo*) along with Fulani herders and fishermen. The political and cultural (adoption of the Fulani language) integration of this peasantry, to which was given the name *Toucouleurs* under colonization, was achieved by the Fulani *jihad* at the end of the 18th century. It reorganized the valley territorially under the authority of a religious aristocracy, the *Toroobe*, united for a time under the central power of the *Almamy*. Control of the lands on the right bank of the Senegal was the object of a secular competition between the Toucouleurs and the Moorish tribes, organized since the end of the 17th century in the form of emirates (Trarza, Brakna, Tagânit). This competition was marked by conflicts and alliances capable of regrouping Toucouleur "countries" and Moorish emirates against other Toucouleur "countries" and other Moorish emirates.

Colonization intervened (at the start of the 20th century) during a phase of intense pressure from the Moors along the major part of the right bank.[34] The population and land pressures in the valley had been partially resolved in the second half of the 19th century by a new *jihad*, that of the Tijani al-Hajj Umar, who led the Toucouleurs as far as the interior delta of the Niger.[35] After having occupied the Futa Toro without too much difficulty, the French would have much more difficulty in establishing themselves in Moorish territory. The resistance of the Moors to colonization would favor a return of the Toucouleurs to the right bank of the Senegal. This push would manifest itself as much in the agricultural domain (pressure on the *walo* lands of the right bank) as in the pastoral domain: Fulani herders penetrated into the interior of Moorish territory.[36] Under colonization this agricultural expansion was favored by the specialization in cereals that was assigned to the Senegal valley in the regional system that was centered on the production of peanuts in Wolof country.[37]

Mauritanian independence created a new situation with the establishment of the political and cultural hegemony of the Moors, the majority in the country. Very soon (1965) the language issue (policy of arabization) gave rise to the first inter-ethnic troubles, for the policy was considered by the non-arabic populations of the river as a new means of perpetuating the domination of the Moors. However, the Toucouleurs continued their traditional policy of alliances and conflicts with the Moorish groups who contested power in the new state political structures, and consequently they were relatively well represented in the state machinery.[38] Although inter-ethnic troubles were recurrent, two facts led to their radicalization in 1989.

The first derives from the evolution within Moorish society of the situation of the *Harâtîn*, an agricultural group of slave origin who represent almost half the arab-speaking population. This landless peasantry,[39] excluded from the modern educational system and from political functions, developed its demands at the end of the 1970s,[40] and its allegiance became a stake in the inter-ethnic competition. The Moors claimed that the *Harâtîn* belonged as Arab-speakers to the politically dominant ethnic group. Certain radical Toucouleur movements,[41] mocking the slave traditions of their own society, attempted to gain their alliance in the name of negritude so as to upset the exclusive power of the Moors. Two measures taken by the Moorish political elites at this epoch illustrate the importance of this stake: in 1981 slavery was officially abolished in Mauritania, and in 1983 a new land law allowed the *Harâtîns* to claim as individual property the common lands that they farmed. As a result, the *Harâtîns* found themselves once again in the Moorish camp in 1989.

A second destabilizing factor is the development of the Senegal River valley,[42] which is modifying its agrarian and land tenure regime. Recession agriculture has been succeeded by irrigated agriculture. The Toucouleur land tenure system, the basis of its social hierarchy, is crumbling, since the *walo* lands have lost their value. The agricultural perimeters of the valley are coveted by speculative farmers from the ruling Moorish milieu and by *Harâtîns*.

In 1989 a commonplace frontier incident gave rise to ethnic riots in both Senegal and Mauritania. Close to 200,000 Moors left Senegal, where they had been involved primarily in trade and business; more than 100,000 Toucouleurs were chased from the right bank; and most of the Fulani herders also left Mauritania. The situation deteriorated further with the repression of the "Toucouleur *coup d'état* of December 1991," which eliminated many Toucouleurs from the high posts that they had occupied in the state apparatus and in the army. The process of ethnic minoritization seems then effectively to have begun.

The Twareg question.

At the moment of the colonial conquest the world of the Twareg was divided into a series of grand tribal confederations, within which political centralization was weak,[43] extending over several saharan and sahelian countries.[44] Territorial control was exercised tribally under the authority of the warrior aristocracy of the *imajeghen*. Pasture zones were distributed among the confederations and the tribes, while matrimonial and political alliances facilitated access to exterior pasture zones. The oases and peripheral sahelian zones were occupied by slave groups[45] who practised agriculture or cultivated date palms. There was also pressure on bordering agricultural populations to obtain agricultural produce and slaves (cf. Bonte 1985 with respect to the Kel Geres confederation).

The Twaregs offered strong resistance to the colonial conquest even though they had only a few firearms. In 1917, furthermore, most of the Twareg world rose up against the colonial authorities, who could only put the movement down with great difficulty.[46] The repression was very severe, physically liquidating part of the *imajeghen* in certain confederations, like that of the Iwellemenden.

This repression was one of the factors in the progressive shrinking of Twareg pasture lands that continues to the present. Another factor is the reversal of power relations between the herders and the southern agro-pastoral populations. During the entire colonial period there was an extension of cultivation northward that penetrated deeply into arable tribal lands. The emancipation of the servile classes in Twareg society[47] accentuated this agricultural pressure. In Niger particularly, Fulani herders also penetrated deeply into Twareg pastoral territory.

Independence completed the break-up of the Twareg world among several countries, where they are in all cases strongly in the minority. Their way of life, the low level of education within their society, and the pressure on land from neighboring populations accentuate their under-representation in the states born from decolonialization. Very soon this situation provoked political and military reactions. Days after Independence the revolt of the Twaregs of Adrar des Iforas marks the rupture between the new states, in this case Mali, and a part of the Twareg world. The dream maintained by certain nostalgic French military of creating a saharan state that would have cut off Algeria, which had become independent in 1962, from its saharan hinterland with its oil reserves contributed not a little to these first reactions.

This pastoral region, reduced and fragmented by the frontiers that were closed with decolonialization, deteriorated further thereafter. To respond to the growing overstocking of cattle, large-scale pastoral hydraulic programs were initiated that divided the pastures into grids with a series of wells.[48] Aside from the fact that this policy helped destroy the last traces of the former territorial limits and the pastoral economy, it had the opposite of its intended effect: overstocking of the pastures increased and led to irreversible degradation around the wells.

The drought of 1973 and succeeding years had heavy consequences for the Twaregs, especially since, particularly in Mali, the distribution of aid was made with extreme ill will on the part of the states.[49] Entire groups were chased from their traditional pastures and had to install themselves as "refugees" in more southerly zones, where they attempted, with great difficulty, to reconstitute their herds. The social fabric is decomposing as a result of these population movements and the definitive liberation of the former slave groups.

The drought accentuated the competition for land. The Twaregs, in contrast to the Fulanis, could not negotiate their reinstallation on new pastures: I have given an example in the case of the interior delta of the Niger. They have also been quite generally excluded from the great development works, most often hydro-agricultural, in the Niger valley, which offered other resources to the populations affected. In Niger they have only benefited to a quite secondary degree from the royalties derived from the exploitation of the uranium at Arlit, even though it is located in their territory.

It was in this context that the Twareg insurrection began, fed in the beginning by migrants or refugees installed in neighboring countries[50] and by the cycle of raids and reprisals that has led to the generalization of the movement in recent years. This movement corresponds to a total social, economic, and cultural crisis in Twareg society, but also to a phenomenon of marginalization that makes the Twareg in most of these states into an ethnic minority condemned to exploit its "exoticism" and particularities for touristic ends.

CONCLUSIONS

In the sahelian context, where the weight of history and state traditions had given ethnic and cultural distinctions a quite distinctive character, recent developments have lent a new weight to this entire dimension. The land stakes and the political dimension of these new ethnic demands have set in motion a dangerous cycle of marginalization of new "ethnic" minorities.

In this case ethnicity is no longer produced by local social and cultural relations that contribute to differentiate neighboring groups or those occupying the same territory. These diverse economic, social, and cultural elements of ethnicity certainly continue to distinguish the groups from each other, but it is the new relationship that they maintain to the power of the state that will essentially contribute to a radicalization of the relations between the local groups.

The elites, whatever the conditions of their formation — technical competence, force of arms, election results in a democratic regime — who exercise this power of the state are led above all to perpetuate it through reliance on the ensemble of relations of kinship and marriage, clientship, redistribution, etc. that attach them to the local groups. It is what has sometimes been called, quite unjustly, "tribalism" in African politics. But, contrary to the usual conditions that produce ethnicity, the result of a series of local conditions differentiating groups, it is now the state itself that produces the conditions of this differentiation and that gives them a radical turn.

Political conflicts over the control of the state apparatus create a new ethnic dimension, and this ethnic dimension translates itself by implacable confrontations between local groups who must each create uncontested territorial bases for their power in the state apparatus. Thus are created the conditions for the wars, too quickly considered to be the products of a secular history and an exacerbated ethnicity, that now devastate the countries of the Sahel.

NOTES

1. It comprises Senegal, Mauritania, Mali, Niger, and Chad; this last country, where I have not had the opportunity to conduct field studies, is not included in the demonstration.
2. Islamic holy wars. The creation of the states was accompanied by a rapid and relatively massive diffusion of Islam, which had started around the 9th to 10th centuries.

3. They speak the Fulani language, but are composed of an aggregate of farming and pastoral populations of the Senegal Valley: Fulani, Sérère, Wolof, Soninke, etc.
4. Ghana, for example, around the Soninke, Mali around the Malinke, and the Songhai, who gave their name to the empire of that name. The Fulani organized the principal *jihads* of the 18th and 19th centuries.
5. Diallo, Touré, Ba, etc.. Rather frequently they are of Fulani origin, which corresponds to the nature of the most recent hegemonies and the spatial dispersion of this population.
6. Thus in Moorish society *bidan* (Whites) are opposed to *sudan* (Blacks), the latter including slaves (*'abid*) and freed slaves (*harâtîn*), who devote themselves exclusively to agriculture.
7. French trading posts in Senegal go back to the 17th century. The occupation of the interior of the country started in the middle of the 19th century. The French occupation of the Sahel was complete by about 1900. The conquest of the Saharan borders would not be over, in Mauritania, till the beginning of the 1930s.
8. It is naturally not exclusive to these sahelian societies but is widespread in the ensemble of African societies.
9. Or wider ensembles, tribal confederations, emirates, etc., that follow the same principle.
10. The difference between these two types of society is not perhaps as distinct as I have presented it if one knows that the title of confederal political chief among the Twaregs, *amenokal*, means "master of the ground" and if one consults my studies on the Moorish emirate (Bonte 1985).
11. One of the best known examples is that of the Dogon land tenure system, which unfortunately I cannot describe in the restricted scope of this study (Paulme 1988; Bouju 1984).
12. For an example in Soninke society consult Pollet and Winter (1971). See also the studies collected by C. Meillassoux (1975) and his work on slavery (1986).
13. It combined rights to water (*bozo* fishers), to agricultural lands (Marka and Fulani, whose *rimaybe* practise agriculture), and to flood pastures (*bourgoutières*), exercised prioritarily by the dominant Fulani herders, who had elaborated precise rules of access to these various resources according to the rhythm of floods and recessions.
14. The rainy season pastures of the cattle herders are the dry season pastures of the camel herders, who move further north into the desert during the rains.
15. The sole uniform juridicial principle exercised during the precolonial period was that of Muslim law, the *shari'a*. It is interesting to note that formally this principle rests identically on the opposition between the common property of the *umma*, the Muslim community, mediated by the political authority, and private property. However, the *shari'a* accords a legal place to customary law, the *'urf*, and

permits easy access, based on the concept of development, to private property.
16. In the case of the *Office du Niger*, local populations had that much less access to a new form of private and individual property to the extent that the colonial administration carried out massive and deadly transfers of workers from distant regions.
17. Along with its port and urban industrial appendages (Dakar, Rufisque, Thiès) for the treatment and exportation of peanuts.
18. The movement is taking place for an important part within the framework of the Muslim brotherhood of the Mourides under a land tenure regime that realizes a synthesis of new objectives (commercial farming) and ancient forms of politico-religious control of access to land.
19. It is there where the Muslim state enterprise (*jihad*) of al-Hajj Umar, in the second half of the 19th century, favored Toucouleur expansion as far as the interior delta of the Niger.
20. This is bringing about a transformation of Moorish animal husbandry. There has been a decline in the breeding of camels and an increase in the breeding of cattle and small animals, which favors a movement of the tribes toward the south. This movement has expanded with the drought.
21. In the inner delta of the Niger, for example, where the Fulani *rimaybe*, under Fulani domination ratified by the Dina, have consolidated their rights over cultivated lands and have cleared pastoral zones, tending to upset the relative equilibrium.
22. This was towards the end of the 1950s and the beginning of the 1960s.
23. This is true even in the Islamic Republic of Mauritania where none of the dispositions of the *shari'a* in this domain (recognition of customary law, easy access to private property) has been kept.
24. This is true independent of political regimes, which are, more-over, extremely variable, including single parties, military regimes, and current democratic experiments.
25. Who had refused to accept the authority of the Fulani Dina, which had established itself in the interior delta of the Niger, and its radical religious reformism.
26. Junior lineages established themselves on the periphery while maintaining ritual and land ties with their lineages of origin, which gave great cohesion and force to the movement (Bouju 1984).
27. Office de Développment de l'Elevage (Herding Development Office) in the Mopti region.
28. It is forbiden in Dogon villages for any one to buy milk, which must only be bartered (one gourd of milk for two of millet after the harvest, one for one in the period preceding the new harvest, when millet is scarce). Whoever contravenes this rule suffers reprisals.
29. The Fulanis have migrated massively into zones further south in Dogon country, particularly toward the region of Sikasso and the areas bordering the Ivory Coast.

30. It is estimated that the delta can support between 1.5 and 2 million cattle and comparable quantities of small animals.
31. The areas of the delta suitable for pasture went from 4,135,000 hectares in 1952 to 2,946,000 hectares in 1972. Similarly the number of animals per hectare went from one to three hectares in 1960 to one to 1.5 hectares in 1970.
32. *Office du Riz* (Rice Office) of the Mopti region.
33. They have been reduced by about one half in the last ten years.
34. The *walo* agricultural lands are still exploited on the right bank by the Toucouleurs, but since the establishment of a defensive system by the Almamys at the start of the 19th century, their villages have been essentially grouped together on the left bank.
35. It brought a massive migration of Toucouleurs lineages and a movement of agricultural colonization that developed particularly in the zone situated south of the present frontier between Mauritania and Mali (Nioro).
36. Particularly in the area of Gorgol, traditionally disputed by the emirates of Brakna and Tagânit, as well as in the Assaba further east.
37. Cereal production in the valley had very early on been focused on barter, particularly with Moorish herders, who exchanged their animals, dates, and salt for cereals.
38. Common adherence to Islam and to Islamic brotherhoods (*turuq*), such as the Tijaniyya, favors this policy.
39. It only has access to land by belonging to a tribe that holds collective rights to it.
40. The al-Hor movement represents a first level of political organization of the scarce *harâtîn* elites.
41. Within the FLAM (Liberation Front of Mauritanian Africans).
42. Two dams, one upstream (Mattali) and one downstream (Diama), regulate the flooding and prevent the influx of salt water in the delta.
43. Various forms of the organization of political power exist in a society so strongly hierarchical ("nobles," *imajeghen*; "vassals," *imghad*; "marabouts," *inislemen*; "freed slaves," *ighawelen*; etc.): in certain cases an *amenokal* ("master of the soil and war chief") is chosen from the principal noble tribe; in other cases power is exercised collegially within the warrior aristocracy.
44. Algeria, Libya, Niger, Mali, Burkina-Faso.
45. "Freed slaves," *ighawelen*; "slaves of the tribe," *iklan n'tawshit*; slaves, *iklan*.
46. The most celebrated episode is the siege of Agadez, where the French garrison was entrenched. It was only lifted under pressure from a major rescue expedition.
47. Much more pronounced than, for example, among the Moorish pastoralists.
48. For this policy in Niger see Bernus 1974.

49. The famous Lazaret camp at Niamey (Niger) thus comprised over 20,000 people, for the most part Malian Twaregs.
50. Libya in particular.

REFERENCES

Bernus, E. (1974). "Possibilités et limites de la politique d'hydraulique pastorale dans le Sahel nigérien," *Cahiers ORSTOM*, série sciences humaines, XI–2: 119–26.

Bonte, P. (1969). "L'élevage et le commerce du bétail dans l'Ader Doutchi-Majya," *Etudes nigériennes*, N° 23.

——————(1975). "L'organisation économique des Touaregs Kel Gress," pp. 166–215, in R. Creswell (ed.), *Eléments d'ethnologie*, Paris, A. Colin.

——————(1985). "Esquisses d'histoire foncière de l'émirat de l'Adrar," pp. 323–46 in P. Baduel (ed.), *Etats, territoires et terroirs au Maghreb*, Paris, Ed. Du CNRS.

——————(1991). "Egalité et hiérarchie dans une tribu maure. Les Awlâd Qaylân, tribu de l'Adrar mauritanien," pp. 145–99, in P. Bonte, E. Conte, C. Hamés et Abd el Wedoud ould Cheikh, *Al-Ansâb La quête des origines. Anthropologie historique de la société tribale arabe*, Paris, Ed. de la Maison des Sciences de l'Homme.

——————et Abd el-Wedoud ould Cheikh. (1983). "Production pastorale et production marchande dans la société maure," in *Contemporary Nomadic and Pastoral Peoples: Africa and Latin America, Studies in Third World Societies*, 17: 31–56.

Bouju, J. (1984). *Graine de l'homme, enfant du mil*, Paris, Société d'ethnographie.

Meillassoux, Cl. (1975). (ed.), *L'esclavage en Afrique* précoloniale, Paris, Maspéro.

Meillassoux, Cl. (1986). *Anthropologie de l'esclavage. Le ventre de fer et d'argent*, Paris, P.U.F.

Paulme, D. (1988), *Organisation sociale des Dogons*, Paris. J.-M. Place (réed).

Pollet E et G. Winter, (1971). *La Société Soninke (Dyahum, Mali)*, Université libre de Bruxelles, Ed. de l'Institut d'Ethnologie.

Chapter NINE

Detour onto the Shining Path: Obscuring the Social Revolution in the Andes

William P. Mitchell
Monmouth University
West Long Branch, NJ, 07764

The Shining Path, or *Sendero Luminoso*, is the popular name of the Peruvian Communist Party. Until the capture of its head, Abimael Guzmán, in the early 1990s, it fought a brutal war against the central government in Lima that at times seriously threatened the government's sovereignty in rural areas. Mitchell shows that the Shining Path's brutality was matched by that of the military. He further argues that such violence results from what he calls a social revolution; a "revolution" that has taken Peru down the path of a not especially competitive industrial capitalism. This path has led to a protracted economic crisis that is the breeding ground of brutal institutions that have impoverished many Peruvians. He contends that a scholarly focus on the Shining Path has directed our attention away from the fundamental social changes and has contributed to a social climate in which force rather than amelioration is seen as the solution to social distress. Mitchell's article poses a grim possibility: is it the case that Peru is the shining path of other late blooming capitalisms?

THE CONSTRUCTION OF AN IMAGE

Until recently, the Shining Path guerrilla war[1] and the cocaine trade have dominated contemporary images of Peru. Journalists, government officials, human rights advocates, political scientists, and — to a lesser extent — anthropologists have understandably focused on the war and its violence.[2] Some have asserted that violence is endemic to the Andes (Poole 1994, Urbano 1991, Vargas Llosa 1983).[3] Others have stressed the cocaine trade and its relation to "narcoterrorism" (Tarazona-Sevillano 1990; see also Gonzales 1991, Ossio 1990), a presumed connection between Shining Path and *coca* production. The particular events reported are often accurate. The war has been real, the military and guerrillas have often been brutal, and some Peruvians have participated in cocaine production. In spite of their accuracy, however, these accounts of war, terror, and cocaine have created a false image by amplifying certain truths at the expense of others.[4]

The war and cocaine have had a disastrous impact on the people of Peru (Urrutia et al. 1987), but they are only two manifestations of the revolutionary transformation of Peruvian society, symptoms of underlying social stress. To focus on Shining Path and *coca* production rather than the general social transformation neglects the systemic changes, thereby distorting our understanding of the Andes and of Shining Path itself. This distortion provides an ideological screen that helps to sustain a climate of repression in which force is used to control what is seen as social evil rather than social upheaval (Poole and Rénique 1991). The military slaughter in 1997 of the Tupac Amaru guerillas who had captured the Japanese embassy in Lima and the secret burial of their bodies without an independent autopsy is an example of this dynamic. Peru, of course, is not the only country where ideological screens are used to support repressive policies. The construction of United States inner cities as crime-ridden rather than in need of resources functions similarly.

Anxiety about the Shining Path war and *coca* production is rooted in social reality, but that concern has been magnified by ideological, national, and disciplinary considerations (see Poole and Rénique 1991). The stake of governments (Peruvian, regional, and international) in containing a movement that threatened to destabilize the Andean region captured the attention of many. Attitudes toward the war have also become political markers in Peru, polarizing opinion and structuring debates over social policy. The frequent portrayals of Shining Path partisans as demoniac crazies (cf. Rosenau and Flanagan 1992, Strong 1992) heightened attention still more, as has the preoccupation of the United States government with domestic cocaine consumption. Research on the war has also been spurred by the general scholarly interest in peasant rebellion and resistance (see, for example, the theoretical works of Hobsbawm 1969, McClintock 1992, Scott 1976, 1985, 1990, and Wolf 1969). Shining Path has consequently engendered more interest, even in scholarly circles, than have changes in peasant household budgets, although the latter tell us more about the social reality that led to the war.[5]

Recent image-makers, mainly government agencies and journalists, have begun to emphasize Peru as a safe source of economic investment. This more favorable picture of Peru began with the election of Alberto Fujimori in 1990, his subsequent neoliberal economic reforms along IMF (International Monetary Fund) lines, including repayment of Peru's international debt in 1991, and the capture of Abimael Guzmán, the leader of Shining Path, in September 1992 and the subsequent decline in most of the outward violence. Both pictures of Peru as a place of violence and as a safe economic haven are distortions, but this paper was first conceived at the height of the war in the late 1980s, and I will concern myself primarily with the picture of violence (see Mitchell in preparation for an extended discussion of the war's aftermath).

Whatever the motivations of individual scholars, research on Shining Path has exerted a generally positive effect on Andean anthropology. To explain the war, scholars have been pushed from some of the more arcane and romantic discussions of *"lo andino"* (the almost primeval Andean) to the real world of conquest, class, repression, exploitation, and social change (Starn 1991).[6] Nonetheless, excessive concentration on Shining Path and *coca* production has emphasized the exotic and the spectacular rather than the mundane existence of everyday people. Most people have not participated in the Shining Path war or the cocaine trade, although they have been greatly affected by them. Nearly everyone, however, has actively participated in the underlying transformation of Peru from a rural country to one in which most people live in cities, a social transformation that Matos Mar (1984) has called the "plebeian flood" (*desborde popular*).

THE UNDERLYING SOCIAL REALITY

It is difficult to translate "*desborde popular*" into a simple English term, but Matos Mar is referring to the rapid population growth after World War II and the subsequent migratory and cultural "flood" that has changed Peru from a country dominated by the Lima elite into one transformed culturally and socially by peasant migrants to Lima. Much of this metamorphosis is related to expanding capitalism: the decline of peasant farming, the intensification of the nonfarm economy, the commodification of labor, and the shift from communal to individual systems of production (Matos Mar 1984, Mitchell 1991a). Further manifestations of the "flood" (and the capitalist expansion) have been the spread of the Spanish language, literacy, and the spectacular growth of Protestantism. Negative consequences have been increasing poverty, the rapid growth of crowded cities, the spread of diseases of poverty and crowding (e.g., cholera, typhoid, and tuberculosis), and the growth of political and economic violence. Shining Path and *coca* production are only part of this picture.

To understand these changes it is necessary to examine the economic pressures that have beset rural communities, the traditional subjects of anthropological inquiry. Instead of viewing these populations as isolated, however, we must see them as parts of larger economic and social spheres. We must look at the political economy of local production (Mitchell 1987, Montoya 1980, Wolf 1982). From this perspective, the transformation in Peru is the result of internal and external pressures on peasant farm production and income. Population has grown dramatically, but poor environmental resources and national economic policies depressing peasant income have limited the ability of peasants to expand farming to feed their larger families. Many have entered the nonfarm economy in consequence. The rapid growth of population has also produced a high percentage of young people pushed out of their rural communities into an economy that has little place for them. They have become a large and often disaffected group of depeasantized youth (Favre 1984).

I explore these points with data on the residents and migrants of Quinua, a district located an hour by road from Ayacucho, the city where Shining Path began. Quinua has a population of about 6,000 people living in a central town and 14 hamlets. The community has changed strikingly since I began my work there in 1966 (table 9.1). Peasants have increasingly shifted from farm to nonfarm production; today nearly every family has some member who works primarily in craft manufacture, trade, or similar activity. Most people born in the community migrate, often permanently, to other areas of Peru and sometimes to other countries. The community sometimes has neglected its irrigation infrastructure but has built schools to facilitate coping with the changed economy (Mitchell 1994). While old people are generally monolingual Quechua-speaking peasants, the young are increasingly educated and bilingual. The elaborate system of fiestas and the accompanying religious-political posts (*cargos*) that helped structure social life (Mitchell and Jaye 1988) has almost disappeared. Many people have converted to Protestantism. Face-to-face

Table 9.1. The Revolutionary Transformation in Quinua, Peru.

Year of 1966	Year of 1987
58-Year Population Doubling Rate	25-Year Population Doubling Rate
Agrarian Focus	Increased commercial Focus
Cyclical Migration	Permanent Migration
Status Relationships (eg, *Ayni, Minka*)	Cash Relationships (eg, wage labor)
Small-scale Trade	Large-scale Trade
Small Weekly Market	Large Weekly Market
Locally Produced Craft Goods	Manufactured Goods
Mostly Barter	Increased Cash Purchase
Some Cash-Cropping	Increased Cash-Cropping
8 Stores (*tiendas*)	38 Stores (*tiendas*)
<50 Commercial Ceramicists	>500 Commercial Ceramicists
10–15 Food Sellers, 2 Half Days/wk	40–80 Food Sellers, 7 Days/wk
Catholicism	Catholicism and Protestantism
Fiesta and *Cargo* System	Diminished *Fiesta-Cargo* System
Peasant Leaders (*Varayoc*)	National Political Forms
Quechua-Speaking	Quechua and Spanish-Speaking
Illiterate Majority	Literate Majority
Economic Inequality	Increased Economic Inequality
Haciendas and Peonage	Peasant owners and Peonage
Status Mechanisms of Social Control	Contract Mechanisms of Social Control
Relatively Tranquil	Increased Personal & Political Violence

Note: Table 9.1. is a model of the differences between the two periods and therefore omits important qualifications. See the text and Mitchell 1991a for a discussion of these complexities.

mechanisms of social control have loosened. Disparities in wealth and property have increased, as has crime against property and person.

Some Quinuenos have actively supported Shining Path, while others have sympathized with them and their call for an end to repression and the creation of a satisfactory social and moral order. Most, however, have simply tolerated or opposed them.[7] Although every Quinueno has been affected by the war, most have resisted being drawn directly into the war by either Shining Path or the military. For many years Quinuenos successfully fought the military demand to create a peasant militia (a civil defense committee), but they finally succumbed in 1990. Instead of war, nearly all Quinuenos have participated actively in the intensification of nonfarm work and the many other changes that have transformed the community and all Peru.

PRESSURES ON PEASANT PRODUCTION

Prior to 1940 Quinua and most rural Peruvian communities subsisted primarily on local resources. Nonetheless, the majority of Quinua peasants — and I suspect most peasants in Peru — did not own or control sufficient land or water to feed themselves for the entire year (Mitchell 1991a: 85–86), and they had to supplement agropastoral production with work on *haciendas* and income earned through occasional cash cropping, artisan manufacture, and trade. They also migrated seasonally to the coast to work in the *guano* mines or cotton plantations, work that earned the bulk of the community's supplementary income. Men (primarily) left Quinua after planting their fields and returned home with cash before the next sowing. Wives and parents sent them agricultural produce while they were away, helping them to subsist on the low wages paid on the coast (see also Caballero 1981: 161–63, Collins 1988, Cotlear 1988, Montoya 1980).

Most Quinua households used (and still use) such migrant and other nonfarm income to pay for food, to buy personal and household necessites and amenities (eg, clothing, medicines, kerosene, school supplies, metal forks and spoons) and to participate in the local fiesta system. They also used the money as capital to purchase agricultural supplies (eg, land, seeds, fertilizers, tools) and the trade goods used in commercial ventures. Up until sometime in the 1940s, these local and nonlocal resources were roughly in equilibrium with population size and economic demand, albeit a demand dampened by repression and ties of dependency (Mitchell 1991b). Most Quinuenos were poor — very poor — but they were able to scrape by.

Conditions changed in mid-century when Quinuenos and other peasants began to experience the combined pressures of population growth and expanding capitalism. The cause of the worldwide decline in infant mortality known as the "health transition" is complex and only partially understood, even for industrial countries. The best predictor of infant mortality in the World Fertility Sample is the educational status of the mother (Brennan 1983, Caldwell et al. 1990, Caldwell and Santow 1990). Whatever the cause, however, infant mortality began to decline in Quinua in the early 1940s, a decline clearly portrayed in municipal mortality records. In these data, there were 241 deaths per thousand births of children less than five years of age in 1955, but only 100 such deaths in 1985 (Mitchell 1991a: 32). Population consequently grew, pushing peasants against the limits of their existing productive system. The birth rate jumped from 12.6 births per thousand population in 1940 to 42.0 births per thousand forty years later in 1980, a function of the youth of the population rather than of increased fertility. The period during which the population would double consequently narrowed from every 58 years in 1960 to every 25 years in 1980 (Mitchell 1991a: 30).

The impact of higher birth rates and declining mortality is graphically portrayed by the increase in the ratio of births to deaths between 1955 and 1985 (table 9.2). In 1955, 1.75 Quinuenos were born for every one who died. This figure soared to 3.33 in 1985. If we regard a death as the opening of a social space, then there were 3.33 applicants for every such space in 1985. These figures illustrate the great pressures that newborns and their parents face: people are forced to find creative solutions to feed themselves and their children.

Table 9.2. Ratio of Births to Deaths: District of Quinua — 1955 to 1985.

	1955	1960	1965	1970	1975	1980	1985
Total Births	145	163	218	231	227	249	260
Total Deaths	83	97	70	125	80	86	78
Ratio: Births/Deaths	1.75	1.68	3.11	1.85	2.84	2.90	3.33

Source: Municipal Records, District of Quinua, data collected by José Oriundo in 1986 and 1987.

Population pressure has created a rural crisis (see also Caballero 1981: 147–72, Collins 1988, Figueroa 1984, Weismantel 1988: 30, 176–77) similar to that experienced during the demographic transition in other areas of the world (Schneider and Schneider 1996), but environmental constraints in Quinua have deterred peasants from significantly expanding their farmland to feed their larger families. Even though Quinua is located on the more productive eastern side of the Ayacucho Valley, most of the terrain is too high and cold or too low and dry for intensive farming (Mitchell 1994, 1997), so that most of Quinua (and, indeed, Peru) is uninhabited (see also Diáz 1969: 23–82). In 1972, as reported in the agricultural census, only 12.2 percent of Quinua's total territory was devoted to farming, and only a small percentage of that 12.2 percent was irrigated (Mitchell 1991a: 43; 1994). Most of the people (90.5 percent in 1961) lived and still live in these two irrigated maize zones (the savannah and valley bottom), small parts of the total territory but the major centers of agricultural production (table 9.3).

Table 9.3. Settlement and Population by Ecological Zone District of Quinua — 1961.

Ecozone	Altitude (Meters)	Productive Regime	Settlements (Percent)	Population (Percent)	Average Settlement Size
Tundra/Paramo	4100+	Herding	0.0	0.0	-0-
Prairie	4000–4100	Herding/Tuber Farming	1.3	0.5	26
Moist Forest	3400–4000	Herding/Tuber & Some Grain Farming	3.8	2.1	37
Savannah	2850–3400	Irrigated Maize Farming	69.6	83.8	81
Thorn Steppe	2500–2850	Non-Intensive Dry Farming	10.1	5.9	40
Valley Bottom	2500	Irrigated Maize Farming	7.6	5.9	52
Unknown	—	—	7.6	1.8	16
Total N			79	5,348	68

Source: Peru 1966: 345–347 and interviews with Virgilio Oriundo in 1983.

Quinuenos have been further hampered from expanding farm production by their inability to muster an effective labor force. Quinua suffers from high dependency ratios (47.4 percent of the inhabitants were less than 15 years of age in 1981) and a scarcity of adult men (women between the ages of 20 to 39 outnumbered the men by 41 percent in the same year), making it very difficult for Quinua farmers (many of them women) to get the laborers needed for agro-pastoral production (Mitchell 1991b, 1994).[8]

Environmental and labor constraints have been exacerbated by a system of private tenure that prohibits free access to idle land. Before the 1970s, *haciendas* controlled much of the land and water needed by politically independent peasants. Quinuenos had to exchange labor for that land and water (Mitchell 1994). They ended many of these restrictions in the 1960s, however, doing so in reaction to the rural crisis even before the Agrarian Reform established by the Velasco regime affected Quinua in 1973 (Mitchell 1994), but Quinuenos are still constrained by a system that limits their use of uncultivated land, much of it owned by nonresident migrants. Although many migrants (or their surrogates) continue to cultivate their lands, others do so poorly or not at all. In the 1972 agricultural census, 16.3 percent of the irrigated lands were listed as having lain in fallow for more than a year (Mitchell 1991a: 72). At least some of these valuable lands had been abandoned (even if only temporarily) by their owners. As migration has increased, more such lands are lying in fallow or are undercultivated, often presided over by aging widows whose children have left Quinua for the cities. Although the law (*Ley de Comunidades*) requires the redistribution of migrant lands in peasant communities such as Quinua, the law is usually not enforced. The Shining Path war has increased field abandonment. People fled the war, abandoning homes and leaving fields in fallow, some of which have been invaded by persistent and difficult-to-plow gramma grasses.

EXTERNAL CONSTRAINTS ON PEASANT INCOME: 1940–1970

The political economy in which production takes place has also constrained Quinuenos, encouraging them to abandon subsistence farming and to enter the nonfarm economy (see also Montoya 1980). Since at least the 1940s, Peruvian governments have tended to put more resources into developing the infrastructure of the export economy (providing credit, roads, electrification, and markets) than into developing the peasant infrastructure (providing irrigation, market roads, transport, credit, and crop loss insurance), a phenomenon also found in neighboring Bolivia (Nash 1992). Not only did government policy favor the coast (which is the center of the export economy) over the highlands (dominated by the peasant economy), but the infrastructural improvements in peasant areas were also tied to exports (e.g., metals and wool), so that some peasant areas were connected to the growing capitalist economy (e.g., the Mantaro Valley) but others (especially the departments of Ayacucho, Huancavelica, and Apurimac) were less so (Montoya 1980). This unequal development hit the Department of Ayacucho particularly hard, for the roads and railways built into neighboring departments tended to siphon trade, manufacturing, and commercial farming (especially wheat, Ayacucho's major commercial crop) away from Ayacucho. In consequence, this once prosperous department (which left a splendid legacy of many fine colonial houses and churches in Ayacucho City) has experienced a long period of decline (Gálvez and Cano 1974: 170, as cited in Degregori 1990: 29).

Peruvian governments have also subsidized low food costs for the urban labor force (working primarily in the export sector) at the expense of rural farmers by both directly controlling the price of food and by setting exchange rates that have cheapened food imports. Inadequate credit and the poor rural infrastructure, moreover, have raised peasant production and marketing costs, exacerbating peasant difficulties in competing with cheap imported foods (Thorp 1991). The resulting low food prices and reduced demand for peasant production have dampened peasant income (Appleby 1982, Collins 1988: 20–21, de Janvry 1981, Ferroni 1980, Franklin et al. 1985, Long and Roberts 1984: 60–63, Pastor and Wise 1992, Thorp and Bertram 1978; see also Meillassoux 1981 and Nash 1992: 290).

International food exporters such as the United States have further intensified these pressures on the peasant by subsidizing Peru's purchase of foreign grain. Similar subsidies have created problems in other areas of the world as well (Hall 1985, Maren 1993).[9] During the period in which the United States began to subsidize the Peruvian purchase of US wheat, Ayacucho wheat production declined to such an extent that wheat mills almost disappeared from the city of Ayacucho (see also Gálvez and Cano 1974, as cited in Degregori 1986b: 21–22).

Peasant farm income has consequently declined vis à vis the prices of manufactured goods in Peru since at least 1940, making it more difficult for peasants to buy even such basic goods as school supplies for children (Caballero 1981: 212, de Janvry 1981: 240, Pastor and Wise 1992). Between 1961 and 1972 the value of the products peasants sell — maize, potatoes, barley, wheat, beef, mutton, and milk — dropped by 15.2 percent in comparison to the price of the commercial goods they buy — rice, cooking oil, fats, noodles, sugar, beer, cane alcohol, soda, textiles, school supplies, detergents, soaps, candles, kerosene, plastics, and salt (Alvarez 1979, Caballero 1981: 212). Between 1979 and 1988, the relative value of peasant goods fell again by about half (Pastor and Wise 1992: 101). Consequently, peasants must sell more farm products today than fifty years ago to buy the same quantity of manufactured goods, a complaint that has been voiced by the Ayacucho peasant federation (Smith 1991: 22).

Additional stress has been caused by disruptions in the cyclical migration that had helped sustain the local economy. In the 1960s, Peruvian cotton production declined because of weakened international demand caused by the development of synthetic fabrics (Matos Mar 1984: 28–31, Morner 1985: 163–87, Reid 1985: 25–27, Thorp and Bertram 1978: 23–144), reducing employment for temporary laborers from Quinua and other peasant communities. In the mid-1970s, moreover, after the government abandoned its commitment to the Velasco agrarian reform, the cotton cooperatives that had been created by that reform were left without capital to buy seed, fertilizer, insecticide, and temporary labor (see de Janvry 1981: 138, 212–13). By 1983, many cooperatives that had provided Quinuenos with cyclical employment had stopped planting cotton and were selling their soil to brick manufacturers (Mitchell in preparation). Responding to these disruptions in cotton work, Quinuenos shifted to cyclical work on wood and fruit production in the tropical forest *montaña*, but this work became increasingly dangerous with the rise of cocaine production in this zone in the 1970s and the devasting impact of the Shining Path war there in the 1980s.

QUINUA'S ECONOMIC TRANSFORMATION

Responding to these ecological and economic constraints on farm production, Quinua peasants have created new sources of income to support their larger families. Because nonfarm income has remained fairly steady in comparison with declining agricultural income (Gonzales de Olarte 1987: 110), peasants have devoted more and more effort to nonagricultural activities in order to eke out the living that would be impossible from agriculture alone. They have come to rely increasingly on commerce, commercial craft manufacture, petty entrepreneurship, and wage labor, a phenomenon found throughout the Department of Ayacucho (Degregori 1986a: 63–64) and Peru (Caballero 1981, Gonzales de Olarte 1987). Consequently, Quinuenos, who have always been linked to the cash economy, are much more so today.

Farming has become increasingly supplemental to the total household economy. The number of commercial ceramicists in Quinua (exporting production to Lima, the United States, Europe, and Japan) has grown from around 50 in 1966 to more than 500 in 1986. Some of these ceramicists have mounted exhibitions in the United States and Europe. In the 1950s Quinuenos produced ceramics to help sustain farming (Arnold 1993). Today many farm to support ceramic production. The number of women selling food on the plaza has grown concomitantly from 10 to 15 women working two half days a week in 1966 to some 40 women working seven full days a week in 1986. The number of fathers listed with nonfarm occupations in Quinua's birth records also jumped from 16.4 percent in 1955 to 36.5 percent in 1985 (Mitchell 1991a: 105).[10]

Quinuenos are also cash-cropping more today than previously, a process of intensification that commenced in the mid-1940s (see also Allen 1988: 30; Cotlear 1988). This increase in cash-cropping is not unique to Quinua: peasants throughout the sierra are substituting cash crops, especially maize and potatoes, for such subsistence foods as quinoa, broad beans, and *cañihua* (Caballero 1981: 182; Cotlear 1988; Gonzales de Olarte 1987: 156). The declining rural-urban terms of trade have fostered this increase. Peasants must produce more cash crops merely to maintain their standard of living. Nonetheless, many farmers have been deterred from cash-cropping by problems in obtaining and repaying agricultural credit (see Poole and Rénique 1992: 19–20) and in the 1980s by the Shining Path war.

Lacking resources to sustain themselves, many Quinuenos have been pushed out of the community, often remaining away permanently. Today, the majority of children born in Quinua live elsewhere as adults, mostly in and around Lima. In genealogical data that I collected in 1966, only 34.6 percent of one informant's kin were living outside Quinua, the town where they had been born. In 1987 more than 50 percent of Quinuenos lived elsewhere. In one rural hamlet 61.8 percent of male children over 19 and 55.4 percent of all children over that age had migrated, primarily to Lima and Ayacucho (Mitchell 1991a: 112). Historically, individuals have generally migrated between the ages of 15 and 25. Now, however, entire families abandon their homes and leave together. Peruvian census data support informant reports: the number of houses reported as unoccupied in the census has increased markedly from 0.9 percent in 1961 to 6.8 percent in 1972 and to 17.2 percent in 1981 (Mitchell 1994, Peru 1966, 1974, and 1983).[11]

The department of Ayacucho has one of the highest rates of out-migration (Degregori 1986b: 19), but similar high out-migration is found throughout rural Peru. This emigration has kept local communities small in spite of high birth rates, while the cities have grown exponentially. Quinua has grown less rapidly than the province of Huamanga (of which Quinua and the city of Ayacucho are a part), the city of Lima, and in fact all Peru (Mitchell 1991a: 36). Over the past century, between 1876 and 1981, Quinua's population increased 71 percent, Huamanga's increased 312, Peru's 531, and Lima's an astounding 3,333 percent (see also Matos Mar 1984: 43-7, 72-3).

Reliance on commerce and migration has led to additional pressures on Quinuenos for cash to pay for transport, education, and appropriate clothing. Less time for household craft production has also had the same effect, encouraging people to buy rather than manufacture their household goods and utensils (Collins 1988: 146). In 1996, when I last visited Quinua, few women were spinning wool in contrast to the near continuous use of the spindle some twenty years ago. Local weaving is more time consuming and expensive than buying manufactured cloth. Symbols of new statuses have also become important, and some people demonstrate their wealth by purchasing such things as infant rubber pants, bicycles (of little use in hilly Quinua) and commercial rather than local maize beer (*chicha*).

Because of these economic changes, economic inequality has increased in Quinua and throughtout Peru (Caballero 1981: 209; Cotlear 1988: 221, table 1; Degregori 1986a; de Janvry 1981: 121; Pastor and Wise 1992). Although many Quinuenos have intensified cash-producing economic activities in a major way, significant numbers have done so less successfully. Lacking capital, credit, education, and sometimes significant family ties, they remain poor and have become even more impoverished. Migrants face similar inequality. Some of them have become part of a new urban, relatively prosperous class of workers, merchants, and entrepreneurs. The majority, however, have remained poor, taking whatever odd jobs they can (*cachuelos*) to survive. They view this situation as an improvement over that in the highlands, where even casual labor is difficult to obtain. Chances of economic mobility, moreover, are greater in Lima than in Quinua or even the city of Ayacucho. Lima also furnishes greater resources of all kinds (medical, governmental, commercial, recreational) and has afforded a refuge for those fleeing the war.

THE ECONOMIC CRISIS: 1970-PRESENT

The national economic crisis that began in the 1970s has pushed Quinuenos — and many Peruvians — ever closer to the edge (Dobyns and Doughty 1976, Reid 1985, Vega-Centeno et al. 1985). The GDP of Ayacucho dropped by 12.3 percent between 1979 and 1985 (Mitchell 1991a: 100, Peru 1987: 25–26). Because of population growth, per capita income declined even further. In the country as a whole, the share of wages in national income declined from 37.7 percent to 28.8 percent between 1980 and 1988, while the profit share rose (Pastor and Wise 1992: 101).

International economic forces have exacerbated the plight of many of Peru's poor. Changes in Peru's official trading relationship with the United States in 1983, for example, reduced textile exports, and some textile plants that had employed Ayacucho and Quinua migrants closed or reduced production (Mitchell in preparation). The neoliberal economic policies of President Fujimori in the 1990s, in many respects a response to the IMF and other international economic bodies, have intensified these pressures (Latin American News Update 1994: 22; Poole and Rénique 1992: 150–55). A small sector located primarily in Lima has made spectacular gains, but poverty has increased for most people (Mitchell in preparation, NACLA 1993, Pastor and Wise 1992, Poole and Rénique 1992: 22–4; Reid 1985, Thorp 1991). Salaries, manual wages, and even informal incomes have fallen precipitously (Pastor and Wise 1992: 94, table 5; Thorp 1991). Many people lost their jobs in the formal sector at the same time that the cost of staples increased precipitously. This poverty has increased more rapidly in Lima than in the rest of the country (Latin American News Update 1994: 22). The percentage of Limeños living below poverty rose from 16.9 percent in 1985–86 to 48.9 percent in 1991.

Although rural areas are protected somewhat from urban inflation and poverty because of barter and because most people have some access to productive resources (Gonzales de Olarte 1987: 103, 106–7), Quinua and its migrants have felt the effects of Peru's economic crisis. General migration, time devoted to schooling and nonfarm production, and the war have made it even more difficult to obtain agricultural laborers. Per capita nonfarm production in Quinua has also suffered. The ceramic industry and many other nonfarm occupations have become saturated, and even established artisans must constantly introduce new designs to develop and maintain market share. It is consequently harder for young people to enter such occupations except as poorly paid assistants.

As migrants' incomes have declined, they have reduced their remittances sent home. These pressures on remittances have also been exacerbated by higher transportation costs. The increased oil prices in the 1970s (resulting from the international oil shock) and in the 1990s (resulting from President Fujimori's economic policies) have increased transportation and shipping costs, so that Quinuenos have been less able to travel and to ship the remittances (food to coastal migrants in return for manufactured goods) that had been part of their productive system (Mitchell in preparation).

The impact of this rural economic deterioration can be seen in statistics from Cusco, where peasants were eating less sugar, rice, milk, cheese, and meat in response to the inflationary spiral of the 1980s (Gonzales de Olarte 1987: 141). They reverted to eating the agricultural products grown in their fields. Data on beer consumption in Ayacucho in 1983 are also illustrative. In that year, an especially poor one, heavy debt payments (Matos Mar 1984: 49) and extensive natural disasters (caused by a severe *el niño* weather disturbance, characterized by heavy rain on the coast and little in the highlands) caused the Gross Domestic Product (GDP) to fall 12 percent (Ortiz de Zevallos 1989: 15). It is hard to imagine Peruvians forgoing beer consumption, a vital component of social and ceremonial life (Mitchell 1991b), but beer sales in the Ayacucho area (which includes Quinua) dropped by 10 percent between 1982 and 1983 (Zanabria et al. 1987: 39). Beer sales increased rapidly after 1983, an increase attributed by the authors of the study to increased political as well as economic tensions in Ayacucho. I believe, however, that a significant portion of the increased beer sales was probably due to the huge influx of military personnel into the department, a group notorious for excessive drinking and for abuses committed while drunk.

The Shining Path war has created its own crisis (especially in the departments of Ayacucho, Huancavelica, Apurimac, and Junin), aggravating the underlying trends (Mitchell 1996, in preparation, Poole and Rénique 1992: 20; Urrutia Ceruti 1987: 19–23). The war disrupted agricultural production as many frightened people abandoned their farms and villages. Food prices rose in Ayacucho as a result of this decreased production, while the price of commercial goods rose more rapidly than in the rest of the country (Urrutia Ceruti 1987: 23).

Perhaps one million Peruvians were displaced by the war (Coral 1994: 23). Between 1980 and 1991, the total number of inhabitants in Ayacucho fell by 3.5 percent, and the rural decline was an extraordinary 23.3 percent (Degregori 1996: 16). Some people left of their own volition (if one can speak of volition in a context of terror), but others were forced to leave by the military, who began to move people to strategic hamlets after 1984 (Degregori 1986b: 49). Others fled the threats and killings of Shining Path and the military.

After the mid-1980s some Quinua hamlets were abandoned entirely (Mitchell 1996). Herders fled high altitude grazing lands, leaving their homes and potato fields to live in the relative safety of the central town, Ayacucho City, or Lima. Farmers living in isolated hamlets abandoned their homes to live in the central town, commuting to their fields on foot. Others, concerned about the vulnerability of their children to recruitment by Shining Path or to military abuses, sent them to live with family in Lima. In one sub-hamlet, 23 of the 86 homes (or 27%) were abandoned during the war, most of them during 1990–1992, when the threats and killings in Quinua were at their height. The remaining families consist primarily of old people, widows, young children, and orphans. The old people are distraught because they find it is difficult to cultivate their fields with the reduced labor pool. They are far poorer than they were previously. As the overt violence began to decline after 1992, some people have begun to return to Quinua and Ayacucho. Nonetheless, many young adults were still afraid to return home even for visits in 1996.

THE SOCIOCULTURAL TRANSFORMATION

The economic and social stress in Quinua and throughout Peru have made it difficult for Quinuenos to live as they had in the first half of the century — tied to their community, celebrating the saints, and worshiping the mountain god and other local deities. Quinuenos have always had to deal with repression and change, but the rapid and profound changes of the last fifty years have probably been the most difficult since the early colonial period. In their struggle to cope, they have created a new economy, forged new identities, and radically changed their sociopolitical organization. A few have chosen revolution.

The increased commodification of labor is one of the most important changes. Quinuenos today rely more on cash relationships to obtain labor and other resources, reducing the importance of the traditional status ties (e.g., *ayni, minka*, the *faena* or corvée labor and fiestas) they had used previously (Mitchell 1991b). They had even freed their labor from the semi-feudal haciendas before the agrarian reform of the 1970s, taking advantage of the same economic forces that had plagued the peasantry but that had also undermined the economic and political power of the haciendas (Mitchell 1994).

As they have entered the cash economy, Quinuenos have adopted an incredible faith in the power of education (Mitchell 1994, see also Degregori 1989: 10–18, 1990: 37–40, 128–29, and *passim*, Montoya 1980: 309–10). The elite class in Peru has maintained its domination not only by control of force and the means of the production (especially land, water, and labor) but also through the control of cultural symbols (language, clothing) and education (Degregori 1989: 12). Consequently, like most Ayacuchanos, Quinuenos believe that Spanish and literacy provide an escape from slavery and trickery (*engaño*) and improve the ability of children to secure work (Degregori 1989: 11).

Almost all Quinua children now attend school. In 1966 most of the adult population was illiterate and spoke only Quechua, but the process of creating the present-day literate and bilingual population (speaking Quechua at home and Spanish to outsiders) was well under way (Mitchell 1991a: 121). In the 1981 census, only 16 percent of the adults more than forty years of age were literate, compared to 87 percent of their children ages 10 to 14 (Mitchell 1991a: 121). Quinuenos have even emphasized schooling over farming, sometimes devoting scarce labor resources to building schools rather than to expanding irrigation, even though more irrigation water would have increased crop production considerably (Mitchell 1994). In 1940, just four schools (going only through the second grade) and four teachers served the entire district. By 1987, there were ten primary schools, a secondary school, three nursery schools, and two artisan schools caring for 2,171 students and employing seventy-seven teachers. Some young people have also left Quinua to attend university.

Quinuenos have changed in other ways. Women must work harder than ever in the fields to compensate for absent or murdered husbands and adult sons. They have also forged new religious identities. In fewer than twenty years Quinuenos have abandoned much of the fiesta system, a system that had been associated with agrarian production as a mechanism to recruit farm labor (Mitchell 1991b). The 18 fiestas celebrated in the central town in 1966 have been reduced to one, that for the patron saint (the Virgin of Cocharcas). The associated peasant political system (the *varayoc*) has also vanished. Many people have questioned the expense as well as the theological underpinnings of the fiesta and peasant political systems, converting to Protestantism in the process.

CHANGING SYSTEMS OF SOCIAL CONTROL

The economic and sociocultural transformation in Quinua has loosened traditional mechanisms of social control (see also Favre 1984: 33 and Seligmann 1992 and 1995). Modifications in social control are difficult to measure, and I do not wish to create a stereotyped past of harmony and obedience in contrast to an anarchic present. Although people complain, for example, that children no longer show the respect for adults that they once did, the deviations appear to be largely of form rather than substance. Children still show considerable respect for most adults. Nonetheless, significant changes have taken place (table 9.4).

Table 9.4. Changing Systems of Social Control, Quinua, 1966–1996.

Social Control Mechanisms	1966	1996
Gossip	+	+
Llamar La Atención ("Shaping Someone Up")	+	+
Face-to-Face Ties	+	−
Geographic Mobility	−	+
Irrigation Sanctions	+	−
Familial	+	−
Godparenthood (*Padrinazgo*)	+	−
Reciprocal Ties	+	−
Priest and Nuns	+	0
Protestant Ministers	−	+
Haciendas	+	0
Peasant Political Leaders (*Varayoc*)	+	0
Police	−	+
Military	−	+
Peasant Militia (Quinua's Established in 1990)	−	+
Municipal Authorities	+	+
Courts	+	+
School	−	+

+ = PRESENT (STRONG); − = PRESENT (WEAK); 0 = ABSENT
Note: The categories are ranked relatively from the beginning of the period to the end, so that for example the police presence in Quinua was weaker in 1966 than in 1996.

Gossip is still the major informal control on behavior, and Quinuenos continue to remind family and ritual kin of the need to obey social rules in a formal manner known as "llamar la atención" (a process similar to the American "shaping someone up"). Other communal mechanisms of social control, however, have declined in importance. Because people move frequently, face-to-face ties are fewer and Quinuenos are able to escape the consequences of their actions more readily than was previously possible. Today, women are reluctant to enter into trial marriage, preferring civil marriage, becasuse they realistically fear that their husbands may abandon them and their children and establish new families on the coast. I experienced the use of travel to escape local social controls when one of Quinua's early

Protestants asked me to serve as godfather at the Roman Catholic baptism of his children in 1973 and 1974. I was unaware of his Protestanism (he kept his religious affiliation hidden from most people), but he escaped the censure of his coreligionists by insisting that we hold the baptism in the city of Ayacucho rather than in the Roman Catholic church in Quinua.

Institutions tied to agrarian production (water distribution, family, systems of reciprocity, godparenthood) have also lost some of their control functions with the declining importance of farming. Denying irrigation water (Mitchell 1976) to people who earn most of their livelihoods as ceramicists has less impact than denying it to full-time farmers. The family still exerts a strong influence on behavior, but a son who earns most of a family's monetary income in outside employment has greater freedom and power than another child dependent on parental farm resources. Sometimes this economic power is used almost tyrannically. One wealthy man who lives in Lima dominates his mother and siblings who depend on him financially, using them and his nieces and nephews as unpaid servants. His mother, afraid he will stop sending remittances, will not chew *coca* leaves (a customary and important peasant practice disdained by nonpeasants, see below) in his presence and when visiting him sucks on sugar instead.

The systems of reciprocity that had been central to social relations in Quinua have also become less important in controlling behavior (Ansión 1985: 70–1). Because of the increased commodification of labor, people are no longer tied to others extensively in reciprocal relationships and are consequently freed of many social constraints on their behavior. Godparents (*padrinos*) do not exert the authority over godchildren that they once had. A woman abused by her husband can no longer get her marriage godparents to whip the miscreant, although the godparents might still chastise him verbally.

Some social control institutions have disappeared completely. Priests and nuns are no longer resident in Quinua, although Protestant ministers have assumed some of their control functions — and probably more successfully. The demise of haciendas, however, has eliminated a major institution of political control and repression (Favre 1984: 33). *Hacendados* (and their henchmen) had a pervasive impact on behavior, as they were tied to the peasantry not only through force but through agrarian production, dependency, reciprocal relationships, and ritual kinship (Mitchell 1991b). Some *hacendados* were also important actors in the local political structure. Although I do not have the evidence for Quinua, Seligmann (1992 and 1995) has argued that the agrarian reform and the demise of *haciendas* in the community of Huanoquite near Cusco created a political vacuum that later facilitated the entry of Shining Path (see also Degregori 1996, Starn 1992b: 99).

The loss of peasant political leaders (*varayoc*) has also greatly reduced community sanctions. In their heyday this ritual and prestige hierarchy of some thirty to forty men and their wives helped maintain order and adherence to social norms. They acted as a police force and sometimes whipped people who did not conform to community standards (Mitchell 1991a: 149–55). I do not wish to idealize the peasant political leaders, for they were often drunk and sometimes criticized (see, for example, Mitchell 1991a: 152). Nonetheless, every Quinueno that I asked about them has told me that the peasant leaders wielded considerable power and that everyone feared them.

The police and military have assumed many of the vacated social control functions of the *hacendados* and the peasant leaders, but their sanctions do not permeate social life in the same way. Prison (and even death) is a powerful sanction, but peasant leaders and *hacendado* ritual kin, acting in a face-to-face climate, and calling on widely-shared values and kin ties in addition to the ever-present threat of force, checked behavior more pervasively. The peasant militia (*comites de autodefensa*) that were introduced into Quinua in 1990, however, are tied to the community by extensive social ties and occupy the social space once held by the *varayoc* (the peasant leaders). In consequence, even though they have committed many human rights abuses that have seriously divided the community, the peasant militia have been effective agents of local social control and played a key role in the defeat of Shining Path (Degregori 1996).

CRIME, VIOLENCE, AND COCAINE

Increased crime and violence have also accompanied the economic crisis and the loosening of social controls. Crime has increased in Quinua, as well as in Ayacucho (Zanabria et al. 1987) and Peru (Starn 1992b: 97–8), and there is less security of property and person than previously. When I first went to Quinua in 1966, fighting, theft, cattle rustling, rape, and wife beating were common enough for me to have been aware of them without any special investigation of the topic (see Bolton 1973 for a discussion of aggression and crime elsewhere in Peru). Women feared unknown or powerful men, and more than one peasant woman told me that men are likely to abuse them sexually. Peasant farmers worried about the theft and destruction of crops, and they moved to huts in distant fields to protect the ripening harvest. They secured their homes with guard dogs, and they deterred cattle thieves by constant supervision and by petitioning the mountain god (*urqu tayta*) to protect the cattle. Wealthy Quinuenos, moreover, feared revolutionaries and land invasions.

Quinuenos, however, generally felt more secure in 1966 than they do today (see also Starn 1992b: 97–8). In the 1970s, even before the Shining Path war, Quinuenos had begun to experience greater insecurity and they encountered occasional armed robbery, especially from unknown travelers along the highway. In 1974, the jeweled crown worn by the image of the patron saint (the Virgin of Cocharcas) and other wealth were stolen from the church, a theft of devastating proportions and one that has remained unsolved to this day. Insecurity increased still more in the 1980s. I do not have the data for Quinua, but police reports of family violence (*delitos contra familia*) throughout Peru rose by a factor of 32.5 between 1980 and 1987 (600 cases to 18,900) (Webb and Fernández Baca 1990: 226; see also Urrutia Ceruti et al. 1987). While the total figures for family violence are still small, and the data are largely from urban areas, the increase is one measure of increased stress in Peru.

The high incidence of crime is visible in Peru's cities (MacGregor et al. 1985). Quinua migrants, like everyone else, suffer increased burglaries and pickpockets even in the city of Ayacucho (Urrutia Ceruti 1987: 25; Zanabria et al. 1987). In Lima, homes and shops have been increasingly fortified with broken glass on perimeter walls and metal bars over windows. It is common for pharmacies to be completely barricaded from customers by metal bars, transactions being conducted through a small opening between the bars. Although people have not taken such extreme measures in Quinua, Quinuenos are aware of them, disturbed by them (one man told me he was ashamed by the "fortification" of Peru, even inventing the word "*rejaización*" to describe it), and see them as one sign of the increasing social disintegration around them. White collar crime, economic crimes, the abuse of authority and position have increased concomitantly, causing many to despair of the sociopolitical system. The promises of President Fujimori and of Shining Path to remoralize the country have been received favorable by many Peruvians.

The war, of course, has aggravated insecurity. With good reason, Quinuenos fear the military, guerrillas, and peasant militia. In 1984, the military roused fourteen young men from bed in Quinua, tortured and murdered them (Mitchell 1991a: 12). In that same year, an entire peasant family was murdered by an unknown group, although many suspect that the peasant militia from neighboring Acos Vinchos had killed them to avenge a land dispute. In 1990, Shining Path killed a Quinueno for participating in the civil defense patrols (Amnesty International 1991: 24). Twenty-four Quinuenos were killed in the community between 1990 and 1992 (Mitchell 1996). In one case, a bus driver's assitant was pulled from his car by a masked group and murdered around the archelogical site of Huari. Many accuse the peasant militia of this and the other killings, claiming the young man was assassinated for talking against the militia. Others, however, deny the accusations or claim that the young man and other people killed were subversives.

Some Peruvians have also entered the cocaine trade, the one boom amid economic chaos (Kawell 1989, Matos Mar 1984: 55–6; Poole and Rénique 1992: 20–1; see also Nash 1992: 277). It is difficult to determine the exact number of people involved in the cocaine trade, but 31 percent of the prison population of Ayacucho in the late 1980s had been charged with drug offenses (Zanabria et al. 1987: 47). Rumor suggests that a few Quinuenos have entered the trade, using it to obtain income the way others have used ceramics. In the early 1970s, one young person exploring his future asked me to serve as a cocaine courier to the United States. Others joked about the possibility, indicating at least the course of their thinking. Most of the Quinuenos that I have spoken to about the matter, however, eschew the commercial cocaine trade and view it as both wrong and dangerous, in contrast to their more complex and tolerant attitudes towards the customary chewing of the leaf. Like commercial ceramic production, the cocaine trade has local roots, reaching back to the ubiquitous trade in the *coca* leaves chewed by peasants (in a customary and nonaddictive manner) and used in medicines and ritual (see Allen 1988, Pacini and Franquemont 1986).

THE RISE OF SHINING PATH

The Shining Path war has been another outcome of increasing poverty, a very young population, and the loosening of social controls over behavior. Some scholars have argued against an economic interpretation of Shining Path. Some have pointed to the role of the 1970s agrarian reform and its associated social mobilization and loosening of rural social controls as important in the development of Shining Path and other political movements (Seligmann 1992, 1995, Stokes 1995). Ossio (1990: 23–4) has argued that an economic explanation of Shining Path is unsatisfactory because its adherents are usually better

Table 9.5. Level of Schooling of Those Imprisoned in Lima for Terrorism and Other Crimes, 1983–1986.

Type of Crime	Level of Schooling (in Percentages)							
	Illiterate	Some Primary	Secondary		University		Professional/ Graduate	No Data	Total N
			Some	Complete	Some	Complete			
Terrorism[a]	1.1	16.4	16.9	27.9	29.5	1.1	4.9	2.2	183
Assault/Robbery	0.0	23.4	46.3	24.4	2.5	0.0	0.0	3.4	205
Illegal Drug Trade	4.1	30.0	21.2	30.7	6.6	0.0	1.5	5.9	410
Other Crimes	2.4	24.4	48.6	14.6	2.4	0.0	2.7	4.9	410

Source: Data adopted from Chávez de Paz 1989: 41. See footnote 12 for important caveats concerning methodological problems with these data.
[a] The term *terrorism*, a direct translation from the Spanish, is a judicial classification that primarily represents people accused of Shining Path activity.

Table 9.6. Occupations of those Imprisoned in Lima for Terrorism and Other Crimes, 1983–1986.

Type of Crime	Percentage in Each Occupation										Total N
	Students	Blue Collar	Farming	White Collar	Street Vendor	Profes-sional[a]	Unem-ployed	Artisans	House-Wives	Other[b]	
Terrorism[c]	24.6	24.0	14.8	12.0	10.4	5.5	3.3	2.7	1.1	1.6	183
Assault/Robbery	6.3	44.9	1.5	21.0	11.7	0.0	1.0	7.3	1.5	4.9	205
Illegal Drug Trade	2.6	25.0	5.6	24.1	10.7	0.5	2.0	4.4	7.3	17.8	410
Other Crimes	1.7	46.8	0.5	21.4	9.8	1.2	2.9	4.9	1.7	9.1	410

Source: Data adopted from Chávez de Paz 1989: 49–50. See footnote 12 for important caveats concerning methodological problems with these data.
[a] The category of "Professional" includes members of the professions and police and military officials.
[b] The category of "other" includes industrialists, large merchants, and lower police and military officials, as well as other categories.
[c] The term *terrorism*, a direct translation from the Spanish, is a judicial classification that primarily represents people accused of Shining Path activity.

educated and from more prosperous backgrounds than most provincials. Existing data seemingly support these assertions (see tables 9.5 and 9.6). Thus, 35.5 percent of those arrested and convicted of "terrorism" between 1983 and 1986 had some university or professional education compared to only 2.5 percent of those in prison for assault and robbery, and 7.7 percent of all adult Peruvians (the economically active Peruvian population over the age of 15) (Chávez de Paz 1989: 40–8).[12]

Degregori (1986b: 18, 41; 1990: 17, 28–31, 34–5) has also emphasized that one cannot mechanically cite the poverty of Ayacucho to explain Shining Path, but that special historical events facilitated its development. The road and rail systems extended into other areas of the sierra led to the economic decline and political fragmentation of Ayacucho (see above and Degregori 1986b: 21–2; 1990: 28–9, and Montoya 1980). The decline in the agrarian economy, moreover, weakened the power of large landowners, creating a power vacuum that was filled by Shining Path (Degregori 1990: 45, Seligmann 1992, 1995).[13] The opening of the University in Ayacucho in 1960 and its special role in the city, especially its participation in the movement to defend free school tuition in 1969, fostered the development of a revolutionary cadre and ideology (Degregori 1990: 41–7 and *passim*; see also González 1985). Finally, according to Degregori, the authoritarian ideology of Shining Path was easily adopted by peasants because it is congruent with an Andean authoritarian tradition in which peasants look to external moral and political guides (Degregori 1989: 13–6).

Both Ossio and Degregori are correct. Shining Path partisans appear to be members of provincial elites and special historical events facilitated the development of the revolution in Ayacucho. Their arguments, however, do not falsify the proposition that economic causation underlies the development of Shining Path (a point that Degregori acknowledges). Very real economic stress underlies all the changes in Ayacucho, including Shining Path.

Economic causation is rarely simple ("I am poor; therefore, I rebel"), but is mediated by such factors as age structure, gender, marital status and number of children (Chávez de Paz 1989: 30–4), as well as by relative deprivation, racism, discrimination, and the loosening of social controls. Personal experience is also important. The complexity of such causation, of course, makes it difficult to sort out the reasons why some people turn to crime, some to violent revolution, some to nonviolent activism, some to acceptance of fate, and some to working harder at a craft or trade.

The age structure of Peru is an important consideration in any explanation of Shining Path. More than half the population of Ayacucho

City — and of all Peru — is less than 18 years of age (Urrutia Ceruti 1987: 18). In Peru, young people have the highest rates of unemployment (*Quehacer* 1988: 21). Young people, moreover, are most receptive to experimentation and rebelling against the establishment (Easterlin 1980) and 79.8 percent of those imprisoned for "terrorism" are less than 30 years of age (table 7, Chávez de Paz 1989: 25–9, *Quehacer* 1988: 21). Nearly all the Tupac Amaru guerillas that seized the Japanese embassy in Lima in 1996–1997 were teenagers. The situation in Peru would be very different if half the population were over the age of fifty!

Most Shining Path partisans appear to be depeasantized youth — young people pushed out of their communities into a national society that has no place for them. There are many such people in Ayacucho City and throughout Peru — young adults who are unable to achieve the social and economic positions for which they were educated (Chávez de Paz 1989, Degregori 1986b: 37; Favre 1984, Mitchell 1979, Poole and Rénique 1992: 40–1, 61–2). Some indication of the problem is readily obtained in conversation with Lima taxi drivers, who invariably report that they had been trained for some profession where they cannot find work. Although those imprisoned for "terrorism" are generally well educatd, 85.8 percent of them had incomes below the official poverty line (Chávez de Paz 1989: 55). Unemployed or underemployed, they have a hard time scraping by. They often rent rooms in homes or in *correlones* (corridors with single-room dwellings), or live with their parents or relatives as dependents.

They are marginalized people, occupying incongruent statuses (see Mitchell 1979 for a discussion of status inconsistency in Peru). Although accorded high prestige in their home communities, they are considered contemprible *cholos* or *serranos* in the national setting (Degregori 1989, 1990: 205–6; Mitchell 1979). Many develop ambivalent feelings about both their natal homes and the national culture (Degregori 1990: 186–7, 205–7). Even those who are successful in confronting racism and who are able to work in their professions are torn by the conflicting pull of Lima and their provincial homes, frequently having to decide whether to oppose the traditional order (peacefully or violently) or joint it (see Degregori 1990: 114). Shining Path furnishes some of these young people an explanation of their plight and a guide to changing the social order (Degregori 1986b, 1990: 187).

Although most Shining Path partisans appear to be unmarried men without children (table 9.7; Chávez de Paz 1989), women have played key roles (Degregori 1990: 145–50). A larger percentage of women are imprisoned for "terrorism" and drug trafficking (16.4% and 19.3%, respectively) than are imprisoned for assault and robbery (only 3.4%) (table 9.7). The important role of women in Shining Path, as well as in earlier rebellions in Ayacucho (Degregori 1990: 145–7), may be rooted in strong traditions of female independence as peasant land owners, market vendors, small scale commercial entrepreneurs, and guardians of family finances. They have to struggle to maintain that independence in the national culture.[14]

Table 9.7. Sex, Age, and Family Characteristics of those Imprisoned in Lima for Terrorism and Other Crimes, 1983–1986.

Type of Crime	Percentage in Each Category				
	Women	Under Age 30	Unmarried[a]	Childless	Total N
Terrorism[b]	16.4	79.8	70.5	63.9	183
Assault/Robbery	3.4	77.1	56.1	48.8	205
Illegal Drug Trade	19.3	48.6	40.7	29.3	410
Other	3.2	66.1	46.3	36.8	410
Total	10.7	64.1	49.8	40.4	1208

Source: Data adopted from Chávez de Paz 1989: 49–50. See footnote 12 for important caveats concerning methodological problems with these data.
[a] Unmarried includes those not in consensual relationships as well as those not officially married.
[b] The term *terrorism*, a direct translation from the Spanish, is a judicial classification that primarily represents people accused of Shining Path activity.

Most unmarried, depeasantized young men and women have not become violent revolutionaries (Degregori 1989: 7; Mayer 1994). Instead of war, violence, or the cocaine trade, most of Peru's depeasantized youth have opted to work ever harder to get by. They take whatever job they can, piecing various incomes together to make do. Many have also channeled their anger into such nonviolent groups working for change as agrarian federations, student activist organizations, unions, and communal kitchens. The proliferation of these institutions may explain the resistance to Shining Path in the Department of Puno (Poole and Rénique 1992: 70–8), as well as Bolivia's resistance to general social breakdown (June Nash, personal communication, 3/14/93; Nash 1992). The rural vigilante groups known as *rondas campesinas* organized by peasants in northern Peru to deal with theft and rural disorder may serve a similar function (Starn 1992b: 108–9).[15]

Quinuenos and other Ayacuchanos have expressed their horror of the war in both ideology and art. To deal with the trauma of the many deaths in the war they have reached to old beliefs, reporting a resurgence of *pistacos* or *nacaq*, light-skinned and frequently bearded people who kill Indians and sell their rendered fat to Lima to run airplanes and other machinery (Ansión 1987). Many have responded with religious beliefs prophesying that a horrible Armageddon will usher in the millennium (Mitchell in preparation). They have also expressed their horror in music. *Flor de Retama*, a song (*huayno*) popular in the 1980s, condemns the murder of students and others by the military, identifying those murdered in the city of Huanta with the flower of the broom plant (*retama*) and describing their blood as richly perfumed with jasmine and dynamite (see also Starn 1992b). One young artisan from Quinua, who was later murdered by the military, made *retablos* (a triptych type of art) vividly depicting the horrors of the war.

SUMMARY

The ecological and economic squeeze on production described above has stimulated Peruvian peasants to find creative solutions to feed themselves and their families. Some Peruvians have turned to theft, violence, cocaine production, and revolution, but most have not. Although every Peruvian has been affected by the war, most have gone on living and coping in very ordinary ways. In doing so, nearly all of them have actively participated in the expansion of capitalism and the consequent intensification of nonfarm work and the "plebeian flood" that has revolutionized all Peru.

Popular images of Peru in the 1980s, however, were not of the social transformation but of war, violence, and cocaine. In an analysis of clippings from *The New York Times* that I have maintained over the years on all aspects of Peru, 59.3 percent of the coverage concerns war and violence and another 8.1 percent is about the drug trade (table 9.8).[16] These images convey political information. They are selective pictures that direct us away from peasant society, away from the poor and dispossessed, leading us to such political questions as how the Shining Path movement and cocaine production can be contained or stopped. The transformation in Peru is thus constructed as a police and military matter, rather than one in which social conditions are primary. Since the capture of Abimael Guzmán, the leader of Shining Path, in September of 1992, and the subsequent subsidence of Shining Path military activities, moreover, we have had even spottier accounts of the social conditions in Peru, even though evidence suggests (Burt and López 1994) that most Peruvians still live in dire poverty and that Shining Path may only be going through a period of local consolidation.[17]

Table 9.8. Analysis of Newspaper Coverage of Peru.

Year	Primary Focus of Story						Total N
	Shining Path War	Other Violence	Drug Trade	Business Investments	Socio-Economic Conditions	Other	
1983	11	0	0	0	1[a]	2	14
1984	20	2	5	0	1	0	28
1985	22	0	0	8	2	8	40
1986	24	6	1	1	2	5	39
1987[b]	ND	ND	ND	ND	ND	ND	ND
1988[b]	4	1	1	0	6	4	16
1989	5	1	3	2	2	2	15
1990	5	1	5	0	1	6	18
1991	ND	ND	ND	ND	ND	ND	ND
1992	30	14	5	1	5	21	76
Total	121	25	20	12	20	48	246
Percent	49.1	10.2	8.1	4.9	8.1	19.5	100.0

Source: The data are from clipping files on Peru from *The New York Times*. The clippings were not collected systematically, but represent all material on Peru on the days (generally daily) that I read the paper. The clippings were analyzed by Jane Freed.
ND=NO DATA
[a] Letter to the editor
[b] I was out of the country in 1987. For the same reason 1988 covers only June through December.

By emphasizing Shining Path terror and underemphasizing that of the military, these images of Peru distort reality still more. Because newspaper reporters frequently rely on official sources, they tend to stress Shining Path depredations. The systematic, everyday abuses by the military (the theft of a watch, the sexual abuse of a woman, the systematic detention and abuse of the powerless, the disappearance of a poor person) tend to go underreported, as opposed to the military's spectacular but not-as-frequent massacres. In contrast to what one would assume from newspaper accounts, at least some Quinuenos see the military as having been equally or even more abusive than Shining Path. In 1996, one hamlet that had suffered a large number of attacks and killings by the peasant militia had begun to organize against the militia, denouncing them publicly. The attitudes of some relatively well off Quinua migrants are indicated by an apocryphal anecdote laughingly related at a party in Lima in 1983 (a particularly gruesome year), after a trucker who had just arrived from Ayacucho told us of the headless body he had encountered: When the guerrillas (*terrucos*) come into a home, they ask "who owns these potatoes?" The owner replies: "I do," to which the guerrillas say "give us half of them." When the antiguerrilla forces (*sinchis*) come into the home and ask "who owns these potatoes," and the peasant responds "I do," the military tell him — "give us them all!"

In spite of military massacres and abuses, however, the term "terrorists" is used widely in Lima (but less so in Ayacucho) as a synonym for Shining Path partisans. It is never applied to the military. This emphasis on Shining Path brutality promotes repressive military tactics and hides the racism underlying a strategy of war in which the people of the coast (constructed as mestizo, modern, and worthy) have attacked and massacred the people of the highlands (constructed as Indian, backward, and brutish). The process is similar to that in the United States where drug use is seen as an African-American phenomenon, although the majority of drug users are white (Staples 1994). Many Ayacuchanos say "To be Ayacuchano is to be guilty" (see, for example, Urrutia Ceruti 1987: 24). To be a student at the National University of San Cristóbal de Huamanga (the university in Ayacucho where Shining Path began) brought with it in the 1980s a risk of detention and sometimes murder. Even in Lima, young Ayacuchanos have suffered disproportionately, often the objects of dragnets, arrests, and torture. Police and military violence has also been directed at students and faculty at public universities that serve the poor, such as the University of San Marcos, rather than at private institutions that cater to the elite.

These same images of violence and war support policies that repress dissent and restrict the activities of those working for social change. In Peru, it was possible during the war to jail, abduct, and kill peasant leaders and human rights activists with relative impunity if they were labeled as Shining Path partisans, terrorists, or guerillas (Americas Watch 1992: 80–2; Amnesty International 1992: 41–3; Gorriti 1992b, Mitchell 1996, in preparation, Poole and Rénique 1992). In 1989, for example, peasant protest against low agricultural prices was one of the factors that led to the arrest of the president of the Agrarian Federation of Ayacucho on charges of "terrorism" (Amnesty International 1989b: 27–8). In Quinua in 1996, the mayor and the head of the peasant militia quickly labeled any opponent a "terrorist," much the way civil rights workers have sometimes been branded as communists in the United States. The ideological use of the war is quite apparent here, for Shining Path has been least successful in those areas with strong institutions working to redress intolerable social conditions (Woy-Hazleton and Hazleton 1992: 214). It is for this reason that Shining Path has threatened, attacked, and killed social change activists (Poole and Rénique 1992: 14, 28–9).

The focus on Shining Path has even distorted our understanding of Peruvian politics and the Peruvian left (Poole and Rénique 1991). Shining Path is only one of many political parties on the left, many of which have opposed Shining Path and its revolution. The emphasis on Shining Path has turned our attention away from the many groups (agrarian federations, labor unions, communal kitchens, human rights activists, student federations, political parties, mothers clubs, milk programs) actively working for change (Andreas 1985, Poole and Rénique 1992).

Focus on the war and cocaine production has also absolved the United States government and international agencies of responsibility for their contribution to the crisis (see, for example, de Janvry 1981, Pastor and Wise 1992). Issues of economic justice are lost in the rhetoric of Shining Path terror and the evils of the drug trade. These and similar images create a climate in the United States that fosters military solutions for social crisis not only in Peru but throughout the Third World.

Shining Path has also constructed events to justify armed revolution (Degregori 1989). Shining Path materials have tended to glorify violence and death, referring for example to the purification of the blood bath (Degregori 1989, 1990: 178, 202). Abimael Guzmán (Smith 1991: 24), the group's leader, and the Committee to Support the Revolution in Peru (1992) have emphasized the semifeudal nature of Peru and have pointed to the poverty, injustice and many deaths that occur as a result of the existing system. With the demise of the hacienda system and the increased commodification of local labor relations, however, it is questionable if Peru can be described accurately as a semifeudal society at the present time. Nonetheless, it is certainly true that Peruvian poverty and the unequal distribution of wealth within the country have caused many deaths. Even the 26,000 deaths in the first twelve-years of the war are less than the number of children who had died of malnutrition and dysentery during the same period. What these constructions of Shining Path ignore, however, are the many groups working peacefully for social change, as well as the misery caused by the war itself. Shining Path presumes to speak for "the people" in defense of its assassinations of police, the military, local functionaries, development workers, and others, but that claim, like similar ones of the Peruvian state, uses ideology in the service of power. Who are "the people" and how do we know them? What gives "the people" or "the state" the right to kill me or anyone?

Emphasis on cocaine production has similarly diverted attention from peasant experience and culture. Destruction of *coca* fields not only affects the livelihood of prodcuers, but disrupts peasant consumption of the leaf. There is little evidence to support elite assertions that *coca* chewing is harmful, although ample data show its centrality to peasant society and culture (Allen 1988, Pacini and Franquemont 1986). Some studies have even suggested that *coca* consumption benefits blood sugar level and carbohydrate metabolism, helping peasants subsist on otherwise inadequate diets (Burchard 1976, 1978). If these studies are correct, disruption of the *coca* trade harms not only the culture of peasants but their ability to survive biologically.

The ethnocentrism underlying United States *coca* policy can be gauged by imagining American outrage if Peru or another country were to launch a program of tobacco eradication in the United States — even though in this case (unlike Peru) the export of cigarettes is promoted by the United States government!

CONCLUSIONS

Shining Path and cocaine production are important aspects of contemporary Peru that must be studied and understood, but only as part of the larger social context. The war has had a devastating impact on the lives and culture of Peruvian peasants, and I would urge everyone to protest the dirty war of the military and of Shining Path against peasants and others in the emergency zones. The commercial cocaine trade has had similarly nasty consequences, placing lives at risk and undermining the probity of police and government (NACLA 1989). The *cocaine* trade, moreover, like the primary export trade generally, has had few income-generating effects and has done little to raise the general prosperity of the country.

While we study these issues, however, we need to focus on the general social transformation of which they are only parts. We must exercise similar caution when analyzing revolution, crime, and general social distress in other areas of the world as well. The social conditions underlying the revolution in Chiapas, for example, are remarkably similar to those in Peru (Burbach 1994, Collier 1994). Although framed in simple terms in the popular imagination, the lives of Peruvian peasants are much more complex than can be understood if we define them only by the war and cocaine. They are human beings trying to cope as best they can (often with wit and grace), struggling against intolerable social conditions, and creating the "plebeian flood" in the process, the "flood" that is the underlying revolution in the Andes and, indeed, in much of the world studied by anthropologists.

ACKNOWLEDGEMENTS

This paper was read in a different form to the Columbia University Seminar on Cultural Pluralism and to the symposium "Indigenous Identity and Ideology: A Zone of Contention," held at the *91st Annual Meeting of the American Anthropological Association*, San Francisco, CA. I am grateful to the Monmouth University Grants and Sabbaticals committee, the Wenner Gren Foundation for Anthropological Research, the Freed Foundation, the National Science Foundation, and the Fulbright Hayes Committee for support of various aspects of this research. I wish to thank Jane Freed for her research assistance and Monica Barnes, María Benavides, Jane Freed, Barbara Jaye, June Nash, Nicholas Mitchell, Steve Reyna, Linda J. Seligmann, and Eric Wolf for having commented on the manuscript.

NOTES

1. Shining Path (*Sendero Luminoso* in Spanish) is the popular name of the Communist Party of Peru — in the Shining Path of Mariátegui (*Partido Comunista del Peru — por el Luminoso Sendero de Mariátegui*). It is not a peasant movement, as has sometimes been claimed, but a hierarchical political party with roots in the urban intelligentsia that disdains peasant culture and organization (Chávez de Paz 1989, Degregori 1986b, 1989, 1990, 1992, González 1985, Harding 1988, Poole and Rénique 1991, 1992, Woy-Hazleton and Hazleton 1992). Nor is it the only Peruvian communist party (Brown and Fernández 1991, Degregori 1992: 34–35, Gorriti 1992a: 154–159) or active revolutionary group, although until the capture of the Japanese embassy by partisans of the group in 1996, we have heard far less of MRTA (Revolutionary Movement-Tupac Amaru) than of Shining Path. Most literature has been critical of Shining path, but Andreas (1985), the Committee to support the Revolution in Peru (1992), and Leupp (1993) vigorously defend their tactics.

2. One can only provide a select bibliography of the war. In addition to numerous newspaper articles and reports in the Peruvian journal *Quehacer*, human rights groups have published frequent reports on Peru: Americas Watch (1986, 1987, 1988, 1992), Amnesty International (1989a, 1989b, 1989c, 1989d, 1990, 1991, 1992), Diez Canseco (1985), and Kirk (1991). Other important works include: Berg (1986, 1988, 1992), Bourque and Warren (1989), Chávez de Paz (1989), Degregori (1986a, 1986b, 1989, 1990, 1992, 1996), DESCO (1989), Favre 1984, Ferguson (1988a, 1988b), Gorriti (1990), Harding 1988, Isbell (1987, 1988, 1992), Kerr (1992), Manrique (1989), Mayer (1991, 1994), McClintock (1983, 1984, 1988, 1992), McCormick (1987), Mitchell (1996), NACLA (1991), Ossio (1990), Palmer (1984, 1985, 1992), Poole and Rénique (1991, 1992), Seligmann (1992, 1995), Spalding (1992), Starn (1991, 1992a), Urrutia Ceruti *et al*. 1987. See Poole and Rénique (1991) for a discussion of the construction of Shining Path by United States scholars.
3. See Mayer's (1991, 1994) critique of this position.
4. The North American Congress on Latin America (NACLA) report on Alan Garcia (NACLA 1986) provides a significant exception. In this report, Shining Path is placed entirely in the larger social context. McClintock (1984, 1988) has also stressed the general social changes.
5. Some reviewers (eg, Gonzales 1992 and Korovkin 1992), for example, criticized my book, *Peasants on the Edge* (1991a), for not dealing more directly with Shining Path, even though my stated aim was to deal with the social transformation in Peru, rather than with Shining Path.
6. Ritual, ceremony, and belief are part of that real world, but apart from the requisite introductory remarks, scholars have often treated these topics as if the people of the Andes are archaic (and often harmonious) holdovers from some ancient past and as if they exist apart from their class and exploitative context. See my critiques (Mitchell 1982, 1987, 1991b) and those of Starn (1991, 1994).
7. See Berg (1986, 1988, and 1992) for some of the few first-hand reports on peasant attitudes toward Shining Path and for useful distinctions concerning the types of support people have given Shining Path.
8. Because similar sex (and possibly age) ratios have an ancient history, going back at least to the forced male migration of the colonial period (Mitchell 1991a: 35), they do not in themselves explain the contemporary crisis, but they have contributed to it.
9. Maren (1993) gives an impassioned description of the disastrous impact of imported food on contemporary Somalia, made all the more poignant for his having worked in Somalia as a USAID official. See the work of Sen (1990–1991) for a general discussion of the political economy of hunger.
10. The percentage of fathers working in nonfarm occupations is probably higher than indicated by my statistics because I took a conservative position in classifying employment as nonfarm work (Mitchell 1991a: 229, note 2).

ON A SHINING PATH

11. The Peruvian census is often unreliable, but is useful in showing general trends.
12. Although anecdotal evidence supports Chávez de Paz's conclusions, these data and those presented in tables 5, 6 and 7 are problematic. They represent information in judicial records about people adjudicated and imprisoned for "terrorism" and other crimes (Chávez de Paz 1989). Because the outcome of Peruvian judicial procedures is notoriously dependant on the class and occupation of the accused, the prison population probably does not represent the entire "criminal" population. In particular, the military have targeted university students, professors, and social activists as "terrorists," but it is questionable whether all the targeted people are Shining Path partisans. Accusations of "terrorism" are often used in Peru to control dissent. The study may be measuring the characteristics of the targeted population (higher education and more prosperous backgrounds) rather than the general membership of Shining Path. Nonetheless, the data of Chávez de Paz are the only concrete information we have on the possible nature of the Shining Path rank-and-file.
13. The Roman Catholic Church, more conservative than in other areas of Peru, was the only significant force still allied to the old order of large landowners (Degregori 1990: 153–155).
14. The Buechlers' describe a market woman in La Paz who changed from European to Chola style clothing (clothing that has traditional associations), doing so to solidify her position in the market and to preserve her independence against abuse from men (Buechler and Buechler 1996, Chapter 10).
15. These vigilante groups are independently organized groups of peasants found primarily in northern Peru (Starn 1992b). They are different from the peasant militia organized by the military that are sometimes also called *rondas campesinas*, but which are better called civil defense committees, *comites de autodefensa* or *montoneros* (Degregori 1986b: 49, 1996). Neither the civil defense committees nor the vigilante groups, of course, can be considered nonviolent.
16. See, for example, *The New York Times* of 20 November 1992, p. 3, which focuses on the war and damage done to Shining Path by the capture of Abimael Guzmán, but says nothing of the social conditions in Peru. When *The Times* does address the social conditions, moreover, it is usually in the context of the war rather than the reverse.
17. Shining Path leaders are also involved in a dispute between Abimael Guzmán, who has called for peace talks with Fujimori, and Oscar Ramirez Durand, the highest leader of the group outside prison, who emphasizes continuing military action (Burt and López 1994). The rank and file appear to be equally divided between support for the two men, but the Ramirez group has increased its military actions and is also focusing on political work among the poor to rebuild its social base. Sporadic confrontations between Shining Path and the military were still occurring in remote areas of the Central Highlands in 1996 and 1997.

REFERENCES

Allen, Catherine J. (1988). *The Hold Life Has: Coca and Cultural Identity in an Andean Community.* Washington: Smithsonian Institution Press.

Alvarez, Elena (1979). Politica agraria y estacamiento de la agricultura, 1969–1977. Ponencia presentada al Primer Semenario sobre Agricultura y Alimentación en el Peru. (Cited in Caballero 1981: 212.)

Americas Watch (1986). *Human Rights in Peru After President Garcia's First Year.* New York: The Americas Watch Committee.

——————(1987). *A Certain Passivity: Failing to Curb Human Rights Abuses in Peru.* New York: Americas Watch.

——————(1988). *Tolerating Abuses: Violations of Human Rights in Peru; An Americas Watch Report.* New York: Americas Watch.

—————— (1992). *Peru Under Fire: Human Rights Since the Return to Democracy.* New Haven and London: Yale University Press.

Amnesty International (1989a). *Peru Country Action; Mailing #1.* San Francisco: Amnesty International.

——————(1989b). *Peru: A Human Rights Emergency.* London: Amnesty International.

——————(1989c). *Peru: Human Rights in a State of Emergency.* New York: Amnesty International.

—————— (1989d). *Peru: The Cayara Massacre.* London: Amnesty International.

——————(1990). *Peru Campaign, Final Mailing.* San Francisco: Amnesty International USA.

—————— (1991). *Peru: Human Rights in a Climate of Terror.* New York: Amnesty International.

——————(1992). *Peru: Human Rights During the Government of President Alberto Fujimori.* New York: Amnesty International.

Andreas, Carol (1985). *When Women Rebel: The Rise of Popular Feminism in Peru.* Westport, CT: Lawrence Hill & Company.

Ansión, Juan (1985). "Violencia y cultura en el Peru." In *Siete ensayos sobre la violencia en el Perú*, Felipe MacGregor, José Luis Rouillón, and Marcial Rubio Correa, editors. pp. 59–78. Lima: Asociación Peruana de Estudios e Investigaciones para la Paz, Fundación Friedrich Ebert.

—————— (1987). *Desde el rincón de los muertos: El pensmiento mítico en Ayacucho.* Lima: GREDES (Grupo de Estudios para el Desarrollo).

Appleby, Gordon (1982). "Price Policy and Peasant Production in Peru: Regional Disintegration During Inflation." *Culture and Agriculture* 15: 1–6.

Arnold, Dean E. (1993). *Ecology and Ceramic Production in an Andean Community.* Cambridge: Cambridge University Press.

Berg, Ronald H. (1986). "Sendero Luminoso and Peasantry of Andahuaylas." *Journal of Interamerican Studies and World Affairs* 28: 165–196.

—————— (1988). "Retribution and Resurrection: The Politics of Sendero Luminoso in Peru." Paper presented at the Annual Meetings of the American Anthropological Association, Phoenix, Arizona.

——— (1992). "Peasant Responses to Shining Path in Andahuaylas." In *Shining Path of Peru*, ed. David Scott Palmer. pp. 83–104. New York: St. Martins Press.
Bolton, Ralph (1973). "Aggression and Hypoglycemia Among the Qolla: A Study in Psychobiological Anthropology." *Ethnology* 12 (3): 227–257.
Bourque, Susan C. and Kay B. Warren (1989). "Democracy without Peace: The Cultural Politics of Terror in Peru." *Latin American Research Review* 24: 7–34.
Brennan, Ellen R., ed. (1983). *Mortality Patterns in Anthropological Populations*. Detroit: Wayne State University Press.
Brown, Michael F. and Eduardo Fernández (1991). *War of shadows; The Struggle for Utopia in the Peruvian Amazon*. Berkeley, CA: University of California Press.
Buechler, Hans and Judith-Maria Buechler (1996). *The World of Sofia Velazquez: The Autobiography of A Bolivian Market Vendor*. New York: Columbia University Press.
Burbach, Roger. (1994). "Roots of the Postmodern Rebellion in Chiapas." *New Left Review* 205 (May/June): 113–124.
Burchard, Roderick (1976). *Myths of the Sacred Leaf: Ecological Perspectives on Coca and Peasant Biocultural Adaptation in Peru*. Ph.D. Dissertation, Department of Anthropology, University of Indiana.
———(1978). "Comment on 'Coca chewing and High Altitude Stress: Possible effects of Coca Alkaloids on Erthropoiesis'" by Andrew Fuchs. *Current Anthropology* 19: 283–284.
Burt, Jo-Marie and José López Ricci (1994). "Shining Path After Guzmán." *NACLA Report on the Americas* 28 (3, Nov/Dec): 6–9.
Caballero, José María (1981). *Economía agraria de la sierra peruana; antes de la reforma agraria de 1969*. Lima: Instituto de Estudios Peruanos.
Caldwell, John C. et. al., ed. (1990). *What We Know About Health Transition: The Cultural, Social and Behavioral Determinants of Health. The Proceedings of an International Workshop, Canberra, May 1989*, vols. 1 & 2. Canberra: The Highland Press, Australian National Univ., Health Transition Centre.
Caldwell, John C. and Gigi Santow, eds. (1990). *Selected Readings in the Cultural, Social, and Behavioural Determinants of Health. The Health Transition Series #1*. Canberra: The Highland Press, Australian National Univ., Health Transition Centre.
Chávez de Paz, Denis (1989). *Juventud y terrorismo: características sociales de los condenados por terrorismo y otros delitos*. Lima: Instituto de Estudios Peruanos.
Collins, Jane (1988). *Unseasonal Migrations: The Effects of Rural Labor Scarcity in Peru*. Princeton: Princeton University Press.
Collier, George (1994). "Roots of the Rebellion in Chiapas." *Cultural Survival Quarterly*, Spring: 14–18.
Committee to Support the Revolution in Peru (1992). *A Response to Amnesty International: The Revolution in Peru is Profoundly Liberating*. Berkeley, CA: The Committee To Support the Revolution in Peru.

Coral, Isabel (1994). Desplazamiento por violencia política en el Perú, 1980–1992. Lima: Instituto de Estudios Peruanos, Documento de Trabajo No. 58.

——————— (1994). El proceso del desplazamiento en el Peru. *In* III encuentro interinstitucional sobre despilazamiento en la region central. S. Peña Guerra, ed. pp. 20–32. Huancayo, Peru: Grupo de Trabajo de la Region Central Sobre el Desplazamiento.

Cotlear, Daniel (1988). "La economía campesina en las regiones modernas y tradicionales de la sierra." *Allpanchis* 31: 217–244.

Degregori, Carlos I. (1986a). *Ayacucho, raíces de una crisis*. Ayacucho: Instituto José María Arguedas.

——————— (1986b). *"Sendero Luminoso": Parte I: Los hondos y mortales desencuentros; Parte II: Lucha armada y utopía autoritaria*. Lima: Instituto de Estudios Peruanos.

——————— (1989). *Que dificil ser Dios: ideología y violencia en el Sendero Luminoso*. Lima: El Zorro de Abajo Ediciones.

———————(1990). *Ayacucho 1969–1979: El surgimiento de Sendero Luminoso*. Lima: Instituto de Estudios Peruanos.

———————(1992). "Origins and logic of Shining Path: Return to the past." In *Shining Path of Peru*, ed. David Scott Palmer. pp. 33–44. New York: St. Martin's Press.

Degregori, Carlos Iván (ed.) (1996). *Las rondas campesinas y la derrota de Sendero Luminoso*. Lima: Instituto de Estudios Peruanos.

de Janvry, Alain (1981). *The Agrarian Question and Reformism in Latin America*. Baltimore: The Johns Hopkins University Press.

DESCO (1989). *Violencia política en el Perú, 1980–1989*. Lima: DESCO (León de la Fuente 110, Lima 17).

Díaz Martinez, Antonio (1969). *Ayacucho: hambre y esperanza*. Ayacucho (Peru): Ediciones Waman Puma.

Diez Canseco, Javier (1985). *Democracia, militarización y derechos humanos en el Perú, 1980–1984*. Lima: SERPO (Servicios Populares) y APRODEH (Asociación Pro Derechos Humanos).

Dobyns, Henry E. and Paul Doughty (1976). *Peru, A Cultural History*. New York: Oxford University Press.

Easterlin, Richard A. (1980). *Birth and Fortune: The Impact of Numbers on Personal Welfare*. New York: Basic Books.

Favre, Henri (1984). "Peru: Sendero Luminoso y horizontes ocultos." *Quehacer* 31–32 (September-October): 25–35. (Also published as "Pérou: Sentier Lumineux et Horizons Obscurs," *Problémes D'Amerique Latine* 72: 3–27, 1984).

Ferguson, Brian (1988a). "A Response to Isbell's 'An Anthropological Dialogue with Violence.'" *COSP Newsletter* 6(2): 8.

———————(1988b). "Rejoinder to Isbell." *Human Peace*.

Ferroni, Marco A. (1980). *The Urban Bias of Peruvian Food Policy: Consequences and Alternatives*. PH. D. Dissertation, Cornell University.

Figueroa, Adolfo (1984). *Capitalist Development and the Peasant Economy in Peru. Cambridge Latin American Studies*, vol 47. Cambridge: Cambridge University Press.

Franklin, David et al. (1985). *Consumption Effects of Agricultural Polices: Peru; "Trade Policy, Agricultural Prices and Food Consumption: An Economy Wide Perspective." Report Prepared for US AID/PERU*. Raleigh, North Carolina: Sigma One Corporation.

Galvez, Modesto and Lucía Cano (1974). *El sistema latifundista en Huamanga, Ayacucho*. Bachiller en Antropología, Universidad Mayor de San Marcos, Lima. (As cited in Degregori 1989: 21–22).

Gonzales, José E. (1991). "Guerrillas and Coca in the Upper Huallaga Valley." In *The Shining Path of Peru*, David Scott Palmer, ed. pp. 105–125. New York: St. Martin's Press.

Gonzales, Michael J. (1992). "Review of *Peasants on the Edge; Crop, Cult, and Crisis in the Andes* (William P. Mitchell)." *American Historical Review* (December): 1637–1638.

Gonzales de Olarte, Efraín (1987). *Inflación y campesinado; Comunidades y microrregiones frente a la crisis*. Lima: Instituto de Estudios Peruanos.

González, Raúl (1985). "Violencia e insurrección en el Perú." In *Siete ensayos sobre la violencia en el Perú*, Felipe MacGregor, José Luis Rouillón, and Marcial Rubio Correa, editors. pp. 137–151. Lima: Asociación Peruana de Estudios e Investigaciones para la Paz, Fundación Friedrich Ebert.

Gorriti, Gustavo (1990). *Sendero: historia de la guerra milenaria del Peru*. Lima: Editorial Apoyo.

——— (1992a). "Shining Path's Stalin and Trotsky." In *Shining Path of Peru*, ed. David Scott Palmer. pp. 149–170. New York: St. Martin's Press.

——— (1992b). "America's Dance With a Dictator." *The New York Times*, December 27 1992, pp. 11.

Hall, Lana L. (1985). "United States Food Aid and the Agricultural Development of Brazil and Colombia, 1954–73." In *Food, Politics, and Society in Latin America*, ed. John C. Super and Thomas C. Wright. pp. 133–149. Lincoln: University of Nebraska Press.

Harding, Colin (1988). "Antonio Díaz Martínez and the Ideology of Sendero Luminoso." *Bulletin of Latin American Research* 7 (1): 65–73.

Hobsbawm, Eric (1969). *Bandits*. New York: Delacorte Press.

Isbell, Billie Jean (1987). "An Anthropological Dialogue With Violence." *Human Peace* 5(4): 2–8.

——— (1988). "Dialogue With Violence Continued: Isbell Responds to Ferguson." *Human Peace* 6(3): 7.

——— (1992). "Shining Path and Peasant Response in Rural Ayacucho." In *Shining Path of Peru*, ed. David Scott Palmer. pp. 59–81. New York: St. Martin's Press.

Kawell, Jo Ann (1989). "The Addict Economies." *NACLA Report on the Americas* 22 (6): 33–41.

Kerr, S. (1992). "Fujimori's Plot: An Interview with Gustavo Gorriti." *The New York Review of Books*, June 25: 18–22.

Kirk, Robin (1991). *The Decade of Chaqwa: Peru's Internal Refugees*. Washington, DC: U.S. Committee on Refugees.

Korovkin, Tanya (1992). "Review of *Peasants on the Edge; Crop, Cult, and Crisis in the Andes* (William P. Mitchell)." *The Journal of Peasant Studies* 19 (2): 412–413.

Latin American News Update (1994). "Peru." Latin American News Update 10 (6): 21–22.

Leupp, Gary P. (1993). "Peru on the Threshold: A Reply to Hobart A. Spalding." *Monthly Review*, March 1993: 25–30.

Long, Norman and B.R. Roberts (1984). *Miners, Peasants, and Entrepreneurs; Regional Development in the Central Highlands of Peru.* Cambridge: Cambridge University Press.

MacGregor, Felipe, J. L. Rouillón, and M. R. Correa, eds. (1985). *Siete ensayos sobre la violencia en el Perú.* Lima: Asociación Peruana de Estudios e Investigaciones para la Paz, Fundación Friedrich Ebert.

Manrique, Nelson (1989). "Sierra central: Batalla decisiva." *Quehacer* 60: 62–83.

Maren, Michael (1993). "Mana From Heaven? Somalia Pays the Price for Years of Aid." *The Village Voice*, January 19, 1993, vol. 38(3): 21–25.

Matos Mar, José (1984). *Desborde Popular y Crisis del Estado. Perú Problema 21.* Lima: Instituo de Estudios Peruanos.

Mayer, Enrique (1991). "Peru in deep trouble: Mario Vargas Llosa's 'Inquest in the Andes' reexamined." *Cultural Anthropology* 6(4): 466–504.

——— (1994). "Patterns of Violence in the Andes." *Latin American Research Review* 29(2): 141–171.

McClintock, Cynthia (1983). "Sendero Luminoso: Peru's Maoist Guerrillas." *Problems of Communism* 32(5): 19–34.

——— (1984). "Why Peasants Rebel: The Case of Peru's Sendero Luminoso." *World Politics* 37: 48–84.

——— (1988). "Peru's Sendero Luminoso Rebellion: Origins and Trajectory." In *Power and Popular Protest: Latin American Social Movements.* Susan Eckstein, editor. Berkeley: University of California Press.

——— (1992). "Theories of Revolution and the Case of Peru." In *Shining Path of Peru*, ed. David Scott Palmer. pp. 225–240. New York: St. Martin's Press.

McCormick, Gordon H. (1987). *The Shining Path and Peruvian Terrorism.* Santa Monica: Rand Corporation.

Meillassoux, Claude (1981). *Maidens, Meal and Money; Capitalism and the Domestic Community.* New York: Cambridge University Press.

Mitchell, William P. In Prep. *Violence and The Rural Diaspora: Economic Pressures and The Social Transformation of Peru.* (A monograph in preparation that will explore the social transformation, the Shining Path war, and the rural diaspora of Peru.).

——— (1976). "Irrigation and Community in the Central Peruvian Highlands." *American Anthropologist* 78: 25–44.

——— (1979). "Iconsistencia de status social y dimensiones de rango en los andes centrales del Perú." *Estudios Andinos* 15: 21–31.

——— (1982). "Symbols and Structuralism in the Andes: A Case of Theory Obscuring the Facts." *Reviews in Anthropology* 9: 87–96.

——————(1987). "The Myth of the Isolated Native Community." In *Global Interdependence in the Curriculum: Case Studies for the Social Sciences*, Judy Himes, ed. pp. 35–49. Princeton: Woodrow Wilson National Fellowship Foundation.
——————(1991a). *Peasants on the Edge: Crop, Cult, and Crisis in the Andes*. Austin: University of Texas Press.
—————— (1991b). "Some are More Equal than Others: Labor Supply, Reciprocity, and Redistribution in the Andes." *Research in Economic Anthropology* 13: 191–219.
——————(1994). "Dam the Water: The Ecology and Political Economy of Irrigation in the Ayacucho Valley, Peru." In *Irrigation at High Altitudes: The Social Organization of Water Control Systems in the Andes*, William P. Mitchell & David Guillet, eds. pp. 275–302. Washington: American Anthropological Association, publication series of the Society for Latin American Anthropology, volume 21.
——————(1996). "Economic and Political Violence in the Peruvian Diaspora: Theorizing Migration." Paper presented at the Symposium "Fight the Power," Annual Meeting of the American Anthropological Association, San Francisco.
—————— (1997). "Pressures on Peasant Production and the Transformation of Regional and National Identities." In *Migrants, Regional Identities, and Latin American Cities*, Teófilo Altamirano and Lane Hirabayashi, eds. pp. 25–48. Washington: American Anthropological Association, Publication Series of the Society for Latin American Anthropology, volume 13.
Mitchell, William P. and Barbara Jaye (1988). "The Only Game in Town: The Latin American Fiesta System and the York Feast of Corpus Christi." *Fifteenth Century Studies* 13: 485–503.
Montoya, Rodrigo (1980). *Capitalismo y no capitalismo en el Perú; Un estudio histórico de su articulación en un eje regional*. Lima: Mosca Azul Editores.
Morner, Magnus (1985). *The Andean Past: Land, Societies, and Conflicts*. New York: Columbia University Press.
NACLA Report on the Americas (1986). *Garcia's Peru: One Last Chance*. *NACLA Report on the Americas*, vol. 20(3).
—————— (1989). *Coca: The Real Green Revolution*. *NACLA Report on the Americas*, vol. 22(6).
——————(1991). *Fatal Attraction; Peru's Shining Path*. *NACLA Report on the Americas*, vol. 24(4).
——————(1993). *A Market Solution for the Americas? The Rise of Wealth and Hunger*. *NACLA Report on the Americas*, vol. 26(4).
Nash, June (1992). "Interpreting Social Movements: Bolivian Resistance to Economic Conditions Imposed by the International Monetary Fund." *American Ethnologist* 19(2): 275–93.
Ortiz de Zevalos, Felipe (1989). *The Peruvian Puzzle, A Twentieth Century Fund Paper*. New York: Priority Press Publications.
Ossio, Juan (1990). *Violencia estructural en el Peru: antropología*. Lima: Asociación Peruana de Estudios E Investigaciones Para La Paz.

Pacini, Deborah and Christine Franquemont, eds. (1986). *Coca and Cocaine; Effects on People and Policy in Latin America. Cultural Survival Report No. 23.* Ithaca: Cornell University Latin American Studies Program and Cultural Survival.

Palmer, David Scott (1984). "Rebellion in Rural Peru: The Origins and Evolution of Sendero Luminoso." Paper prepared for the Project on Latin American Insurgencies of the Center for Strategic and International Studies, Georgetown University.

——— (1985). "The Sendero Luminoso Rebellion in Rural Peru." In *Latin American Insurgencies*, ed. Georges Fauriol. pp. 67–96. Washington, DC: The Georgetown University Center for Strategic and International Studies and The National Defense University.

Palmer, David Scott, ed. (1992). *Shining Path of Peru*. New York: St. Martin's Press.

Pastor, Manuel and Carol Wise (1992). "Peruvian Economic Policy in the 1980s: From Orthodoxy to Heterodoxy and Back." *Latin American Research Review* 27(2): 83–117.

Peru (1966). *Sexto censo nacional de población; primer censo nacional de vivienda, 2 de julio de 1961, tomo I, volumen de centros poblados*. Lima: Dirección Nacional de Estadística y Censos.

——— (1972). *Segundo censo nacional agropecuario, 4 al 24 de setiembre, 1972, Departamento de Ayacucho*. Lima: Instituto Nacional de Estadística.

——— (1974). *Censos nacionales, VII de población, II de vivienda, 4 de junio de 1972, Departamento de Ayacucho*. Lima: Oficina Nacional de Estadística y Censos.

——— (1983). *Censos nacionales, 1981; VIII de población, III de vivienda, resultados definitivos, vol. A, 3 tomos*. Lima: Instituto Nacional de Estadística.

——— (1987). *Indicadores demográficos y socioeconómicos: Peru 1987*. Lima: Consejo Nacional de Población.

Poole, Deborah (ed.) (1994). *Unruly Order: Violence, Power, and Cultural Identity in the High Provinces of Southern Peru*. Boulder, CO: Westview Press.

Poole, Deborah and Gerado Rénique (1991). "The new chroniclers of Peru: US scholars and the 'Shining Path' of peasant rebellion." *Bulletin of Latin American Research* 10(2): 133–91.

——— (1992). *Peru: Time Of Fear*. London: Latin America Bureau (Monthly Review Press).

Quehacer (1988). "Violencia y pacificacion: Un informe que debe ser escuchado." *Quehacer* 54: 18–28.

Reid, Michael (1985). *Peru: Paths To Poverty*. London: Latin American Bureau.

Rosenau, William and Linda Head Flanagan (1992). "Blood of the Condor; The Genocidal Talons of Peru's Shining Path." *Policy Review* 59 (Winter, 1992): 82–5.

Schneider, Jane C., and Peter T. Schneider (1996). *Festival of the Poor: Fertility Decline and the Ideology of Class in Sicily, 1860–1980*. Tucson: University of Arizona Press.

Scott, James C. (1976). *The Moral Economy of the Peasant: Rebellion and Subsistence in Southeast Asia*. New Haven: Yale University Press.
——————(1985). *Weapons of the Weak; Everyday Forms of Peasant Resistance*. New Haven: Yale University Press.
——————(1990). *Domination and the Arts of Resistance; Hidden Transcripts*. New Haven: Yale University Press.
Seligmann, Linda (1992). "Agrarian Reform and the Shining Path Guerrilla Movement in Peru." Paper presented to the New York Academy of Sciences, Anthropology Section, February 24.
——————(1995). *Between Reform and Revolution: Political Struggles in the Peruvian Andes, 1969–1991*. Stanford: Stanford University Press.
Sen, Amartya (1990–91). *The Political Economy of Hunger*. Oxford: Oxford University Press.
Smith, Michael L. (1991). "Taking the High Ground: Shining Path and the Andes." In *Shining Path of Peru*, David Scott Palmer, ed. pp. 15–32. New York: St. Martin's Press.
Spalding, Hobart A. (1992). "Peru on the Brink." *Monthly Review*, January, 1992: 29–43.
Staples, Brent (1994). *Parallel Time: Growing Up Black and White*. New York: Pantheon Books.
Starn, Orin (1991). "Missing the Revolution: Anthropologists and the War in Peru." *Cultural Anthropology* 6(1): 63–91.
——————(1992a). "New Literature on Peru's Sendero Luminoso." *Latin American Research Review* 27(2): 212–26.
——————(1992b). "'I Dreamed of Foxes and Hawks': Reflections on Peasant Protest, New Social Movements, and the Rondas Campesinas of Northern Peru." In *The Making of Social Movements in Latin America: Identity, Strategy and Democracy*, Arturo Escobar and Sonia Alvarez, eds. pp. 89–111. Boulder, CO: Westview Press.
——————(1994)."Rethinking the Politics of Anthropology: The Case of the Andes." *Current Anthropology* 35(1): 13–38.
Stokes, Susan C. (1995). *Cultures in Conflict: Social Movements and the State in Peru*. Berkeley: University of California Press.
Strong, Simon (1992). *Shining Path: The World's Deadliest Revolutionary Force*. London: Harper Collins.
Tarazona-Sevillano, Gabriela (with John B. Reuter) (1990). *Sendero Luminoso and the Threat of Narcoterrorism*. New York: Praeger.
Thorp, Rosemary (1991). *Economic Management and Economic Development in Peru and Colombia*. Pittsburgh: University of Pittsburgh Press.
——————& Geoffrey Bertram (1978). *Peru: 1890–1977; Growth and Policy in an Open Economy*. New York: Columbia University Press.
Urbano, Henrique, ed. (1991). *Poder y violencia en los Andes*. Cusco: Centro de Estudios Regionales Andinos, Bartolomé de las Casas.
Urrutia Ceruti, Jaime (1987). "La violencia en la región de Ayacucho." In *Los niños de la guerra*, ed. Jaime Urrutia Ceruti et al. pp. 15–25. Ayacucho:

Instituto de Estudios Regionales "José María Arguedas," Universidad Nacional San Cristóbal de Huamanga.

Urrutia Ceruti, Jaime et al., ed. (1987). *Los niños de la guerra*. Ayacucho (Peru): Instituto de Estudios Regionales "José María Arguedas," Universidad Nacional San Cristóbal de Huamanga.

Vargas Llosa, Mario (1983). "Inquest in the Andes." *The New York Times Magazine*, July 31, 1983.

Vega-Centeno et al., Máximo (1985). "Violencia y pobreza: una visión de conjunto." In *Siete ensayos sobre la violencia en el Perú*, Felipe MacGregor, José Luis Rouillón, and Marcial Rubio Correa, editors. pp. 79–112. Lima: Asociación Peruana de Estudios e Investigaciones para la Paz, Fundación Friedrich Ebert.

Webb, Richard and Graciela Fernández Baca (1990). *Almanaque estadístico: Perú en numeros 1990*. Lima: Cuánto S.A.

Weismantel, Mary J. (1988). *Food, Gender, and Poverty in the Ecuadorian Andes*. Philadelphia: University of Pennsylvania Press.

Wolf, Eric R. (1969). *Peasant Wars of the Twentieth Century*. New York: Harper & Row.

——————— (1982). *Europe and the People Without History*. Berkeley: University of California Press.

Woy-Hazleton, Sandra and William A. Hazleton (1992). "Shining Path and the Marxist Left." In *Shining Path of Peru*, ed. David Scott Palmer. pp. 207–24. New York: St. Martin's Press.

Zanabria, Blanca, et al. (1987). "Violencia, Familia y Menor." In *Los niños de la guerra*, ed. Jaime Urrutia Ceruti et al. pp. 27–48. Ayacucho: Instituto de Estudios Regionales "José María Arguedas," Universidad Nacional San Cristóbal de Huamanga.

Index

A

'Abid, 185, 191
Abimael Guzman, 237, 262
Accelerants, of war, 4
Age Sets, 143, 150
Agency, politico-military, 157, 163, 165, 167, 168
Agrarian land reform (Mauritania), 189, 190
Anarchist Syndicalism, 102
Anglos, 93, 95, 99
Augustin Garza, 94, 97, 98
Ayacucho, 242, 244

B

Bidan, 179, 180, 185, 190, 191, 192, 194
Blackbirding, 83
Bodi, 135, 138, 140, 143
Bume (see Nyangatom), 142

C

Cannibals, 71
Capitalism, 3, 8, 9, 235, 262
Cattle Raids, 138
Charles K. Gravis, 88, 99, 100, 103
Civil society war, 4
Civil war, 4

Cocaine, 236, 256, 262, 266
Colonialism, 69, 88, 225, 226
Colonization, 214, 215, 219, 225, 226
Common property, 216, 217, 231
Compadrazgo, 99
Competition in land, 219, 222
Complexes, 24, 26, 31, 39, 40
  military capitalist, 24, 25, 35, 41, 58
  networked, 40
Conflict over land, 217, 223
Crime, 254, 255, 262
Crisis
  national economic, 247
  rural economic, 241, 247, 248
Cultivation, flood retreat, 136, 137
Cultivation, shifting, 136
Culture of violence, 162, 171

D

Dakar, 180, 183
Decolonization, 228
Dehumanization, 163
Depeasantized youth, 238, 260
Desensitization training, 167

Determinants of war, 4
Development policies, 220
Dirty war, 153, 161, 162, 164, 266
Discourse, 113
 of ethnicity ('tribalism'), 108, 109, 110, 111, 113
 of uneven development, 109, 110, 113
Domanial laws, 218
Donor lending, 191
Drought, 192, 193, 202
Duelling, 148

E

Elites, 221, 227, 230
Emigration, 247
Endemic Warfare, 80, 76
Ethiopia, 133
Ethnic cleansing, 87, 104
Ethnic conflict, 181, 202
 Tambiah's theory, 182, 183, 184, 203
 Horowitz's theory, 182, 183, 184
Ethnic minority, 214, 229
Ethnicity, 108, 180, 182, 189, 222, 230
Expansion, territorial, 135
Experiential reality, 171
Export Economy, 243

F

Fields, 26
Fields, feudal, 26, 28

FLAM (African Liberation Force in Mauritania), 189, 190
Foreign debt crisis, 191
Frelimo (*Frente de Libertacao de Mocambique*), 155
Fueds, 74, 78
Fur Trade, 79

G

Government, 2, 11, 12
Guns, 72

H

Haalpulaar, 179, 180, 198, 199
Hacienda, 240
Haratin, 179, 180, 185, 190, 191, 192, 194
Hegemony, 7, 82, 227
Holy Spirit movement, 122
Hudson Bay Co., 79, 84
Huron, 78

I

Ian Smith, 156
Identity, 161, 163, 183, 188, 202, 223
Idi Amin, 111, 114, 115, 116, 120, 126
Internal war, 4, 155, 156
International conflict process, 164
International war, 4
Iroquois, 78

INDEX

L

Lake Turkana, 144
Land grabbing, 194
Land policy, 217
Land tenure, 219
Land tenure system (rule), 216, 219
Large scale irrigation works, 218
Life-world, 10, 160, 161
Linguistic policies, 227
Logics, 24
   mutually reinforcing logics, 24, 28, 34
   of capital accumulation, 24, 28, 34
   of predatory accumulation, 24, 27, 28, 32, 34, 57

M

Magendo, 121
Mago, River, 136
Maure, 179, 189
Mengo, 109
Milton Obote, 111, 113, 114, 116, 126
Monetary relations, 217, 220
Monopoly over trade, 78, 79
Mufatamingi, 114
Mursi, 134, 140, 141, 143
Museveni, 111, 114, 116, 126, 127

N

National economic policy, 238
National Revolutionary Movement (NRM), 114, 115, 122
New Ireland, 71, 77
Nouakchott, 180, 183, 191, 194
Nyangatom, 138, 142

O

Omo, River, 136, 137, 139

P

Partido Liberal Mexicano (PLM), 97, 98
Pastoral production, 224
Peasant income, 238, 243, 244
Plan de San Diego, 87, 89, 94, 96, 97, 98
Police Boys, 73, 75
Political identity, 136, 146, 149, 151
Population growth, 238, 241
Power, decentered, 168
Private property, 217, 218

Q

Quinua, 238, 240, 243

R

Racism, 260
Raiding, 78
Reciprocity, 57, 58
Refugees, 181, 198, 199, 201, 229
Regimes, 26, 41, 45
   domination, 26
   fiscal, 26, 28, 32, 33, 37, 41, 55

Renamo (*Resistencia Nacional Mocambicana*), 156, 158, 160, 162
Repression, 236, 240
Resistance, 163, 168, 226
Rhodesia, 156, 170

S

Segmentary lineage system, 81
Shining Path (*Sendero Luminoso*), 237, 256, 259, 260, 265, 267
Silenced spatiality, 108
Slavery, 215, 216, 227
Social control, 251, 252, 253
Somalia, 80, 81, 82
South Africa, 156, 170
State, 2
States, 4, 5, 19
Structural, 4
Structure of peace, 88, 99, 101
Subjective, 4, 5
Systematic change, 236

T

Tejanos, 87
Teso, 108, 118, 121, 123, 128, 129

Texas Rangers, 89, 91
Trade, 76
Tsetse fly, 136, 139

U

Uganda, 108
  North, 107, 108
  Protectorate, 109, 113
  South, 107, 108

V

Violence, 254,
  family, 255
  police and military, 263, 264
Violent force, 26, 27, 30, 57

W

War of Liberation (1978–79), 108, 114, 116
Weapons, automatic, 142
Wool production, 88, 92